THE *ABBAYE DU SAINT ESPRIT*

Previously published volumes in this series are listed at the back of the book.

VOLUME 21

THE *ABBAYE DU SAINT ESPRIT*

Spiritual Instruction for Laywomen, 1250–1500

by

Janice Pinder

BREPOLS

British Library Cataloguing in Publication Data

A catalogue record for this book is available from the British Library

ISBN: 978-2-503-58681-6
E-ISBN: 978-2-503-58682-3
DOI: 10.1484/M.MWTC-EB.5.118758
ISSN: 1782-3366
E-ISSN: 2294-8406

Printed in the EU on acid-free paper
D/2020/0095/21

For David Garrioch

Contents

Part II

Acknowledgements

This book has been a long time in the making and has incurred many debts along the way. A crucial factor in its completion was my participation in a collaborative research project on virtue ethics in the education of aristocratic women in the late Middle Ages, funded by the Australian Research Council, whose support I gratefully acknowledge. Some early research was made possible by a travel grant from the Australian Academy of the Humanities, and the understanding and cooperation of my main place of work, Monash University Library, has also contributed to getting the book written.

The virtue ethics collaboration contributed enormously to my understanding of the context of moral advice to women in late medieval France, particularly in relation to aristocratic women's networks. I benefited greatly from many conversations with my collaborators, Constant Mews and Karen Green, whose research helped me to elucidate the branch of the *Abbaye*'s history that touched a French aristocratic readership.

It would not have been possible to tell the story of the *Abbaye* without the pioneering work of Geneviève Hasenohr over the last three decades, identifying manuscripts, texts, and sources. My debt to her research is evident in the footnotes to every chapter, and I am very grateful to Mme Hasenohr for her warm personal welcome and for generously sharing her knowledge and copies of some hard-to-obtain papers. I am also grateful to Aden Kumler and Kathryn Hall for sharing their research in advance of publication.

As this project involved the study of a number of manuscripts, I must acknowledge the assistance of staff in many libraries: the Bibliothèque nationale de France, the Bodleian Library, the British Library, the Herzog August Library in Wolfenbüttel, the National Library of Belgium, and the Niedersächsisches Landesarchiv in Osnabrück. Special thanks are due to Mme Christine Le

Bretton at the municipal library in Vesoul, the staff of the library and of the Section romane at the Institut de Recherche et d'Histoire du Texte in Paris, and the staff of the document delivery service of Monash University Library.

I would like to thank Clare Monagle for her penetrating reading of the first draft and constructive suggestions, Tomas Zahora and John Crossley for useful comments on early chapters, and Constant Mews and Renate Blumenfeld-Kosinsky for their close readings of the final version. They have all contributed improvements to the text, whose shortcomings of course remain my own. I also extend warm thanks the History program at Monash University for having welcomed me as an adjunct for many years, providing a stimulating intellectual home and an opportunity in departmental seminars to try out parts of this book. The seminars of the Centre for Medieval and Renaissance Studies have likewise been a site of friendship and lively discussion.

Finally, David Garrioch has contributed in countless ways to thinking about the project, getting the work done, and keeping the author sane. I dedicate this book to him.

ABBREVIATIONS

INTRODUCTION

The growing demand for spiritual reading material in the vernacular languages of northern Europe from the twelfth century onwards is now well documented. Forms of writing which had formerly been available only in Latin — commentaries, biblical paraphrases, didactic and catechetical writings, and works of spiritual advice — took their place alongside saints' lives and prayers in anthologies owned by literate laypeople. An anonymous French writer from the fourteenth century compared the insatiable hunger of the devout person living in the world for different foods and spiritual nourishment in the form of masses, prayers, sermons, to that of a pregnant woman, who often wants to try different kinds of food to satisfy her appetite and soothe her taste so as not to lose the child she has conceived.[1] Bernard McGinn, using the term 'vernacular theology' for such literature, suggested that it, like the new forms of mysticism it accompanied in the thirteenth century, was the product of a conversation between men and women, clerics and laity.[2] This literature of

---

[1] 'Et por ce, tot aussi comme la femme ençainte, qui toute maniere velt ensaier por faire aisis a son apetit et a son goust por ce qu'ele ne perde son enfant, tout autresi cuer deuot qui est ençaint de la grace du Sainz Esperit et a conceu bone volenté et bon propos, et quil couvient vivre au monde et si ne veut pas vivre selonc le monde, si se demente en moult de manieres et quiert diverses refections a son esperit de messes, de sermons et d'oroisons.' (And therefore, just like a pregnant woman, who wants to try all manner [of food] to satisfy her appetite and taste, so she will not lose her child, the devout heart pregnant with the grace of the Holy Spirit, having conceived good will and intention, and having to live in the world but not wishing to live according to the world, makes all kinds of effort and seeks diverse nourishment for her spirit from masses, sermons, and prayers.) *La droite forme de vivre à l'âme* (The correct way of living for the soul); the prologue is edited from BnF, MS fr. 1802, fols 74ᵛ–75ᵛ, by Hasenohr, 'Les Prologues des textes de dévotion en langue française', p. 621.

[2] McGinn, 'The Changing Shape of Late Medieval Mysticism', pp. 203–04. This concept

spiritual advice is distinct from the more basic catechetical treatises and confession manuals associated with the call from the Fourth Lateran Council for
priests to instruct the laity in their faith.[3] It addresses those seeking spiritual
perfection, which had formerly been the preserve of the professed religious but
was increasingly seen as an ambition within the reach of the laity. While the
often-anonymous authors were probably clerics in the main, they shaped their
texts in response to the demands of their lay readers. Sometimes they simply
translated monastic authors, but more often they refashioned the material to
suit lay sensibilities and ways of reading that were being developed through the
new vernacular secular literature.

The exact nature of the conversations that created vernacular theology is
beyond our grasp, although there are hints in the historical record. The case
of the twelfth-century parish priest in Liège, Lambert of Theux, who is said
to have made a verse translation of the Acts of the Apostles and a translation
of the life of St Agnes for his deeply pious parishioners, shows new texts being
created in response to demand.[4] Such evidence is rare, but glimpses can also be
gained from close reading of the products of the conversation that have come
down to us and close study of their manuscript traditions. Choices of material
and form, changes made in the adaptation of source material and adjustments
made in new copies, and where the information is available, the context of their
production and use can all provide insights into the interplay of reader needs
and authorial intent. This book presents a study, edition, and translation of one
such product, examining its complex history from its origins in the thirteenth
century to its final flowering in the Burgundian court of the late fifteenth century. The story of its evolution involves many themes in the growth of lay religious culture, the participation of women in new religious movements, and the
use and transformation of twelfth- and early thirteenth-century monastic formation literature for new audiences.

of vernacular theology is introduced in his introduction to McGinn, *Meister Eckhart and the
Beguine Mystics*, pp. 4–14.

[3] The more basic vernacular didactic texts in French have recently been studied by Waters,
Translating 'Clergie'.

[4] See for example Scheepsma, *The Limburg Sermons*.

The Abbaye du saint Esprit

The subject of this study, the *Abbaye du saint Esprit*, is an example of French vernacular theology. In French speaking areas, the production of such literature was well under way in the thirteenth century. Those who were hastening to answer the need for spiritual guidance in the vernacular drew predominantly on a mixture of patristic authors and monastic authors of the twelfth century, especially Augustine, Isidore of Seville, Bernard of Clairvaux, Hugh of St Victor, and Anselm.[5] They also continually plundered earlier vernacular texts, putting new texts together from pieces of old ones. Some large-scale syntheses of moral advice were produced, often by the confessors of royal patrons, such as the *Miroir de l'ame* composed for Blanche of Castile, or the *Somme le roi* written for Philip III by his Dominican confessor. They were sometimes first composed in Latin before being translated into the vernacular, as was the case of the *Miroir de l'ame*.[6] These long, prestigious works, often of known authorship, tended to be widely copied and show great textual stability in their transmission. That is not the case for the shorter, usually anonymous works; in general, little is known about the circumstances of their production. Most exist in a handful of copies at the most, and the manuscripts in which they are found usually bear no owner identification.[7] Much of what is known about this anonymous literature of spiritual instruction in French is due to the pioneering work of Geneviève Hasenohr, who over the length of a career in manuscript study has done much to map texts and sources, and shine light on individual texts.[8]

Among these shorter, anonymous texts, the *Abbaye* can be considered a success, since it is known from sixteen manuscripts, left traces in other texts, and

---

[5] Geneviève Hasenohr notes the importance of pseudo-Augustinian and pseudo-Bernardine compilations, and of Book II of Isidore of Seville's *Synonyms*, for French vernacular moral didactic literature. Hasenohr, 'Un Enseignement de vie chrétienne du XIIIᵉ siècle et sa postérité', pp. 325–27, and Hasenohr, 'Isidore de Séville, auteur ascétique "français"?'.

[6] Field, 'Reflecting the Royal Soul'.

[7] Sometimes they are gathered in manuscripts owned by religious houses. In these cases, they could be for the religious themselves (particularly in the case of female houses) or be designed to serve the monastery's pastoral mission, like the anthology of vernacular texts held by St Peter's in Chartres, which was described as 'aliqua verbis gallicis ad eruditionem etiam laicorum' (some writings in French for the instruction of the lay): Chartres, Bibliothèque municipale, MS 1036. See Omont, Molinier, and Coyecque, *Chartres*, pp. 322–23.

[8] Some of her most important contributions are collected in Hasenohr, *Textes de dévotion et lectures spirituelles en langue romane*. See especially the notice on the *Abbaye du saint Esprit* on p. 80.

was also translated into English.[9] Based on an architectural allegory that had its roots in twelfth-century monastic renewal literature, it addresses a lay, female audience, proposing the construction of an abbey made of virtues in the heart of the devout person. It is known in English as the *Abbey of the Holy Ghost*, the title of the popular Middle English translation through which it is best known to scholarship. In the French manuscripts it is variously called *Li sermons de l'abeie dou saint espirs, Li livres de la religion dou cuer et de l'abeie, L'abbaye de devotion et de chariteit, Le livre du cloistre de l'ame*, and *La religion du benoit saint esprit*, as well as *L'abaye du saint esperit*, and was seen as important enough to be attributed in different manuscripts to two famous spiritual masters, Hugh of St Victor and Jean Gerson.[10]

The English translation and many of the French manuscripts identify the intended reader as someone who would like to join a religious order but is prevented by circumstances such as marriage or poverty. Although the English translation and some of the French manuscripts address a mixed audience, it seems likely that the text was written originally for a woman. Two of the oldest manuscripts clearly have a female reader in mind:

> Fille, je resgarde que mout de gent uouroient estre en religion et ne puent, ou par povretei ou par ce qu'ils sont retenut par le loien de mariage, ou par autre raison; ce te fas un livre de la religion dou cuer de l'abaie dou saint Esperit, que tu et tuit cil qui ne puent estre en religion corporeil soient en la religion esperituel.

> [Daughter, I see that many people would like to be in a religious order and cannot, either through poverty or because they are held back by the bonds of marriage, or for some other reason; thus I make you a book of the religion of the heart of the abbey of the Holy Ghost, so that all those who cannot be in a bodily religion may be in the spiritual religion.][11]

There are further addresses to the reader as *fille* within the text, and even in those manuscripts where many such addresses have been omitted, one is almost

---

[9] The French version survived in sixteen manuscripts until World War II, when two were destroyed. See the Introduction to Part II for a full list. The English translation made during the fourteenth century survives in twenty-four manuscripts and five incunabula: Consacro, 'A Critical Edition of "The Abbey of the Holy Ghost"', p. 20.

[10] For convenience I will refer to the work as a whole as the *Abbaye du saint Esprit* or the *Abbaye*, but use the title given in the manuscripts in question in the chapters on individual versions.

[11] *M*, fol. 63, cited by Meyer, 'Notice du ms. 535 de la Bibl. Mun. de Metz', p. 49. It is present (slightly altered) in *C*, and also in *L*, *A*, and *VO*. See the list of manuscripts and their sigla in the Introduction to Part II.

always retained: 'Fille se tu vueus estre religieuse tien toi close et garde ton cloistre' (Daughter, if you want to be a religious woman, you should keep yourself close and guard your cloister) (*R* fols 133vb–134ra). Women, both lay and religious, were certainly prominent among its subsequent readers. Two copies were owned by nuns: Cistercian nuns at the royal abbey of Maubuisson and Poor Clares in Amiens. Three others belonged to prominent laywomen: Marie de Berry, Thomine de Villequier, and Margaret of York, Duchess of Burgundy.[12]

The opening identifies the text as a letter of spiritual direction, a very common form among vernacular works of spiritual advice. The text assigns qualities (virtues, graces, and gifts of the Holy Spirit) to the construction of the buildings; for example, Poverty and Humility dig the foundations, Confession builds the chapter house, and Contemplation constructs the dormitory. It then lists the holders of the main offices of the community, which is ruled over by Charity (abbess), Wisdom (prioress), and Humility (sub-prioress). In most versions, it ends with a narrative, telling of the incursion into the abbey of four vices (daughters of the Devil) and the restoration of order by the Holy Ghost. In its conception, the *Abbaye* exemplifies the tendency of much medieval vernacular spiritual advice literature to apply a monastic model to lay piety. It stops short, however, of the practical prescription of many other texts, which provide timetables and forms of prayer to superimpose on everyday activities.[13] The *Abbaye* is concerned more with being than doing; as will be seen in Chapter 1, its subject is the ordering of the interior life, using the allegorical framework to present a set of virtues to cultivate. Desirable forms of behaviour are implied, but actual practice remains flexible. That flexibility may well have contributed to its longevity.

The *Abbaye* is best known to modern readers through mentions in work on the late fourteenth-century English translation and, in the absence of an edition, has only been accessible through transcribed passages in articles. Early work concentrated on the question of authorship — in one manuscript, it is erroneously attributed to Richard Rolle — but three more recent interpretative studies place it in the context of lay religious life in late medieval England.[14]

---

[12] For the Maubuisson manuscript and those owned by Marie de Berry and Thomine de Villequier, see Chapter 4. For the Poor Clares and Margaret of York, see Chapters 5 and 6.

[13] Clark, 'Constructing the Female Subject in Late Medieval Devotion', pp. 160–68, drawing on Hasenohr, 'La Vie quotidienne de la femme vue par l'Eglise' (reprinted and updated in Hasenohr, *Textes de dévotion et lectures spirituelles en langue romane*, pp. 631–711).

[14] On the attribution to Rolle, see Allen, *Writings Ascribed to Richard Rolle*, pp. 335–37. The more recent studies are Carruthers, 'In Pursuit of Holiness Outside the Cloister'; Whitehead,

The French text has remained shadowy, however, and while its textual history is referred to briefly in works on the English translation, chiefly in attempts to identify a source manuscript, there is a tendency to regard the *Abbaye*'s features as products of the time and place of its translation, rather than that of its composition, which must have been a century earlier.[15] It is therefore important to identify the original features of the French text and place them in the context of the religious developments of the second half of the thirteenth century. Seeing the French tradition simply as background to the English translation also ignores its considerable development during the fifteenth century, when three new versions were produced. Yet the complexity of the French textual tradition was made clear by Kathleen Chesney half a century ago, in an article that remains a vital reference for any work on the French *Abbaye*. She established the existence of a number of different versions in a variety of manuscripts spanning the period from the late thirteenth century to the last quarter of the fifteenth, some of which could be linked to aristocratic female patrons, and suggested that the text had been reworked several times for new audiences.[16] To that list of reworkings we can now add a version made for Franciscan nuns in the early fifteenth century.[17]

Three recent scholars devote some attention to the French *Abbaye*, each dealing with a single version. Kathryn A. Hall's doctoral dissertation examines all of the manuscripts known to Chesney, essentially accepting her view of their relation to each other, but its main focus is on the adaptations made to the version for Margaret of York, in which Hall sees some cross-fertilization from the English translation.[18] The most thorough treatment of a stage of the French tradition is in Aden Kumler's study of illuminated manuscripts of spiritual instruction for women. In her chapter on the illuminated *Somme le roi* manuscript (now BL, MS Additional 28162 and MS Yates Thompson 11) which contains a version of the *Abbaye* and other short spiritual treatises accompanied by full-page miniatures, she treats the text in some detail, exploring its

'Making a Cloister of the Soul in Medieval Religious Treatises'; Rice, 'Spiritual Ambition and the Translation of the Cloister'.

[15] Whitehead, for instance, makes perceptive comments on the place of the *Abbey* in the development of vernacular religious literature, but relates it to the late fourteenth century. Whitehead, *Castles of the Mind*, pp. 77–78; Whitehead, 'Making a Cloister of the Soul in Medieval Religious Treatises', pp. 16–19.

[16] Chesney, 'Notes on Some Treatises of Devotion', pp. 13–17.

[17] Pinder, 'Un recueil picard de lectures spirituelles pour des sœurs franciscaines'.

[18] Hall, 'The Abbey of the Holy Ghost'.

relation to both the images and the other texts that accompany it.[19] Nicole Rice's comparative study gives the most comprehensive and nuanced account to date of the ways the English translation modifies its French source, but is only concerned with the version that is closest to the English, and gives the impression that the French tradition stopped at the point where the English translation was made.[20]

All of this work draws on Chesney's article for the history of the French text. Since that article was published, however, four new manuscripts have been discovered, including a much earlier one of the version on which the English translation is based, and further information on some of the manuscripts has become available. It is now possible to revise the history of the text, and in particular to reposition Chesney's version *c* as the original from which the others are derived, and her version *a* as an early reworking for a new audience. By studying the differences between versions, and sometimes between individual manuscripts, we can now begin to uncover the processes of adaptation and readaptation to new audiences that made the *Abbaye* a fruitful case study for the development and use of vernacular spiritual advice.

The history of the text is part of a larger story, however. In recent years, work on medieval texts has moved beyond individual text studies towards considering works in their manuscript context, taking into account the material aspects of the manuscript — codicological features including appearance, layout, and structuring of quires — and thematic content, which might give a clue to the reasons for the choice of texts, particularly where evidence of manuscript ownership is available.[21] Many studies have demonstrated the fruitfulness of a 'whole book' approach to multiple-text manuscripts.[22] For the *Abbaye*, which

---

[19] Kumler, *Translating Truth*, pp. 161–237.

[20] Rice, 'Spiritual Ambition and the Translation of the Cloister'; Rice, *Lay Piety and Religious Discipline*, pp. 21–28.

[21] Proclaimed as the 'New Philology' by Stephen Nichols in the 1990 special number of *Speculum* devoted to the subject, it is called 'materialist philology' by Nichols and Wenzel in the introduction to their influential edited volume, *The Whole Book*. This approach is no longer new, as was pointed out already in 2004, in Echard and Partridge, *The Book Unbound*, p. xii.

[22] The title of the Nichols and Wenzel volume cited in the preceding note has provided a label for an approach, used by subsequent students of miscellany manuscripts, represented for example in Bell and Couch, *The Texts and Contexts of Oxford, Bodleian Library, ms. Laud misc. 108*. A similar development has taken place in French scholarship, and can be seen in Mikhaïlova-Makarius, *Mouvances et jointures du manuscrit au texte médiéval*; Leroux, *La Mise en recueil des textes médiévaux*; Collet and Foehr-Janssens, *Le Recueil au Moyen âge*; Van Hemelryck and Marzano, *Le Recueil au Moyen Âge*.

is never the sole text in a manuscript, this approach is particularly pertinent and has already been used to good effect in Nicole Rice's short studies of some manuscripts containing Middle English religious advice works, including the *Abbey of the Holy Ghost*, and Aden Kumler's study of MS Additional 28162 and MS Yates Thompson 11.[23] Allied with this approach and moving beyond the individual manuscript, textual study has been enriched by tracing text networks, in the way used for example by Wybren Scheepsma in his study of the Limburg Sermons, a fourteenth-century collection of Flemish devotional texts whose networks intersect with those of the *Abbaye*.[24]

I use a combination of these approaches in Part I of this book, examining the differences between the base version of the *Abbaye* and its successive reworkings against the ownership, construction, and content of the manuscripts it appears in, and the transmission networks it is implicated in through those manuscripts. The first chapter provides a broad contextualization of the *Abbaye* within Latin and vernacular traditions, showing its origins in monastic formation literature of the twelfth and early thirteenth centuries and links to vernacular traditions among Cistercian nuns, and identifying thematic and rhetorical features it shares with other vernacular works of spiritual advice. The triangulation of networks of textual transmission, content analysis of individual manuscripts, and close reading of the *Abbaye* and related texts in Chapter 2 allows me to argue that the *Abbaye* was originally created in an urban environment in northern France or southern Flanders, in a context of experimentation with new forms of religious life among the laity where features of beguinal life and prayer were familiar and viewed with approval. Chapters 3 to 6 follow the subsequent reworkings of the text in a series of curated miscellanies, considering in each case evidence of the audience and purpose of the miscellany, the nature of the alterations made to the *Abbaye*, and its relation to the other texts with which it appears. In Chapters 3 and 4 the *Abbaye* enters the ambit of moral education of aristocratic women of high rank, both nuns and laywomen. Chapter 3 is concerned with the *Sainte abbaye*, long considered the original version of the text because of the early date of one of its manuscripts, arguing that it is an adaptation made for Cistercian nuns and their royal visitors. It re-examines the prestigious Maubuisson manuscript in which it is found and uncovers a trace of its continuing circulation among royal women in a copy made for the chaplain of the dowager queen Blanche de Navarre. Chapter 4 continues to follow the reception of the *Sainte abbaye*, examining an adaptation made for

[23] Rice, *Lay Piety and Religious Discipline*, pp. 136–40. Kumler, *Translating Truth*, pp. 161–237.

[24] Scheepsma, *The Limburg Sermons*, pp. 370–78.

a noblewoman at the beginning of the fifteenth century and transmitted in a collection of moral and spiritual works accompanying the *Miroir des dames*, a work of moral advice originally composed for Philip IV's queen, Jeanne de Navarre. Chapter 5 sees the *Abbaye* return to its urban roots with an adaptation for Franciscan nuns in Picardy, while in Chapter 6 it appears once again in the service of a powerful woman's spiritual self-fashioning and representation, with the late fifteenth-century version created for the Duchess of Burgundy, Margaret of York.

Part II provides editions of the five distinct states of the text, with an English translation of the earliest version. Although all states of the text visibly share an underlying structure, and repeat some content, there can be no question of a single edition; to attempt one would be to create an artificial entity which no medieval reader ever encountered.

To provide a reference point for the following chapters, I conclude this introduction with a summary of the text's history, as it appears from the surviving manuscripts. It is outlined as simply as possible here; full details of the manuscripts and their relationships are provided in Part II.

French Manuscripts and Groups

The *Abbaye du saint Esprit* survives in thirteen known manuscripts. Two others perished in the Second World War, and fragments of the text are recombined in a further manuscript. Working from the nine manuscripts known to her, Kathleen Chesney established four groups which she saw as a series of successive reworkings, each one adding to what was in the preceding one, and numbered them *a–d*. For her, *a* was the original, and *b* and *c* roughly contemporary reworkings for different audiences, with *d* then building on *c*. Chesney's argument for the priority of version *a* rested on an assumption that the process of adapting a text would involve addition rather than deletion, and on the fact that *Y*, dated 1295, seemed to be the earliest witness to the text. The discovery of manuscript *C*, however, which is almost contemporary with *Y* but gives the text of Chesney's version *c*, throws doubt on that argument. The transcription quoted above, published by Paul Meyer of the beginning of the copy in the lost manuscript *M*, which he dated to the late thirteenth or very early fourteenth century, indicates that it, too, was an early witness to Chesney's version *c*.[25] It seems then, from the surviving manuscript evidence, that at the end of the thir-

---

[25] Meyer, 'Notice du ms. 535 de la Bibl. Mun. de Metz', p. 43.

teenth century two closely related redactions of the *Abbaye* existed in different places and went on to have different, separate histories.

One redaction, α, was already dispersed over a wide geographic area by the beginning of the fourteenth century, which suggests that it had already been circulating for some time. The earliest known copy was in a manuscript made in Metz around the turn of the century, and a copy apparently derived from the Metz manuscript was made in Liège in the early fourteenth century. Just before that, another copy was made in the diocese of Cambrai, and two more were made in the first half of the fourteenth century, one in Metz and one somewhere in the region of Paris. This stage of the text I have labelled α_1. Later in the century, a copy of α_1 made its way across the Channel and was translated into Middle English. Two further French developments of this redaction were produced during the fifteenth century: one radical reworking in Picardy early in the century (γ), and one in Ghent in 1475 (α_2). Neither of those can be linked to any existing manuscript of α_1.

The other redaction, β, seems to have been confined to the Paris region. It first appears in a manuscript dated to 1295 and is known to have been housed in the royal abbey of Maubuisson in the fifteenth century. A faithful copy of the text as it appears in that manuscript was made in the late fourteenth century for Pierre Basin, chaplain of the dowager queen Blanche de Navarre. These two manuscripts form the group β_1. A new version, identifiably based on this redaction but with some modification, was included in a collection of ethical and spiritual works for a noble lay woman in the first decade of the fifteenth century (β_2). The collection survives in four copies, three of which are associated with the family of Jean, Duke of Berry.

The geographic dispersion of the early copies and the variety of readings they contain suggest that the text had already been in circulation for a few years, probably in the form of unbound quires.[26] The original could therefore have been composed in the 1270s or 1280s. It is likely that the original was closest to α. While β was certainly very early, the wide geographic distribution of α and its continuing influence weigh in its favour. In Chapter 2 I will argue that it bears the strongest traces of the original audience of the *Abbaye*.

---

[26] On the circulation of short texts in unbound quires, some of which survived through being incorporated in manuscript compilations, see Hasenohr, 'Les Recueils littéraires français du XIIIe siècle'.

Part I

Chapter 1

THE CLOISTER OF THE SOUL
AS A LAY RULE OF LIFE

In this chapter I consider the *Abbaye* as a whole, rather than its individual variants, and situate it within Latin and vernacular traditions of spiritual formation literature. I seek to move beyond the simple search for sources to consider more broadly the processes of transformation engaged in by vernacular writers as they forged new works from the raw material derived from monastic patristic writers such as Augustine, Bernard, and the Victorines. Scholars have described the *Abbaye* as a sermon, a lay rule, a letter of spiritual direction, and a meditation. Two of these terms, sermon and rule, are used in versions of the text itself and the rubrics of manuscripts it was copied into. All these descriptions encompass a notion of teaching, reflecting the generic term for vernacular spiritual writing found in many inventories and wills: *enseignement*. To gather together its teachings on the development of the spiritual life the *Abbaye* adapts an allegorical framework derived from monastic formation literature of the twelfth century. This Latin cloister allegory tradition, which will be described below in more detail, maps virtues onto the spaces of daily life in a monastery, such as the chapter house, refectory, and dormitory, to teach about the ordering of the interior life. This chapter explores these two aspects of the *Abbaye*, framework and teachings, and attempts to throw light on the composition process and materials used by the original author. As is the case with many medieval texts, we do not have direct access to that author's work, only to later copies, so we cannot say for certain what

form it took. In this discussion, I therefore focus on features that are common to most of the versions.[1]

The *Abbaye* has been classed in the genre of lay rules of life, which by their very nature — applying the concept of a rule, drawn from the monastic sphere, to the lay world — blur the boundaries between monastic and lay. The way the *Abbaye* does this, however, is different from most other vernacular rules. Rather than setting out a programme of daily activity for the devout laywoman to perform in her own home, it constructs an imagined space through its adaptation of the monastic cloister allegory, drawing on several traditions. This creates a framework that functions on two levels. It affords a set of spaces for the author to bring together (gather) teachings on aspects of the spiritual life that he judges necessary for, or of interest to, his audience. For the audience, it provides a structure for recalling the content after reading. Such a framework would have been very familiar to lay audiences from preaching.[2] Indeed many would have experienced texts like the *Abbaye* through hearing them read aloud, and would therefore have processed the content in the same way as listening to a sermon.

To make sense to its audience, however, the framework must be constructed from elements they know about, and which have meaningful associations for them. As recent scholars of the *Abbaye* and its English translation have noted, the Latin cloister allegories were written for monks whose daily lives were lived out within the spaces referred to in the texts, while for the lay readers of a vernacular text like the *Abbaye*, the nexus between the real spaces of daily life and the allegorical spaces is broken.[3] In the cloister allegories written for monks, the physical spaces of the monastery could act as cues to recall the spiritual content of the allegory as the monks passed through them in the course of their daily activities. The vernacular allegory, however, evokes different spaces from those surrounding its lay readers, and therefore requires of them an effort of imaginative construction, which relies on details provided in the text and any familiarity they might have with the broader aspects of life in a monastery. The architectural framework provided for a lay audience is therefore necessarily more archetypal, less concerned with the minutiae of monastic life. This has been

---

[1] Quotes from versions of the *Abbaye* are from the editions in the second part of this book (designated by the version number: α_1, β_2, etc.) unless they refer to a significant manuscript variant reading.

[2] For the use of allegorical and other mnemonic structuring techniques in sermons, see Rivers, *Preaching the Memory of Virtue and Vice*.

[3] Whitehead, *Castles of the Mind*, p. 79; Kumler, *Translating Truth*, p. 236.

noted in relation to the German vernacular cloister allegories, where Gerhard Bauer points out the absence of more specialized monastic spaces, those with which lay people, presumably, would be less familiar.[4] This observation is borne out for the *Abbaye* by the locations used in the Latin cloister allegories that it does not take up — the place for hand-washing, the parlour, the warming room — which would arguably be less familiar to people outside a monastery than the major spaces of chapter, refectory, and dormitory. Indeed, some vernacular authors of works on the interior life preferred to construct allegories on the more familiar domestic spaces of the house or the castle. Another departure by the *Abbaye* from the Latin cloister allegories also indicates that it is privileging the ways lay people relate to religious foundations: the identification of God the Father as founder rather than supreme abbot. Founding a monastery was a favoured means for the lay elite to participate in the salvific work of monasticism while remaining in the world.[5]

The disconnection of the metaphorical space of the abbey from the lived environment of the readers moves the operation of the allegory to a more imaginative and symbolic level. Part of the framework's appropriateness rests on the desire of the reader (as constructed by the author in the text) to be part of the monastic project, and to be included among those who are eligible to undertake work towards spiritual perfection. For such a reader, the framework allows the act of reading itself to be an imaginative performance of the content — the reader, directly addressed several times, can situate herself among the nuns of her spiritual cloister and participate in the drama of the incursion and expulsion of Satan's daughters.[6]

The content gathered in each of the allegorical spaces reveals a familiarity with monastic culture, possibly mediated through collections of texts for preachers, and with its expression in the vernacular, suggesting a clerical author with an interest in the pastoral care of women. The earliest versions suggest an author who assumes that his audience will not be put off by learned references in Latin, although most of them are translated and none of the theology they support is complex. The text constructs the audience as laywomen who desire to participate in a regulated life and aspire to spiritual perfection. This much can be gleaned from an examination of the common elements of the *Abbaye*. For a more specific

[4] Bauer, *Claustrum animae*, p. 305.

[5] Pinder, 'Love and Reason from Hugh of Fouilloy to the *Abbaye du Saint Esprit*', pp. 81–82.

[6] Here I draw on Mary Suydam's application of performance theory to medieval devotional texts: Suydam, 'Beguine Textuality'.

picture of its reception and use, we must turn to the actual instances in which the *Abbaye* was copied, which will be the work of Chapters 2 to 6.

Early scholars felt that although the *Abbaye* did not correspond exactly to any known Latin texts, there must have been a Latin original, now lost. Today we are less inclined to think that religious writing in the vernacular must be directly based on a Latin model, but even were we not, the structure of this text should warn against the likelihood of a single source. As John Conlee observed in his brief summary of the English translation, *The Abbey of the Holy Ghost*, the structure of this text is a fusion of three distinct parts: the construction of the abbey, which focuses on the buildings; the peopling of the abbey, which allegorizes the nuns; and the narrative of the four daughters of Satan, which recounts the infiltration of the abbey by discordant elements and the restoration of order.[7] Each of these parts has its own set of relations to other texts. In the first part of the chapter I examine these sets of relations, which provide an example of the synthesis of content from multiple sources which was often involved in the adaptation of monastic material for lay use.

As noted earlier, the text also has affinities with the genres of the letter of spiritual direction and the lay religious rule, presenting a rule of life for women analogous to a monastic rule. In this it is echoing a tradition going back to Jerome, but also present in many other vernacular religious works. In the second part of the chapter I turn to the relations between the *Abbaye* and other vernacular rules of life, examining some examples of the teaching material gathered in the spaces afforded by the allegorical framework. Subsequent chapters will examine the variants of this material in the individual versions of the *Abbaye* in the context of the manuscript anthologies in which they are reproduced.

The Abbaye and Latin Cloister of the Soul Traditions

The first part of the *Abbaye*, the construction of the buildings, situates it in a tradition of allegories of the cloister of the soul, itself part of a wider tradition of architectural allegory. This tradition has been comprehensively described by Christiania Whitehead, while ways in which the *Abbaye* differs from that tradition have been discussed more recently by Aden Kumler.[8] Neither of these

---

[7] Conlee, 'The Abbey of the Holy Ghost and the Eight Ghostly Dwelling Places', p. 140. Aden Kumler describes this three-part structure as 'a cloister allegory in three acts: construction, installation and reformation'. *Translating Truth*, p. 196.

[8] Whitehead, 'Making a Cloister of the Soul in Medieval Religious Treatises'; Whitehead, *Castles of the Mind*; Kumler, *Translating Truth*, pp. 201–05.

discussions goes into the specifics of the resemblances between the Latin and French texts, so it is appropriate here to briefly outline the Latin cloister allegory in order to assess its relation to the *Abbaye*.

The allegorical monastery first appears in the twelfth century, in Hugh of Fouilloy's *De claustro animae*.[9] Hugh was prior and reformer of the Augustinian house of Saint-Laurent-au-Bois at Fouilloy, close to Corbie, in Picardy.[10] He wrote a number of shorter instructional works for novices, but *De claustro animae* is his longest and most developed work. It reflects the central concern of twelfth-century religious renewal, that observance should reflect and be nourished by an interior life that conforms to the spirit of the Gospels. The treatise consists of four books: the first two deal with the literal sense of the religious life and its practicalities, while the third and fourth present the allegorical and anagogic senses. It is the third book, in which Hugh attempts to give shape to the interior life, that has provided the model for subsequent cloister allegories. It lists the structures of the monastic enclosure — cloister, guest house, chapter house, refectory, dormitory, oratory — and elaborates on each in turn, equating various parts with virtues, spiritual qualities, and types of behaviour. As Whitehead notes, Hugh's allegory provides a mnemonic framework for knowledge about the interior life, at the same time investing the daily routine and setting that provide the framework with more spiritual meaning.[11]

De claustro animae was widely copied, and it seems to have been appreciated as a manual of spiritual formation, giving rise to a number of adaptations.[12] But it was probably the early thirteenth-century reworking of Hugh's text by another Augustinian, John, prior of Saint-Jean-des-Vignes near Soissons, that had the greatest consequences for the uses of the allegory of the cloister in the vernacular.[13] Taking Book III and parts of Book IV, he reduced the allegory to the bare bones of its architectural framework and expressed it as a set of simple

[9] Hugh of Fouilloy, *De claustro animae*.

[10] Gobry, 'Hugues de Fouilloy'. Gobry dates the treatise to around 1153.

[11] Whitehead, 'Making a Cloister of the Soul in Medieval Religious Treatises', pp. 4–5.

[12] There are 176 surviving manuscripts: Gobry, 'Hugues de Fouilloy', col. 882. See also Baron, 'Note sur le *De Claustro*'. On the influence of the *De claustro*, see Whitehead, 'Making a Cloister of the Soul in Medieval Religious Treatises', pp. 4–5, and Pinder, 'Love and Reason from Hugh of Fouilloy to the *Abbaye du Saint Esprit*', pp. 68–72. The *De claustro* was often erroneously attributed to Hugh of St Victor, which helps to explain the heading of β$_2$: *Le livre du cloistre de l'ame, que Hue de Saint Victor fist.*

[13] Bauer, *Claustrum animae*; Oury, 'Le "De Claustro Animae" de Jean, prieur de Saint-Jean-des-Vignes'.

equivalences arranged as a set of steps for the soul to reach union with God, short enough to be delivered as a sermon.[14] He took verse 2. 4 of the Song of Songs, 'Introduxit me rex in cellam vinariam, ordinavit in me caritatem', as his opening theme. A number of vernacular translations were made of this work. Besides the German and Dutch translations listed by Gerhard Bauer, there are two French versions.[15]

At about the same time as John was writing *Introduxit me rex*, William of Auvergne composed a similar work, also called *De claustro animae*, which survives in fourteen manuscripts.[16] This work is not derived from that of Hugh of Fouilloy but may well have been inspired by it. It is very similar in intention, adopting a reforming tone and making frequent comments to connect the allegory with real monastic life. The structure is very similar, although the buildings are introduced in a different order, and the abbot is Charity, rather than Reason (Hugh) or Intellect (John). While not achieving the popularity of Hugh's *De claustro*, and apparently not inspiring any vernacular translations, William of Auvergne's allegory did leave some vernacular traces. The French translation of *Introduxit me rex* found in BnF, MS fonds français 423 and BL, MS Additional 15606 seems to have used some elements of William's work, notably in identifying the abbot of the spiritual cloister with Charity. An Anglo-Norman cloister allegory may have based its ordering of the buildings on William's while also using elements of *Introduxit me rex*.[17]

A comparison of the first part of the *Abbaye* with the texts of the Latin cloister tradition reveals a number of parallels, not so much with Hugh's *De claustro*, but with the much shorter text derived from it, *Introduxit me rex*. The first sequence of four elements (foundations, walls, cloister, chapter house) is the same. After that the two texts have another five elements in common (refectory, chapel, dormitory, infirmary, cellar), although not in the same order. While one could argue that these commonalities can be explained by the necessary fea-

---

[14] Bauer, *Claustrum animae*, p. 289. There is an edition of *Introduxit me rex* on pp. 377–87. In the citations below, numbers refer to the line numbers in Bauer's edition, followed by the page number.

[15] See Bauer, *Claustrum animae*, p. 293. The two French versions are a fairly faithful translation in BL, MS Royal 16 E XII, fol. 148ra, and Munich, Bayerische Staatsbibliothek, MS cod. gall. 914, fol. 94rb, and a freer adaptation in BnF, MS fr. 423 (also online at <beta.biblissima. fr/ark:/43093/mdata0857cfa4e2f675ed37008a6fa963084fff24ec36>), fol. 142vb, and BL, MS Additional 15606, fol. 156va.

[16] Oury, 'Le "De Claustro Animae" de Jean, prieur de Saint-Jean-des-Vignes', p. 432.

[17] Published by Hunt, 'An Allegory of the Monastic Life'.

tures of the shared framework, there are also some close parallels in matters of detail. The stones making up the walls are in both texts said to be good works. 'Muro etenim bonorum operum' (6, p. 377). In the chapel (*oratorium*), 'jubilus canit' (73–74, p. 381), recalling *Jubilation*, the assistant to the choir-mistress *Oroison*, in the *Abbaye*. Another common element, the monastery clock (*horologium*, *orloge*), has a similar set of associations in the Latin and French texts, although they do not correspond exactly: the *horologium* is 'sollicitudo divine laudationis' (116, p. 384), while in the *Abbaye* it is 'jalousie et amors de perfeccion'.[18] Finally, the 'religion espirituel' of the *Abbaye* finds a parallel in 'Cella est religio spiritualis' (3, p. 377).

While these similarities suggest strongly that the author of the original *Abbaye* knew *Introduxit me*, it is not the only Latin cloister with which the *Abbaye* has parallels. Some details not present in *Introduxit me* are shared with William of Auvergne's *De claustro*. Two of the monastic buildings, the granary and the cellar, occur in the *Abbaye* and William's cloister, but not in Hugh's or in John's adaptation. As in William's cloister, the oratory of the *Abbaye* is devotion and the dormitory is contemplation. The relation between *devotio* and *contemplatio* is expressed by William as the spatial relation between the oratory and dormitory, which positions the dormitory (*contemplatio*) above the oratory (*devotio*). In the *Abbaye* a similar positioning of the granary above the cellar places meditation above devotion, and the identification of contemplation with the dormitory is justified by that room's elevation. The bells of William's oratory are sighs and laments, as are the *clochettes* which, echoing the words of a secular song, awaken the heart to love of God in the *Abbaye*. Finally, the abbot of William's *Claustrum* is Charity, like the abbess of the *Abbaye*. It seems likely then that the original author of the *Abbaye* took overall inspiration and a basic structure from *Introduxit me rex* but was also familiar with William of Auvergne's *De claustro* and, like the author of the *Introduxit me* French translation, incorporated some details from it. The two Latin texts were sometimes copied together, which would make it easy for an adapter to draw on both.[19]

---

[18] I translate these terms by 'clock', although in the thirteenth century, as David Landes points out, *horologium* could refer to any device for telling the time and can only reliably be taken to mean a mechanical clock in the fourteenth century: Landes, *Revolution in Time*, p. 53. Among the *Abbaye* manuscripts, *R* and *Y* both contain the phrase 'auloge de religion qui chiet aus matines', and the use of the verb *cheoir*, 'fall', suggests a water clock: Dohrn-van Rossum, *Die Geschichte der Stunde*, p. 60.

[19] Both texts appear in Tours, Bibliothèque municipale, MS 399 and Città della Vaticano,

Perhaps the best way to think of the way the *Abbaye du saint Esprit* relates to the Latin cloister tradition is to use the idea elaborated by Mary Carruthers of allegory as a tool for composition.[20] The *Abbaye* has been classed among building allegories, with the suggestion that the architectural structure of the monastery simply provides a convenient set of places for storing information that the reader can then retrieve at will.[21] But the monastic art of memory as expounded by Carruthers is predominantly an art of invention that aided composition. In the monastic context, it functioned as a tool for meditation, a way of building prayer. It was built upon by preachers as an aid to constructing sermons, both to aid the preacher to remember and order his material, and to help the listener to make sense of it.[22] Looked at from the point of view of the author of the *Abbaye*, the framework of the monastery suggested by the Latin cloister tradition provides a set of loci within which to elaborate ideas on the spiritual life and to gather authorities. Furthermore, these loci are available to each subsequent *remanieur*, providing the possibility of an infinite set of variations — a process which will be explored in the later chapters on successive moments in the manuscript tradition of the French *Abbaye*.

A Feminine Cloister

The discussion of the *Abbaye*'s relation to existing textual traditions has thus far focused on the allegory of the abbey buildings, which occupies the first part of the text. The second part, the list of nuns who hold offices in the abbey, starting with the abbess and ending with the sacristan, does not correspond directly to any of the Latin texts we have mentioned. Hugh of Fouilloy does evoke some of the obedientiaries of the monastery in his elaborations of individual monastic spaces; for example, in the section on the chapter house he names the abbot as Reason, who presides over the chapter in which virtues accuse each other of their possible excesses. In the guest house, Charity opens the door, Cheerfulness receives the guests, Affability feeds the hungry, and Humility serves the weary.[23] The buildings, nonetheless, provide his main structuring

---

Biblioteca Apostolica Vaticana, MS Latinus Reginensis 444: see Bauer, *Claustrum animae*, pp. 362–63.

[20] Carruthers, *The Craft of Thought*, esp. p. 9.

[21] Whitehead, 'Making a Cloister of the Soul in Medieval Religious Treatises', pp. 4–5.

[22] Rivers, *Preaching the Memory of Virtue and Vice*, pp. 4–5.

[23] Hugh of Fouilloy, *De claustro animae* III. 5, cols 1091d–1092a.

metaphor. Later writers, however, exploited the possibilities afforded by the personnel of the monastery to create an allegorical structure of their own; an allegory of monastic office holders first appears in a thirteenth-century Latin text, generally entitled *Claustrum Animae cum dispositionae officiorum et officialem suorum*.[24] But this text is still not an abbey of nuns; despite their feminine grammatical gender, the virtues that constitute these monastic officers are portrayed as monks.

The feminine abbey peopled by virtues seems to be a creation of the thirteenth century. There are two examples earlier than the *Abbaye du saint Esprit*, both associated with Cistercian women's communities and with outstanding figures in women's vernacular theological writing.[25] The earlier of the two is a cloister passage associated with Beatrice of Nazareth (1200–1268), a Cistercian nun who had been educated by beguines. In Part II, Chapter 7 of the *Vita* of Beatrice, the anonymous hagiographer describes a spiritual exercise she practised: she built a cloister in her heart and peopled it with virtues.[26] This chapter may have been based on a vernacular text written by Beatrice herself, as was Chapter 12, which translated and adapted her treatise on mystical ascent, *Seven Manieren van Heiliger Minnen*.[27] It is likely that these vernacular texts reflected oral teaching that Beatrice gave the nuns under her care.[28] The offices listed in Beatrice's cloister are similar to those of the *Claustrum Animae cum dispositione officiorum et officialem suorum*, but their holders, as well as being female, are different virtues. Beatrice's abbess is Reason, like the abbot in *De claustro animae*. The prioress of her abbey is Wisdom, and the sub-prioress is Prudence. The supreme authority, however, rests with the abbot, who is God.

The Saxon beguine Mechthild of Magdeburg (1212–*c*. 1282), in the seventh chapter of *The Flowing Light of Godhead*, a work of theological reflection on her mystical experience, describes a vision in which virtues appear as nuns in a spiritual convent.[29] Mechthild's allegory is quite independent from Beatrice's;

[24] The manuscripts are listed in Bauer, *Claustrum animae*, p. 313, n. 11.

[25] What follows recapitulates the discussion of these two texts found in Pinder, 'Love and Reason from Hugh of Fouilloy to the *Abbaye du Saint Esprit*', pp. 73–74.

[26] Reypens, *Vita Beatricis*, pp. 81–83.

[27] Pedersen, 'Can God Speak in the Vernacular?', p. 191. The author of the *Vita* claimed to have based his text on Beatrice's writings, and Pedersen identifies the cloister chapter as one of the passages whose style differs from the hagiographer's own.

[28] Pedersen, 'The In-carnation of Beatrice of Nazareth's Theology', p. 64, n. 8.

[29] Mechthild of Magdeburg, *The Flowing Light of Godhead*, trans. by Tobin. The interpretation of the work as theological reflection is Amy Hollywood's, in *The Soul as Virgin Wife*, p. 57.

although the basic framework is the same, the office holders represent different virtues. In her abbey, the abbess is Love, the prioress is Peace, and the sub-prioress is Amiability. Like Beatrice's abbey, Mechthild's is ultimately subordinate to a male, divine authority, in this case a provost named Divine Obedience. This chapter, whose overall emphasis is on harmony, restraint, and uncomplaining obedience, was written after Mechthild retired late in life to the Cistercian nunnery of Helfta, and it may reflect a new consciousness on her part of the virtues needed to maintain a harmonious community.[30]

The appearance of these two independent versions of a feminized cloister allegory indicates that by the late thirteenth century it had become a productive framework for composing spiritual teaching for pious women, teaching which may often have taken place orally within convents. It is interesting that both versions come from Cistercian women's communities, given that in France at least, a number of Cistercian male communities possessed copies of Hugh of Fouilloy's *De claustro animae*, and one of the earliest manuscripts of the *Abbaye* is associated with a Cistercian women's community.[31] Their links with extra-monastic women's piety are equally interesting. The works of both Beatrice and Mechthild are emblematic of a new form of vernacular theological writing produced by women in the thirteenth century, in Flanders, the Rhineland, and Saxony, which emphasized contemplative union with Christ, often expressed in the language of courtly love.[32] Many of these writers are described as beguines, a term that covers a range of ways in which women elected to live a life of prayer and simplicity in small households or larger groups, often caring for the sick or performing textile work.[33] Mechthild for most of her life lived as a beguine, and Beatrice spent part of her childhood with the beguines of Zoutleeuw.[34] As we will see in Chapter 2, the early manuscript tradition of the *Abbaye* places it among works written for, and sometimes by, beguines.

---

[30] Whitehead, *Castles of the Mind*, p. 71.

[31] Peltier, 'Hugues de Fouilloy', p. 35, n. 34. The connection of *Y* with the royal abbey of Maubuisson will be discussed in Chapter 3.

[32] See Barbara Newman's essay, 'La mystique courtoise: Thirteenth-Century Beguines and the Art of Love', in Newman, *From Virile Woman to WomanChrist*, pp. 137–81.

[33] There is now an extensive literature on beguines; the best overviews are McDonnell, *The Beguines and Beghards in Medieval Culture* and Simons, *Cities of Ladies*.

[34] The only sources of biographical information are, for Beatrice, the *Vita Beatricis* (see above, note 26) and for Mechthild of Magdeburg, *The Flowing Light of Godhead*, trans. by Tobin.

The Four Daughters of Satan Narrative

The third textual element of the *Abbaye*, the closing narrative episode of the four daughters of Satan, has no analogues, as far as I know, in Latin or French. The introduction of a narrative element is certainly a departure from the Latin cloister tradition, although narrative allegory is a very important form in both Latin and vernacular writing, both religious and secular. There is, however, a German and Dutch vernacular text about a feminine cloister that parallels the second and third parts of the *Abbaye*. As in the *Abbaye*, the Holy Ghost plays an active role and is reflected in the title of the text. Preserved in four manuscripts from the fourteenth and fifteenth centuries, *Des hilghen gheystes closter* tells how the Holy Ghost built a convent for his beloved daughters, who are all virtues (Humility, Wisdom, Love, Chastity, Temperance, Mercy, Mildness).[35] In the first part he calls them to him and assigns to each her office in the community. In the second, he departs for a while, leaving the nuns, his daughters, to look after themselves (in one version, he warns them not to go out while he is away). Then Satan, who is described as a powerful local lord, sends his daughters to beg for admission, and once admitted, they set about taking over the convent. The good nuns pray for help and the Holy Ghost returns, drives out the interlopers, and remains in the cloister. A note at the end explains that this work has a spiritual sense and teaches people to make a cloister of virtues in their soul.

The outline of the narrative is strikingly similar to the *Abbaye*, although there are several differences. Neither the personified virtues that make up the office holders of the convent nor the vices that represent the daughters of the Devil are the same. In the German/Dutch text the vices are the seven deadly sins, while the four daughters in the French version are Envy, Presumption, Murmur or Detraction, and False Judgement; the latter three sins are allied with pride and, along with envy, particularly dangerous to communal harmony.[36] But although the virtues and the offices they are assigned in the German/ Dutch text do not correspond exactly to those of the *Abbaye*, the governing trio is still Love, Wisdom, and Humility (Humility is abbess, Love prioress, and Wisdom procuress). There is clearly a connection between the French *Abbaye* and the German/Dutch version. The presence of the *Abbaye* in bilin-

---

[35] The manuscripts are listed in Bauer, 'Herzklosterallegorien', p. 1158.

[36] Detraction, envy, and boastfulness are among the vices to be guarded against in the early thirteenth-century work of spiritual advice for nuns, *Liber de modo bene vivendi ad sororem*, and its English translation, *The manere of good lyvyng*, ed. by Mouron.

gual areas like Metz and Liège on the one hand, and the fact that the text was also known in Dutch-speaking areas close to the same linguistic border (the Dutch manuscript is from Brabant) on the other, make plausible the idea that both the German and French texts may be descendants of a work created on the borderland of either the French and Dutch or French and German speaking areas.[37] It is tempting to see in the symmetry and coherence of the German/ Dutch text an original creation, on which the daughters of the Devil episode in the French text might be based. The late dates of the German and Dutch manuscripts, however, make it impossible to say that this version predated the French, although it may have been circulating orally at an earlier date. It is also possible that the influence went in the opposite direction, and that the German/Dutch text represents an effort to impose greater coherence on the rather loosely attached parts of the *Abbaye*.[38]

This analysis of the framework of the *Abbaye* shows its author tapping into three allegorical traditions built on the setting and practice of monastic life: the architectural allegory of the cloister tradition stemming from Hugh of Fouilloy, the personification of virtues in a female convent known in women's religious communities in the thirteenth century, and a narrative of vices and virtues that may reflect an existing tradition, or may be an original creation. The synthesis of these three elements provided the template for future reworkings of the text. But even for the original author, they were just the frame within which to gather teachings about the interior life. It is to those teachings we now turn, and to the *Abbaye*'s position in the landscape of vernacular religious texts.

The Abbaye as a Rule of Life

The prologue of the most widely distributed version of the *Abbaye* (α) and the traces in the manuscript tradition of internal addresses to a spiritual daughter place it in the line of letters of spiritual direction to nuns and anchoresses. Many vernacular prose texts of religious instruction, including a number that are copied in manuscripts alongside the *Abbaye*, are framed in this way.[39] Among these, many take the form of a rule of life for people living in the world. They gener-

---

[37] In a similar way to the *sermon du paumier*, which was sometimes transmitted in the same manuscripts as the *Abbaye* — see Scheepsma's discussion in *The Limburg Sermons*, pp. 370–78.

[38] This seems to have been the case with a text based on the English *Abbey*, the *Charter of the Abbey of the Holy Ghost*. Boffey, 'The Charter of the Abbey of the Holy Ghost'.

[39] See, for example, the introductions quoted in nn. 43 and 44 of Hasenohr, 'Les Prologues des textes de dévotion en langue française', p. 601.

ally attempt to impose the routine of monastic prayer and ascetic practices on the person living in a lay household, with a greater or lesser degree of adaptation to the demands of their circumstances.[40] Several features of the *Abbaye* align it with these works, but it also differs from them in important ways.[41]

The prologue indicates that the text is intended as a guide for those who, living in the world, wish to live in a regulated way. Some textual clues indicate that it was thought of in this way from the beginning — the early MS *M* and the copy in *A* call it 'la religion du cuer'— 'religion' meaning in this case something like 'form of life'. It is still being presented as a rule in the fifteenth-century copy in *X*, which calls it 'le rieulle du benoit saint Esprit' (the rule of the blessed Holy Spirit). But unlike the majority of rules for lay people, the *Abbaye* offers little in the way of concrete prescriptions of behaviour.[42] There is no mention, for instance, of the practice recommended by many vernacular guides of meditating on the Passion following the monastic timetable of daily prayer.[43] What it does offer is limited to advice on guarding the senses (the four sides of the cloister) and a very brief reference to decorum, relating to the behaviour taught by the novice mistress, Honesty: 'Demisiele Honestés sera maisteresse de nosvisces et enseignera a honestement vivre et aller et a saintement parler en tel manière que tout cil qui les verront i prignent bon example' (Lady Honesty shall be novice mistress and teach them to live and behave honestly and have holy speech, in such a way that those who see them can follow a good example) (α_1). This simple evocation of proper deportment echoes advice presented more amply in many other lay rules of life, which in most cases goes back to monastic sources.[44] Both the regulation of external behaviour and the regulation of the senses are also common themes in advice on the examination of conscience found in other vernacular texts, sometimes expressed in very similar words to the *Abbaye*.[45] But in general the *Abbaye* operates on a more abstract level, order-

[40] Hasenohr, 'La Vie quotidienne de la femme vue par l'Eglise', pp. 41–43.

[41] Hasenohr has described it as a 'règle de vie féminine' in 'Un Faux Pierre de Luxembourg', p. 177.

[42] Nicole Rice, borrowing from Bourdieu, contrasts the French *Abbaye*'s 'regulated improvisations' with the English version's more prescriptive and regulatory approach: Rice, *Lay Piety and Religious Discipline*, p. 21.

[43] For instance, *Comment on se doit maintenir selonc les heures du jour qui sont contenues en la passion Ihesu Crist*, in BL, MS Royal 16 E XII (*R*), fol. 306.

[44] Important sources were the *Speculum monachorum* by the twelfth-century Cistercian Arnoul de Bohéries, and the *Synonyma* of Isidore of Seville. See Hasenohr, 'Un Faux Pierre de Luxembourg', and Hasenohr, 'Isidore de Séville, auteur ascétique "français"?'.

[45] See the *Règle des cœurs ordonnés*, whose prescribed examination of conscience includes

ing the interior life according to the virtues, rather than governing external behaviour. In this it remains in keeping with the spirit of the Latin works for novices that inspired it, according the same spiritual autonomy to its lay readers as Hugh of Fouilloy and his followers assumed in their charges.[46]

Not all vernacular rules of life were concerned solely with precepts governing daily behaviour. In its focus on underlying virtues and principles, the *Abbaye* has much in common with another 'proto-rule' of lay religious life, the *Regle des fins amans*.[47] The *Regle*, written somewhere in northern France towards the end of the thirteenth century — so at approximately the same time as the *Abbaye* — is addressed specifically to beguines.[48] It does contain some practical prescriptions for dress and behaviour, but much of it, like the *Abbaye*, deals with virtues the reader should cultivate, reflecting what Barbara Newman has called 'a beguinal ethos', that is, a shared set of attitudes which expressed the beguine's intimate friendship with Christ in terms of courtly love, and placed it within an exclusive circle of *fins amans*.[49] Some of those virtues are the same and have similar roles in both texts. Both texts present themselves as rules within

an examination of outward behaviour 'en maintieng, en aler, en venir, en vir, en oïr, en parler, en ouvrer ou en aultre' (in conduct, in going, in coming, in seeing, in hearing, in speaking, in working, or in other matters): Hasenohr, 'Un Enseignement de vie chrétienne du XIIIe siècle et sa postérité', p. 352. A passage from the *Somme le roi* presents a striking parallel with the *Abbaye*, although its emphasis is somewhat different: 'Aprés, doit l'en encore aler es .V. sens dou cors ou l'en peche mout souvent, ou par les eulz en folement reguarder, ou par les oreilles en folement escouter et oïr volentiers mesdisenz, losengiers, menteurs et autres folies; ou par la boiche en folement parler, en trop boire et en trop mengier' (Next, we should proceed to the five senses of the body, by which we often sin, either by the eyes in frivolous looking; or by the ears in frivolous listening and willingly listening to slanderers, flatterers, liars, and other foolishness; or by the mouth in frivolous talk, and eating and drinking too much), *Somme le roi* 56. 311–14. This is one of three similar passages on the senses; the others occur at 55. 81–86, p. 265 and 58. 84–88, p. 334. All quotes from the *Somme* are from Laurent d'Orléans, *La Somme le roi par Frère Laurent*, ed. by Brayer and Leurquin.

[46] Jeroen Laemers has described Hugh of Fouilloy's *De claustro animae* as providing a template for ordering the mind, as a basis for acquiring virtue: Laemers, 'Claustrum animae'.

[47] Rice suggests that the *Règle* is one of the *Abbaye*'s sources, pointing to similarities between the two, but there is no evidence to establish a relationship of dependence in either direction. Rice, 'Spiritual Ambition and the Translation of the Cloister', pp. 235–36.

[48] Edited by Christ, 'La Regle des fins amans' (citations are from this edition), and analysed by Newman, *From Virile Woman to WomanChrist*, pp. 139–43. The manuscript edited by Christ was from Picardy, although the text may have been originally composed in Paris: Christ, 'La Regle des fins amans', p. 183.

[49] Newman, *From Virile Woman to WomanChrist*, p. 139.

an imaginative construct — the order of *fins amans* on the one hand, and the order of the Holy Ghost on the other — which positions the lay reader in relation to an already existing regulated life: courtly love and monastic religious life respectively. The relationship of the *Abbaye* to the *Regle* will be discussed in more detail in Chapter 2.

In its use of the construction metaphor, already present in its Latin sources, the *Abbaye* is also in tune with vernacular religious literature written close to its time. The metaphor was particularly suited to descriptions of self-fashioning, as in the *vita* of the Cistercian nun Alice of Schaerbeck (d. 1250) written at the abbey of Villers near Liège, which says that she strengthened her spiritual edifice by laying a foundation of humility and building on it a layer of obedience. Many works of religious advice variously exhort their reader to build herself a house or a castle, usually in the conscience, with recurring combinations of virtues in similar building motifs.[50] Two texts we will have occasion to look at more closely in Chapter 3 demonstrate the common stock on which all these texts of advice draw. The *Miroir des dames*, composed in the first half of the fourteenth century, advises the queen to construct her house with precious stones made, like those of the *Abbaye* (and of *Introduxit me*), from good works.[51] The *Droite forme de vivre a l'ame* tells its reader to construct a castle whose walls should be made from patience and fortitude to resist attacks with arrows of piercing words and catapult balls of tribulation. This same combination occurs in the *Abbaye*, where Patience and Fortitude construct the pillars that will strengthen the abbey's walls against the winds of tribulation and stinging words. The *Regle des fins amans* also uses construction metaphors, without extending them to a whole building. It speaks of four pillars which support the order, Purity, Poverty, Humility, and Charity, which is also equated with cement (in the *Abbaye*, faith is the cement which binds the stones of good works).

For the *Abbaye*, the metaphor also carries associations with reform. Anne Lester argues that in the thirteenth century, the construction metaphor is underpinned by a close association in the minds of readers between actual rebuilding and reform, pointing to the use made of Francis of Assisi's reconstruction of dilapidated churches to signify his reforming activity.[52] The *Abbaye*

---

[50] Kumler, *Translating Truth*, p. 188, notes that construction metaphors permeate the *Somme le roi* but are not collected within a sustained architectural allegory.

[51] On the *Miroir* and its Latin source, the *Speculum dominarum* of Durand de Champagne, see Durand de Champagne, *Speculum dominarum*, ed. by Flottès-Dubrulle; Mews and others, 'Introducing the *Miroir des dames*'.

[52] Lester, 'Suburban Space and Religious Reform'. The reference to Alice's life is on p. 74.

makes explicit reference to the transformative building activities of the mendicants when it says the pleasant sites they occupy were often formerly very ugly, covered in weeds and filth.[53] Most of its readers, particularly the earliest ones, would have been familiar with the sight of mendicant friars rebuilding ruined sites on the fringes of towns. The reference thus gives a contemporary resonance to the metaphor, drawn from the Latin sources, of the wasteland of the conscience which must be cleared before laying the foundations of the inner abbey.

The final part of this chapter turns to two themes that remain important through all the versions of the *Abbaye* in its advice on the construction of an ordered interior life: enclosure and discipline, on the one hand, and the soul's ascent to God, on the other. These two reference-points of monastic writing are particularly prominent in advice to nuns and carry over into vernacular advice to lay women. They play out in the *Abbaye* in ways that demonstrate the process of using concepts central to monastic formation literature that are also familiar to lay people as a salient feature of monastic life.

Enclosure and Discipline

Enclosure in a monastic context refers to a secure space free from distraction and harm, within which the inhabitants of the monastery remain and from which members of the outside world are excluded. The concept is expressed in a number of ways in the *Abbaye*. The cloister (that is, the four-sided space surrounded by monastic buildings) is evoked as a closed space. In fact, its most salient characteristic is that it is enclosed: 'Pour ce a il a non cloistres qu'i[l] est clos et doit estre clos et bien gardés' (α_1). The four sides of the cloister are associated with four faculties: thought, sight, hearing, and speech. The cloister is to be guarded, or kept, by keeping these faculties under control.

> Fille, se tu vulz estre bien relegieuse si te doit tenir close bien garder ton cloistre. Clorre les ex de legerement regarder. Clorre les oreilles d'autrui mal oïr, la bouce tenir de parler et de rire, le cuer clorre de toute mauuaise pensee. Qui bien gardera et tenra ces .iiii. choses, ele sera bone nonmee et bien religieuse.

> [Daughter, if you want to be a religious woman, you should keep yourself close and guard your cloister. Close your eyes to frivolous looking, your ears to listening to ill of others, hold back your mouth from speech and laughter, close your heart to all

---

[53] 'Sovent est avenu qu'il a mout de biaus lieus, ou as prescheeurs ou as meneurs, qui soloient estre mout lais et mout hideus' (*R*, fol. 132va), 'Sovent est avenus et bien avons veut que orait bel lieu, ou de prechours ou de freres menours, ou il soloit avoir urteil et ordeure' (*A*, fol. 50ra).

wicked thoughts. She who guards and keeps these four things will be called good and truly religious.] (α_1)

This passage reflects a number of concepts already found in monastic literature. One of these is the widespread teaching on the custody of the senses, which was already being applied in vernacular texts as well. According to this teaching, the senses are the doors and windows of the soul; when they are not firmly closed, there is danger. For example, the Cistercian abbot John of Ford (1140/50–1214) warns in a sermon to keep eyes, ears, lips, and all senses of the body under guard, lest death break in and steal the soul's treasure.[54] The *Abbaye* draws explicitly on this notion that the senses (eyes, ears, mouth) are the entrances to the cloister when it says that the portress, *Paors* (Fear of God), must make sure that no evil enters 'parmi la porte de la bouce, ou des iex, ou des oreilles' (through the door of the mouth, or of the eyes, or of the ears) (α_1). The story of the incursion of the daughters of Satan gives a vivid illustration of what happens when *Paors*'s guard is relaxed. This general advice was also explicitly associated in monastic literature with enclosure and the etymology of 'cloister', as is shown by an anonymous twelfth-century text from Peterhausen, quoted by Aden Kumler in her discussion of the cloister passage in *Y*:

Nonne tibi videntur fores tunc bene clausae, quando os a loquendo, aures a vano auditu, manus a malis operibus, pedes vero a vago incessu cohibentur? Velit nolit, monachus tali claustro religatus erit. Fores, inquit, clausae erant. Hinc primo videtur claustri nomen exortum, quod utique, sicut diximus, manere semper debet intus et exterius undique clausum.

[Do not the doors seem well closed to you then, when they restrain the mouth from speaking, the ears from vain listening, the hands from evil works, and indeed the feet from aimless walking? Whether he wishes or not, the monk shall be bound in such a cloister. The doors, he says, were shut. From this, the name of 'cloister' seems to have first arisen, because certainly, as we said, it must always remain, within and without, closed in every respect.][55]

The parallel with the *Abbaye*, even at the verbal level, is striking, as Kumler notes. But that need not suggest a direct borrowing; these teachings circulated widely in Latin and were taken up very widely in vernacular texts. Later ver-

[54] 'Hinc oculos, hinc aures, hinc labia, hinc omnes denique corporis uestri sensus fida munitae custodia, ne qua mors possit irrepere et ad thesaurum reconditum mittere manum suam.' John of Ford, *Super extremam partem Cantici canticorum sermones CXX*, ed. by Mikkers and Costello, line 172, p. 59.

[55] Kumler, *Translating Truth*, p. 204. Translation given by Kumler.

sions of the *Abbaye* show adapters also dipping into this pool to elaborate the cloister passage with variations and examples.

Another commonplace of monastic literature reflected in the cloister passage is that guarding the cloister or keeping it (in the sense of remaining inside) is one of the signs of a good monk. Grounded in Benedict's recommendation of stability, it was so familiar that it could be given a figurative meaning. Alexander Neckam, in his moral work *Solatio Fidelis Animae*, provides a series of recommendations on keeping the mind as well as the body in the cloister, beginning each one with 'Claustrum bene custodit, qui...'.[56] The phrase used in all versions of the *Abbaye*, 'garde ton cloistre' (which, like 'claustrum custodit', covers the two meanings of protect and keep to), is clearly echoing Latin admonitions of this type.

The notions of the guard of the senses as a general moral safeguard, and of keeping the cloister as a requirement of the professed religious, are constants of monastic literature and not exclusively directed at women. In advice for women, however, guarding the cloister was more likely to mean protection against incursion than prevention of wandering. This is reflected very clearly in the statutes of the Sisters of Mary Magdalene in Strasburg, written in 1232: 'sic eciam claustrum firma et diligentissima custodia clausum et custoditum, ne aliquis detur locus diabolo' ('Thus indeed the cloister is to be kept closed and protected by strong and diligent guard, lest the place be given over to the devil').[57] In much spiritual advice for nuns and anchoresses, the enclosed physical space the woman inhabits is equated with the closure of her virginal body, and keeping to the cloister and guarding its entrances become a figure for preserving her virginity. The *Abbaye*, however, departs from this tradition. Although it equates the cloister with a body whose entrances to the world are closely guarded, it does not explicitly make it a virginal body; in fact, it does not mention virginity anywhere as a condition for the holy life. This looks like recognition of the nature of its primary audience, who may well be married women or widows.

Nonetheless, the way the two notions, guarding and staying in the cloister, are framed in the *Abbaye* suggests a close identification with advice to women religious. The *Abbaye*'s graphic account of the Devil's breach of the cloister could serve as an elaboration of the Strasburg statute quoted above. Furthermore, the

---

[56] *Solatium fidelis animae* (*Tractatus Moralium super Genesim qui dicitur Solatium fidelis anime*). Canterbury, Cathedral Library, MS Lit. B. 6, fols 2ra–29vb. I am indebted to Tomas Zahora for this reference.

[57] *Constitutiones Sororum Sanctae Marie Magdalene*, Ch. 3, p. 157, cited by Smith, 'Clausura Districta', p. 28.

framing of the cloister passage implies that religious perfection for a woman can be reduced to the guard of the senses. In most versions of the *Abbaye*, the exhortation to guard the senses is framed as an encapsulation of religious discipline for a woman who would be a perfect nun; *religieuse* carries a double meaning: in the passage from the *Abbaye* it can be read as either an adjective meaning 'observing religious precepts' or as a noun, 'nun'. The guard of the senses is popular in twelfth- and thirteenth-century advice to women religious such as the *Speculum virginum*, *De modo bene vivendi*, and the *Ancrene Wisse*, where the admonition to limit sensory contact with the outside world is often associated, as noted above, with teaching on decorum (keeping eyes lowered, speaking little and in a low voice, moving slowly). The cloister passage opens with 'Fille, se tu vulz estre bien relegieuse si te doit tenir close bien garder ton cloistre' (Daughter, if you want to be a religious woman, you should keep yourself close and guard your cloister), and closes with 'Qui bien gardera et tenra ces .iiii. choses, ele sera bone nonmee et bien religieuse' (She who guards and keeps these four things will be called good and truly religious).[58] This echoes a suggestion in the *Speculum virginum* that keeping enclosure through custody of the senses is an essential part of a nun's 'multiform discipline'.[59] Thus the *Abbaye* is relying heavily on the reader's desire to emulate nuns: 'keeping the cloister' is something that good religious do, and for the reader of the *Abbaye*, doing this through guarding the senses is the essence of perfection, just as it was for the nuns of the *Speculum virginum*. The *Abbaye*'s construction is not presented as creating a dwelling place for God, as is the case with some other architectural allegories. However, the goal of union with God is central to its message and forms the second theme to be considered here.

The Soul's Ascent to God

The soul's ascent to God through contrition, confession, tearful prayer, and meditation is the other major thematic thread of the *Abbaye*. It appears in the part organized around the office holders of the abbey, which focuses on individual aspects of that ascent. The loci of cellarer, granary-keeper, choir-mis-

---

[58] Versions of this wording are found in all manuscripts except those of γ.

[59] 'Inclusio tua, Theodora, pro uitando strepitu uel tumultu suscepta multiformis discipline materia est, quinque sensuum exteriorum custodia, interiorum cautela, conseruandi pudoris occasio, intuendae ueritatis introitus.' (Your enclosure, Theodora, to avoid trouble and tumult is supported by a multiform discipline: custody of the five external senses, caution regarding the interior senses, the opportunity to preserve modesty, contemplating the entrance of truth.) *Speculum virginum*, ed. by Seyfarth, 2. 180.

tress, and sacristan are used to draw together teaching about the nature and importance of devotion and meditation, the kinds of experience those adept at contemplative prayer have, and the consolation the soul receives from prayer praising God. The ordering of this material, and thus the sense of spiritual progression, emerges through the amount of elaboration each element receives at its appropriate locus within the structure, rather than being suggested by a prescribed movement through the monastery buildings. Associating devotion and meditation with the responsibilities of the abbey's nuns rather than with an itinerary within its spaces emphasizes their perennial nature, as something to be always kept in the heart and practised every day. Here the *Abbaye* contrasts strongly with the French translation of *Introduxit me* in BnF, MS fr. 423, which links each place and activity to the one that follows, creating a sense of rapid movement from one to the next: 'Emprés componcion doit venir confessions qui est senefié par le chapitre' (After compunction should come confession, which is signified by the chapter house) (fol. 143va), 'Aprés confession doit on corre a oreisons' (After confession one should run to prayer) (fol. 143vb), and 'Quant arme se part d'oreyson, aler s'en doit en refeitour qui senefie sainte liçon' (When the soul leaves prayer, it should go to the refectory, which signifies holy reading) (fol. 143vb).

The elements of ascent to contemplation are associated with the office bearers of the abbey whose roles receive the greatest elaboration in the text overall: *Meditation* (the keeper of the granary), *Jubilation* (assistant to the choir-mistress, prayer), and *Jalousie* (the sacristan). It is instructive to look more closely at them, as they afford a glimpse of the way the *Abbaye* draws on and adapts a common stock of vernacular adaptations of monastic teaching.

Meditation

Teaching on meditation is assembled under the building of the granary and the person of the granarer. It addresses those who are aiming for spiritual perfection, which once would only have been accessible to those in a religious order: 'C'est li commencement de toute perfection quant cuers se set metre en bien penser a Diu' (It is the beginning of all perfection, when the heart is able to begin thinking about God) (α_1). This goes beyond the counsel of perfection through regulation of behaviour expressed in the cloister passage. The notion of meditation offered by the *Abbaye* is close to the monastic concept of meditation on Scripture (rather than, for example, meditation on one's own sins). Its definition is, in the wording of *R*: 'une vertu qui est bien penser a Dieu et a ses fes et a ses dis, c'est es escriptures' (a virtue which consists of thinking

about God and his deeds and words, that is, about scripture) (fol. 137ra). In the monastic practice of *lectio divina*, of which meditation formed a part, the reading of scripture was often conceived of as taking nourishment and described in terms of chewing and ruminating.[60] Although the *Abbaye* does not use those terms, the metaphor of nourishment is not far away, since Meditation is keeper of the abbey's food store.[61] Meditation is linked to the Eucharist through the allegory of the wheat that the granary keeper gathers together, which is Christ's body, the grain from which the bread of the Eucharist is made. This is the only place in the *Abbaye* where the Eucharist is mentioned, but it has some close affinities with Guiard of Laon's sermon on the twelve fruits of the Eucharist, which will be discussed in Chapter 2.

The bulk of the passage on meditation, however, is concerned with meditation as a stage in the soul's ascent to God and draws on Dionysian theology — indeed, on the form of Dionysian theology articulated in the thirteenth century by Thomas Gallus, which emphasizes ardent love.[62] Some of this passage is similar to advice on prayer from the widely copied digest of moral teaching for lay people, the *Somme le roi*, which gives a clearer picture of some of the sources the *Abbaye* uses. It is worth pausing to examine the passage in detail, as it illustrates both the complexities of vernacular authors' access to and treatment of biblical and theological sources, and the differences between the kinds of prayer the *Somme* and the *Abbaye* are advocating.

The passage in the *Abbaye* asserts that meditation is superior to verbal prayer and indeed transcends it: 'Et tout aussi que li fruis vaut miex des fuelles, tout aussi vaut miex une boine pensee en sainte meditation que moult de paroles dire en oroison' (And just as the fruit is worth more than the leaves, one thought in holy meditation is worth more than saying many words in prayer) (α_1). But the author goes a step further, moving from the idea that non-verbal meditation is better than verbal prayer to that of the silent prayer which occurs when one is rapt in contemplation: 'Et si di encore plus, que quant cuers est pris et eslevés en oroison il ne puet bien dire. Et tant a afere de penser a ce qu'i[l] sent et qu'i[l] voit et qu'il ot, qui ne puet mot dire et parole li faut; si se test por mieus crier et pour mex parler aprés' (And I say it is even more than this, that when the heart is engrossed and lifted up in prayer, it cannot speak. It is so occupied by what it feels and sees and hears, that it can say nothing, and words fail it; thus it is silent the better to cry out, and in order to speak better afterwards)

---

[60] See the examples quoted in Leclercq, *The Love of Learning and the Desire for God*, p. 73.

[61] This definition occurs in some form in all manuscripts of the *Abbaye* except those of γ.

[62] McGinn, *The Flowering of Mysticism*, pp. 78–87.

(α_1). To support this, there is a quotation from Psalm 32. 3 (31. 3), with an interpretation said to come from 'la glose': 'Et de ce dist David: *Quoniam tacui dum clamarem*. Et la dist la glose, li grans cris que nous crions a Diu si est li grans desiriers que nous i avons' (And of this David said: *Quoniam tacui dum clamarem*. And there the gloss says that the great cry we cry out to God is the great desire that we have) (α_1).

This last passage is puzzling as it stands: Firstly, the verse of the psalm is taken out of its penitential context and truncated in a way that changes its meaning. The Vulgate reads 'Quoniam tacui, inueterauerunt ossa mea: dum clamarem tota die'. Secondly, the gloss does not correspond to any in the printed edition of the *Glossa ordinaria*, which all treat 'clamarem' as referring to the laments of the sinner rather than the cry of the soul desiring God. However, its working becomes clearer when we set it beside the much more elaborated passage on prayer from the *Somme le roi*. In the *Somme*'s chapter on prayer (*Oroison*), the subdivision on *devocion de cuer*, which the author glosses as single-minded prayer ('eslever le cuer a Dieu senz penser ailleurs'; raise the mind to God without letting it wander elsewhere), there are some close parallels with the *Abbaye* passage.

Like the *Abbaye*, the *Somme* establishes a hierarchy in the elements of prayer; in the *Somme*, the words of prayer are placed lower than heartfelt devotion. To do so, it uses a variation of the same metaphor that in the *Abbaye* separates words and meditation:

> Tele différence comme il a entre la paille et le grain, entre le bren et la fleur de fourment et entre la pel et la beste, tel différence a il entre le son de l'orison et la devocion dou cuer.

> [The same difference that there is between the straw and the grain, the bran and the wheat flour and between the skin and the beast is found between the sound of prayer and heartfelt devotion.] (*Somme* 58. 204–05)

The author extends the metaphor, saying that God is not a goat that eats leaves — indeed he cursed the tree that produced only leaves (a reference to the barren fig tree of Luke 13. 6–9) — and elaborates on the idea that empty words of prayer are displeasing to God.[63] In this parallel we can see two different reali-

---

[63] This passage is reworked in *Le vergier de la sainte ame*, a text on prayer in the *Abbaye* manuscript *C*, which suggests forcefully that the person who mouths prayers without proper devotion is literally making a goat of Christ: 'car vois de bouche sanz desirier de cuer ne vaut nient plus que mouuoir les leures sans parler [...]. Einsi tient nostre sire pour chieure. Car aussi com paist la chieure des feuilles de larbre sans plus, Sil veut il paistre nostre seingneur de feilles,

zations of what must have been a common teaching on prayer which discouraged the mouthing of empty words. It appears that this common teaching was illustrated, in the manner of good preaching, by a metaphor, which is given full treatment in the *Somme* but abbreviated in the *Abbaye*.

The next step, on prayer that comes from the heart, presents a more complex picture of sources. The author of the *Somme* uses the same idea of the cry from the heart, supported by scripture and gloss, that we find in the *Abbaye*, but the details of the psalm and the gloss are different:

> Qui veut donques veraiement Dieu prier, il doit a Dieu crier du parfont du cuer, comme fesoit David qui disoit ou Sautier: 'Sire Dieux, oiez ma voiz, que je crie a vous dou parfont de mon cuer'. La farveur d'amour est le cri dou cuer, ce dit sainz Augustins. Tiex voiz et tiex cris li plest, non mie noise de paroles acoutrees.

> [Whoever would pray truly to God must cry out to God from the depths of the heart, as David did, who said in the Psalter: 'Lord God, hear my voice, I cry out to you from the depths of my heart'. The fervour of love is the cry of the heart, says Saint Augustine. Such a voice and such cries please Him, not the din of accumulated words.] (*Somme* 58. 221–24)

This time, it is Psalm 130. 1–2 (129. 1–2) that is paraphrased. The gloss, attributed to Augustine, looks at first sight to be different too. It appears to be taken from Augustine's commentary on Psalm 37, where we find:

> Qui tacuerunt? De quibus dictum est: quoniam abundauit iniquitas, refrigescet caritas multorum. Frigus caritatis, silentium cordis est; flagrantia caritatis, clamor cordis est. Si semper manet caritas, semper clamas; si semper clamas, semper desideras; si desideras, requiem recordaris.

> [Who are the people who have fallen silent? Those of whom the Lord said, With iniquity increasing mightily, the love of many will grow cold. The chilling of charity is the silence of the heart; the blazing of charity is the heart's clamor. If your charity abides all the time, you are crying out all the time; if you are crying out all the time, you are desiring all the time; and if you are desiring, you are remembering rest.][64]

Cest a dire de ces parolles sanz deuocion et desirier de cuer' (For sounds from the mouth without desire from the heart is worth no more than moving the lips without speaking [...]. Thus [this person] takes our lord for a goat. For just as the goat eats leaves and nothing else, he wants to feed our lord nothing but leaves, that is, word without devotion and desire from the heart) (fol. 23ʳᵇ).

[64] Augustine, *Enarrationes in Psalmos*, ed. by Dekkers and Fraipont, lines 13–18, p. 392 (Psalm 37. 14). English translation from Augustine, *Expositions of the Psalms*, trans. by Boulding, p. 157.

However, although the *Abbaye* attributes its comment to 'la glose', it is possible that Augustine's commentary is the source of both versions. The *Somme*'s 'La farveur d'amour est le cri dou cuer' is clearly a translation of 'flagrantia caritatis, clamor cordis est', while 'si semper clamas, semper desideras' is plausibly the source of the *Abbaye*'s 'li grans cris que nous crions a Diu si est li grans desiriers que nous i avons'. Augustine was the source for much of the *Glossa ordinaria*'s glosses on the Psalms, and indeed in version β_2 of the *Abbaye*, the reference to 'la glose' is replaced by one to Augustine. What both these vernacular texts seem to reflect is a loose tradition uniting the concept of the cry of the heart with fervour or desire for God, backed by a psalm containing reference to a cry and Augustine's gloss. Neither text quotes the psalm that matches the commentary, although both psalms contain the word *clamor*. It is likely that in this and many other instances, the authors were relying either on memory or on works of reference that contained key words and abbreviated references.

The differences between the two passages in the *Somme* and the *Abbaye* are as interesting as the similarities. The *Somme* advocates a conventional kind of fervent devotion, while the *Abbaye* goes on to link the preferred kind of prayer to contemplation. The continuation of the Meditation section draws explicitly on the theology of contemplation with a supporting quotation from pseudo-Dionysius:

> Et de ce dist S. Denis in *Mistica Theologia*: *Quantum superius ascendimus quantum contemplantibus nobis verba coartancur. Et postea: sine uoce erit totus vinctus immobili.* C'est a dire, quant cuers est bien soulevés et par grant desirier d'amor il ne puet dire ce qui sent, qu'il est si merveilleus et si esbahis que parole li faut.

> [And of this Saint Denis said in *Mystica theologia*: *Quantum superius ascendimus quantum contemplantibus nobis verba coartancur. Et postea: sine uoce erit totus vinctus immobili.* That is to say, when the heart is lifted up by desire of love, it cannot speak what it feels, because it marvels and is so astounded that speech fails it.] (α_1)

Here it looks as though the author of the *Abbaye* has copied the citations ready-made from another treatise. The use of *et postea* in the pseudo-Dionysius passage suggests that it was taken whole from another treatise that quoted the *Mystica Theologia*, as does the fact that the wording does not correspond to either of the best-known Latin translations of pseudo-Dionysius's work.[65]

---

[65] The first part of the quote is closer to the Eriugena translation ('verba contemplationis invisibilium coartantur' rather than 'sermones conspectibus intelligibilium contrahuntur'), while the second is closer to Sarrazin ('totus sine voce erit, totus unietur ineffabili' rather than 'totus sine vocus erit, et totus adunabitur voce carenti'). Chevallier, *Dionysiaca*, p. 589, col. 1,

The Meditation passage concludes with a summary of teaching on the relation between meditation and other stages of prayer. Using an allegory based
on Psalm 4. 8, 'A fructu frumenti, vini, et olei sui, multiplicati sunt', it sets out
a progression that starts with meditation (wheat), goes on to devotion or tearful prayer (wine), and culminates in consolation (oil), which illuminates and
inflames the soul.

Jubilation

The peak of contemplative prayer is elaborated in the passage on Jubilation,
who is assistant to the choir-mistress, Prayer. In it the culmination of prayer is
seen from the angle of *jubilatio*, the soul's outpouring of joy at contact with the
divine. This passage comes earlier in the text than the one on meditation, which
underlines the absence of linear progression in the *Abbaye*, since meditation
could be considered as an earlier part of the process leading to jubilation. The
passage first gives a definition of *jubilatio*, and follows it with an example, elaborated to a different extent in different versions of the *Abbaye*, of the experience
of 'spiritual' people (*genz esperituels*). All versions use the same definition and
attribute it to Gregory the Great:

> Jubilations, ce dist sains Grigoires, si est une tres grans joie qui est conceue en ame
> par grasce aprés orison par amor et par ferveur d'esperite, qui ne puet estre dou tout
> moustree ne dou tout celee.
>
> [Jubilation, Saint Gregory said, is a great joy conceived in the soul by grace after
> prayer by love and by fervour of the spirit, which cannot be entirely shown nor
> hidden.] (α_1)

It is probably drawn from a passage in the *Moralia in Job*:

> Iubilatio quippe dicitur cum cordis laetitia oris efficacio non expletur, sed quibus-
> dam modis gaudium prodit, quod ipse qui gaudet, nec tegere praeualet, nec explere.
>
> [For it is called 'exultation', when the joy of the heart is not fully expressed by the
> power of the voice, but when he who rejoices makes known in certain ways the joy
> which he can neither conceal, nor fully express.][66]

p. 590, col. 3. No copy of the *Abbaye* has these exact words for the second part, however; the
passage seems to have posed problems to scribes from an early date. At some point a scribe interpreted it as 'vinctus immobilis', which underlies the readings of *Y* and *C*.

[66] Gregory the Great, *Moralia in Job*, ed. by Adriaen, p. 1422. I am indebted to Constant
Mews for this reference. English translation from Gregory the Great, *Morals on the Book of Job*,
trans. by Bliss and Marriott, p. 289.

Gregory's point about the inefficacy of words is not expressed in the French translation of the definition, but the idea is clear throughout the passage. The association with song as an alternative to speech is established through the identity of Jubilation as the choir-mistress's assistant. The example, which is drastically abbreviated in some versions, tells of people who express their joy through involuntary song and movement.

The concept of *jubilatio* was not foreign to vernacular spiritual instruction. Similar definitions are also found in other works, such as the *Sermon du palmier*, an allegorical text contemporary with the *Abbaye* and copied beside it in a number of manuscripts (*M*, *C*, *A*, and *R*), which has:

> Et quant ele le sent venu en sen cuer par grasce — si a si grant joie qu'ele ne le puet dire ne taisir du tout.

> [And when she [the soul] perceives that he [the Lord] has come into her heart by grace — she experiences such joy that she can neither express it nor keep silent.][67]

This definition occurs in the description of the nightingale, the bird that sits on the fifth branch of the tree of contemplation, whose song through the night represents the soul waiting in desire for the sight of God. There is a similar passage in a devotional text in an early fourteenth-century Picard collection, Lund, Universitetsbibliotek, MS Medeltidhandskrift 53, fol. 106[r]: 'Quant li ame sent en li le bonté Dieu et les grasces des douls sentemens que Dieux li a fait elle est si au coer ferue et navree que recryer li couvient et joie mener et canter amoureusement' (When the soul perceives the goodness of God within her and the graces and sweet feelings that God has given her she is struck to the heart and wounded, so that she must rejoice and sing like a lover).

Jubilation also appears in the sermon on the twelve fruits of the Eucharist referred to above, where the ninth fruit is described as 'lightness of heart'. This is a movement of the heart culminating in the inarticulate joy of ecstatic union with the divine, here called *jubilus* and defined in the earliest known manuscript in almost the same words as in the *Abbaye*: 'De cest esmouvement vien joie de cuer ke on apele jubilus. Ceste joie ne puet on dire ne ne doit on taire' (From this movement comes joy in the heart, which is called jubilus. This joy cannot be told of, nor should it be silenced).[68]

The concept continued to be used in later texts. It also appears in the *Miroir des dames*, the French translation of the *Speculum dominarum* written by

---

[67] Christ, 'Le Livre du Palmier', lines 151–52.

[68] BnF, MS fonds français 6447, fol. 361ra.

Durand de Champagne for Jeanne de Navarre, wife of Philip IV, in the early fourteenth century, which was copied together with the *Abbaye* in an early fifteenth-century collection of religious advice for a noblewoman. Here, rather than denoting the experience of contemplative union in this world, jubilation is related to the joy of those who dwell in Paradise, but it is clearly Gregory's definition being used again, and the words echo those of the *Abbaye*, although they are following the Latin *Speculum*: 'Jubilacion est une ioie de cueur qui est si grant que nul ne la puet exprimer ne par parole ne par autre signe souffissement montrer' (Jubilation is a joy in the heart so great that no one can express it in words or adequately show it by any other sign).[69]

Jalousie

Space for another reflection on prayer is provided by the final office to be listed, that of the sacristan, who is *Jalousie* (Zeal/Desire). This final passage on the office holders of the *Abbaye* seems to be anchored as much in the world of the lay reader as in the monastic world she is being asked to emulate, blending secular and monastic imagery as it intertwines references to the urban landscape and secular song with biblical references. It revolves around images of wakefulness and waking, blending references to ecclesiastical and secular timekeeping. First come the three kinds of call to wake: the cockcrow of the countryside, the horn of the town watch, and the bell of the monastery. A fourth kind exists for 'contemplation et [...] sainte beguignage' (α_1, α_2, β_1), which is love and desire for perfection. The rest of the passage is permeated with references to the Song of Songs, not always explicitly quoted, but signalled through language that would be familiar to readers of other vernacular spiritual texts. Like many religious who are up and praying before the bell has rung, the zealous heart is woken by love, and not a lazy layabed: 'benoite soit l'arme que amors esveille et qui n'est endormie ne parceuse' (blessed be the soul woken by love, for it is neither asleep nor lazy) (α_1). This makes sense in relation to the monastic imagery of getting up to pray, but 'endormie ne parceuse' also carries an allusion to the Song of Songs, as the parallel between this passage and one in a thirteenth-century treatise on contemplative prayer makes clear:

[69] BL, MS Additional 29986, fol. 146va. The *Speculum Dominarum* has: 'Jubilum dicitur quando ineffabile gaudium mente concipitur quod nec abscondi potest, nec sermonibus aperiri, et tamen quibusdam moribus proditur, quamvis nullis proprietatibus exprimatur' (It is called 'jubilum' when an ineffable joy is conceived in the mind that can be neither hidden nor disclosed in words, and whatever means are used, its properties cannot be expressed): Durand de Champagne, *Speculum dominarum*, ed. by Flottès-Dubrulle, III. 4, p. 307.

L'en trueve en cantiques d'une tele ame qui estoit lasche et pereceuse si ne se voloit
mouvoir ainz gisoit en son lit si cuidoit la trouver son ami mes ne il trouva mie si
com ele dist: *In lectulo meo quesivi et non inveni.*

[In the Song of Songs one finds such a soul, who was lax and lazy, and thus did not
wish to stir, but rather lay in her bed and thus thought to find her lover there; but
she did not find him at all, as she says: In lectulo meo quesivi et non inveni. (Song
of Songs 3. 1)][70]

The *Abbaye* goes on to cite and explain another verse of the Song of Songs
(5. 2), 'Ego dormio et cor meum uigilat', illustrating the explanation with a reference to a secular love song, in which the singer's heart is awakened to love by
little bells (allegorized as the sighs and laments of the soul at prayer).

Conclusion

The *Abbaye* was one vernacular text among many which attempted to trans-
mit to lay audiences understandings of spiritual development that were originally intended for novices in monastic orders. It shared idioms and sources of
teaching with other, similar works. It has been characterized as a treatise on the
mixed life, extolling active virtues such as charitable giving on the one hand,
while promoting the soul's ascent to God on the other.[71] This no doubt contributed to its continuing appeal in the two centuries after it was first composed, to
both lay and religious audiences. I would suggest that its attractive allegorical
structure of gathering places, well-adapted to its subject matter, was also a factor, since it provided a ready means to vary the detail of the content without
appearing to change the overall shape and character of the text. This meant
that a new reader or readers could possess their own instance of a popular text,
tailored to their own needs. The next five chapters will examine the fashioning
and refashioning of the *Abbaye* in its various contexts, starting with the earliest
and most influential version.

---

[70] This passage, quoted and translated by Kumler in *Translating Truth*, p. 224, is from the
treatise on the love of God found in *Y*, and in Paris, Bibliothèque Mazarine, MS 788, discussed
in Chapter 3.

[71] Consacro, 'The Author of *The Abbey of the Holy Ghost*'; Kumler, *Translating Truth*,
pp. 203–04.

Chapter 2

The Religion of the Heart

There is nothing in the *Abbaye* that allows us to pinpoint its place of composition, but there can be little doubt that it came into being in north-eastern France or southern Flanders, among the fervour for spiritual perfection and apostolic purity that burgeoned there throughout the thirteenth century. This chapter examines the earliest manuscripts of the *Abbaye*, focusing on the *Religion du cuer*, the version found in the α_1 family of manuscripts.[1] The *Sainte abbaye*, version β_1, also occurs in a very early manuscript, but I argue in this chapter that the *Religion du cuer* represents the earliest version of the *Abbaye*. The first path of analysis leads through the evidence of the manuscripts themselves, their geographic distribution, their owners where they can be identified, and what their contents can tell us about the textual communities among which they circulated. The second turns to the text of the *Religion du cuer*, first seeking to discover what it reveals about the world its readers inhabited, and then examining its relationship to other texts produced in the same context of religious experimentation.

The Manuscript Context

The earliest copies of the *Religion du cuer* come from Lorraine, Picardy, and Wallonia, all regions whose urban life was marked by the intense religious

---

[1] In this chapter, when referring to the version of the text represented by the α_1 manuscripts, I will use the designation from the prologue, the *Religion du cuer*.

experimentation of the thirteenth century. Two of the manuscripts, *M* and *A*, were copied in Metz, and a third, *L*, shared with *M* a group of texts, including the *Religion du cuer*, which may have been copied directly from the Metz manuscript.[2] Metz was, by the last decades of the thirteenth century when the earliest of these manuscripts was copied, an important urban centre, which had been independent since 1232. As well as housing a number of traditional monasteries, it had in the third quarter of the century seen an explosion of activity by mendicant orders, and also of groups of women living a semi-religious life outside monastic structures.[3] *L*, even though it was copied elsewhere, came from a similar context. It was written in Liège, an even more important centre for the development of alternative forms of religious life, with nineteen convents of beguines by the 1230s.[4] It was the holy women of the diocese centred on this city whose lives were held up by James of Vitry and Thomas of Cantimpré as exemplars of a new form of feminine piety. The other early copy, *C*, was made in the neighbouring diocese of Cambrai. Although many texts in that manuscript appear to have been adapted to a male audience, some of them explicitly address women, possibly beguines.[5]

The manuscripts *M* and *L* have attracted recent scholarly interest as part of overlapping networks of circulation of beguine literature in Lorraine, Wallonia, and Picardy.[6] A network centred on Metz is reflected in four manuscripts of the

---

[2] *M* and its contents are described in Meyer, 'Notice du ms. 535 de la Bibl. Mun. de Metz' and Långfors, 'Notice des manuscrits 535 de la bibliothèque municipale de Metz et 10047 des nouvelles acquisitions du fonds français de la bibliothèque nationale', which both provide some extensive transcriptions, mostly of the poems. Some further poems are published in Hilka, 'Altfranzösische Mystik und Beginentum', and another in Otto, 'Altlothringische geistliche Lieder'. *L* is described in Bayot, *Poème Moral*, pp. xix–xx. Bayot provides evidence for the dependence of *L* on *M*. *A* is described in Hasenohr, 'Un Enseignement de vie chrétienne du XIIIᵉ siècle et sa postérité', p. 330.

[3] Långfors, 'Notice des manuscrits 535 de la bibliothèque municipale de Metz et 10047 des nouvelles acquisitions du fonds français de la bibliothèque nationale'; McCurry, 'Religious Careers and Religious Devotion in Thirteenth-Century Metz', pp. 329–30. For literary activity in Lorraine, mostly centred on Metz, see Busby, *Codex and Context*, pp. 535–53.

[4] Geybels, *Vulgariter Beghinae*, p. 51.

[5] Hasenohr, 'Isidore de Séville, auteur ascétique "français"?', pp. 311–12.

[6] The most comprehensive study to date of these manuscripts and texts is Hasenohr, 'D'une "poésie de béguine" à une "poétique des béguines"'. See also Reynaert, 'Hadewijch', pp. 219–21, and Scheepsma, *The Limburg Sermons*, pp. 358–79. All of these studies build on late nineteenth- and early twentieth-century manuscript research: the work by Meyer, Långfors, Hilka, and Bayot cited above (note 2), and Christ, 'Le Livre du Palmier'; Christ, 'La Regle des fins amans'; Bechmann, 'Drei Dits de l'ame'; Meyer, 'Notice d'un manuscrit lorrain appartenant a

late thirteenth and early fourteenth centuries. All of them contain both prose vernacular spiritual texts — sermons, short allegorical works, and translations of Latin texts — and lyric poems strongly marked by beguine spirituality.[7] *L*, although from a different linguistic area and predominantly in Latin, was connected with this network as it shared three verse and three prose French texts (including the *Abbaye*) with *M*.[8] Similar collections of prose texts and poems are found in Picard manuscripts of the same period.[9]

The poems and the prose corpus probably have different origins and authorship, although there are many thematic parallels (for instance, prose treatises on meditating on the Hours of the Passion and poems which treat each hour and episode in lyrical fashion). The poems are only found locally, in the thirteenth- and early fourteenth-century manuscripts mentioned above (one corpus in the Metz manuscripts and *L*, and a different one in the Picard manuscripts). They are metrically distinctive, display a high degree of intertextuality, and are strongly marked by affective mysticism. Geneviève Hasenohr suggests local beguine authorship and sees their metre and reuse of verse fragments as the product of local cultures of oral transmission.[10] The prose texts, on the other hand, continued to be copied beyond the fourteenth century and outside the Picard-Walloon-Lorraine linguistic areas. Many, like the *Abbaye*, address a female reader. For the most part they are anonymous and provide few clues about those who wrote them, although their content often suggests a clerical author, and a number are presented as letters of spiritual direction. Many show a strong Bernardine influence, and the Cistercians were active in the pastoral care of cloistered and uncloistered women at the time

une collection privée'. Some of the manuscripts described in these works have since disappeared or changed location; current locations of some are given in Hasenohr's article.

[7] Metz, Bibliothèque municipale, MS 535 (*M*), Munich, BSB, MS cod. gall. 32, Urbana, Univ. Lib., MS 98, Montpellier, Bibl. École de méd., MS 43. See Hasenohr, 'D'une "poésie de béguine" à une "poétique des béguines"'.

[8] In *L* they were grouped together, while in *M* none were consecutive, which suggests that the Liège compiler selected them from the Metz manuscript or one like it. The copies of Philippe de Novare's *Quatre ages de l'homme* in *M* and *L* shared a number of variants against other copies of the same text, suggesting that the Liège version was copied from *M*. Bayot remarks that the Liège copies were of poor quality compared to the Metz versions. Bayot, *Poème Moral*, p. xix.

[9] Lund, Universitetsbibliotek, MS Medeltidhanskrift 53; BnF, MS nouvelles acquisitions françaises 10246; BRB, MS 9411–26. See Hasenohr, 'D'une "poésie de béguine" à une "poétique des béguines"', pp. 927–36.

[10] Hasenohr, 'D'une "poésie de béguine" à une "poétique des béguines"', pp. 936–37. Oliver makes the same suggestion about vernacular poems of petition in the Liège psalters: Oliver, 'Devotional Psalters and the Study of Beguine Spirituality', p. 214.

when they were being composed. The Cistercian abbey of Villers was closely involved not only with Cistercian nunneries, but with beguines in Nivelles and Oignies. With a rich library, it was well placed to disseminate edifying reading material and is seen by modern scholars as a powerhouse of mystical spirituality and a driving force behind the women's religious movement.[11] Cistercian spirituality is strongly evident in the third early manuscript of the *Religion du cuer*, *C*, from the diocese of Cambrai, which brings together many of the prose texts found in the networks described above.[12] The Franciscans and Dominicans, present in the towns of the region from the third and fourth decades of the thirteenth century, also provided spiritual support to beguines, and some of the prose texts may have mendicant authors. Franciscan saints and St Dominic figure in the beguine psalters from the diocese of Liège studied by Judith Oliver, and beguines are recorded living near Franciscan convents, confessing to the friars, and being buried in their churches.[13]

The largely female audience envisaged by the authors of many of the prose texts is borne out by their reception in the manuscript context examined here. The four manuscripts of the Metz network can all be connected with communities of religious women, both cloistered and uncloistered. Montpellier, Bibliothèque de l'École de médecine, MS 43 is likely to have been made for a beguinage.[14] *M* also seems to have been directed at beguines rather than cloistered women. Hasenohr concludes, from a close analysis of the published descriptions and content, that it was a manuscript intended for personal use rather than display, commissioned for a specific audience of beguines.[15] The other two belonged to communities of Benedictine nuns: Munich, Bayerische Staatsbibliothek, MS col. gall. 32 to the abbey of St Glossinde, and Urbana, University Library, MS 98 to the abbey of St Marie. Both manuscripts contain a translation of the Rule of St Benedict adapted for women.

The related manuscript *L* looks as though its primary audience was different. It was purchased by the prior of St Jacques in Liège, Philippe d'Othey, in

---

[11] Scheepsma, *The Limburg Sermons*, pp. 88–90, 97.

[12] Hasenohr, 'Isidore de Séville, auteur ascétique "français"?', p. 311.

[13] Oliver, 'Devotional Psalters and the Study of Beguine Spirituality', p. 205. On the the associations between beguines and Franciscan convents, see Lauwers and Simons, *Béguines et Béguins à Tournai au Bas Moyen Age*; Oliver, 'Devotional Psalters and the Study of Beguine Spirituality', p. 204; Simons, *Cities of Ladies*, p. 180; Farmer, *Surviving Poverty in Medieval Paris*, pp. 144–45.

[14] Hasenohr, 'Un Enseignement de vie chrétienne du xiiie siècle et sa postérité', p. 329.

[15] Hasenohr, 'D'une "poésie de béguine" à une "poétique des béguines"', p. 916.

1422; nothing is known of its first owner, but the contents give some clues.[16] Three quarters of it was made up of Latin texts that would have been useful for a priest engaged in pastoral work: the *Legenda Aurea* and two additional saints' lives, the *Lucidarium*, and two digests of the *Summa Poenitentia* of Raymond of Peñafort — a verse version of the *liber sacramentorum* and a prose *summa penitencie*.[17] This little library of Latin texts would have provided material for preaching and hearing confessions and a handbook for administering the sacraments. The vernacular texts copied at the end of the manuscript (including the six also found in *M*) may also have been useful for sharing and discussing with a lay flock. Two of them were widely copied didactic religious poems, the *Poeme Moral* and the *Chanteploure*. The group of six texts shared with *M* combines elements of the two corpora outlined above, comprising three poems and three prose treatises, one of which was the *Abbaye*. Two of the poems were published by Hilka; one of them begins 'Qui veut droit beguignage avoir' and praises poverty, while the other is an allegory of mystical union.[18] The third poem, published by Otto, uses the language of both courtly love and affective devotion to speak of the soul's love for Jesus, and incorporates references to the Passion linked to the canonical hours.[19] Of the prose treatises, one is the *Quatre ages de l'homme*, by Philippe de Novare, a moral treatise examining childhood, youth, middle, and old age.[20] The other has not been identified outside the two manuscripts and was not edited before their destruction. Its contents can therefore only be guessed at from the incipit and explicit recorded from *L*: 'En non do Peire e do Fil et dou saint Esperit. Je wel ci recordeir une lechon d'amour que une ame raportat de l'escole d'orison dort [*sic*] li Sains Espirs estoit maistre' (In the name of the Father and of the Son and of the Holy Spirit. Here I will record a lesson in love that a soul brought back from the school of prayer of which the Holy Spirit was the schoolmaster) and 'Cis est teils, qui te proie de lui ameir. les .vii. graces vos ai moustreie qui sunt en lui. Por Deus, or l'amons tuit, car il est bien dignes' (He is thus, who asks you to love him; I have shown you the seven graces that are in him. For God's sake, let us all love him, for he is worthy). In *L* the text was described as 'Une lechon d'amour' (A lesson in love), while in *M* it was headed: 'Conment tu saveras a cui tu te dois doner' (How you will know to whom you should give yourself). If the Latin texts indicate that the original

---

[16] For the purchase by Philippe d'Othey, see Bayot, *Poème Moral*, p. xx.

[17] Bayot, *Poème Moral*, p. xvi.

[18] Hilka, 'Altfranzösische Mystik und Beginentum', pp. 145–53.

[19] Otto, 'Altlothringische geistliche Lieder', pp. 587–92.

[20] Philippe de Novare, *Les Quatre Âges de l'homme*, ed. by de Fréville.

compiler of the manuscript was a cleric engaged in pastoral care, the French texts suggest that his flock may have been women, perhaps a group of beguines to whom he acted as spiritual adviser.

The prose texts in the manuscripts from Metz and Picardy are never in exactly the same combination from one manuscript to the next, but many of them recur in manuscripts across the two regions. They provide reading material for a person who desires to deepen her spiritual life and practice, on how to understand the Mass and how to pray, with a particular emphasis on meditation on the Passion, the Eucharist, and contemplative prayer. Some of the works, like the *Abbaye*, are allegories, while others take the form of treatises or sermons. Some are collections of sayings of Bernard, Augustine, and other patristic writers. One of the prose texts, the *Regle des fins amans*, is addressed specifically to beguines; it is found in only one of these manuscripts, but partial copies in later manuscripts suggest that it might have had a wider distribution. There is also some overlap with vernacular prose texts found in the women's psalters from the Liège region that Judith Oliver argues persuasively were made for beguines.[21] Two of the works from this repertoire, the *Sermon du palmier* and a sermon on the twelve fruits of the Eucharist attributed to Guiard of Laon, also circulated on the Dutch side of the linguistic border, where the *mulieres religiosae* were equally active.[22] Many of the texts appear for the first time in these manuscripts, and it is probable that at least some were composed specifically for beguines. That is certainly the case of the *Regle des fins amans*, and it seems likely for the *Sermon du palmier*.[23]

Of the surviving witnesses of α_1, *C*, *A*, and *R* all contain some of this repertoire of prose texts: all have the *Sermon du palmier*. *C*, the oldest of the three, is a large collection of devotional works in prose, some of which have not been found anywhere else. Dating from the beginning of the fourteenth century and produced in the diocese of Cambrai, it may have been made for a male religious community, but much of its content still bears traces of its original female audi-

---

[21] Notably the twelve fruits sermon and Hours of the Cross. See Oliver, 'Je pecherise renc grasces a vos'. The argument for beguine use is also made by Oliver, 'Devotional Psalters and the Study of Beguine Spirituality' and Oliver, 'Devotional Images and Pious Practices in a Psalter from Liège'.

[22] They are, respectively, Sermon 31 and Sermon 40 of the *Limburg Sermons*. The *Sermon du palmier* also circulated in German, English, and Latin, but Scheepsma argues that it was composed originally in French, somewhere close to the French/Dutch linguistic boundary. Scheepsma, 'Het oudste Middelnederlandse palmboomtraktaat', pp. 170–72; and Scheepsma, *The Limburg Sermons*, pp. 129–30. The *Sermon du palmier* was edited by Christ, 'Le Livre du Palmier'.

[23] Scheepsma, *The Limburg Sermons*, pp. 129–33.

ence. It has a copy of the twelve fruits of the Eucharist sermon, in addition to the *Sermon du palmier*. In *C*, the *Abbaye* is followed by another cloister allegory, a translation of *Introduxit me rex*.

A is Lorraine in origin: in fact, probably from Metz, since it also contains a copy of the *Image du monde*, a text which itself was written in Metz. A composite manuscript, its central part consists of three texts addressed to a woman, one of which is the *Abbaye*.[24] It is connected to the Metz textual network through its origin in the city and three shared texts: the *Abbaye*, the *Sermon du palmier*, and a lay rule of life related to one in *M*.[25]

R is a small manuscript for private use containing a large anthology with Franciscan connections: a major item (the only one with a historiated initial) is a prose life of St Francis, based on the *Legenda Maior* of Bonaventure. Its place of origin is unknown. Paul Meyer considered that its language was that of Paris or the surrounding area, and that it was written in the mid-fourteenth century.[26] Its text of the *Religion du cuer* has some affinities with the wording of *L*, but the contents of the two manuscripts are not otherwise related. *R* contains the *Livre du palmier* and the *Regle des fins amans*. This is a different version of the *Regle* from that published by Karl Christ. It contains no reference to beguines, although it retains elements that frame the text as a religious rule. The first part (just over a quarter of the text) is based on the first two chapters of the text printed by Christ, and incorporates material from one later chapter, 'Quatre manieres de penser a Jhesucrist'; the rest is a development which bears no relation to the published *Regle*. This manuscript seems to have been compiled with a mixed audience in mind: the opening of the *Religion du cuer* addresses both men and women, unlike the copies in other manuscripts. Another text, in the form of a letter, is addressed to a man ('Biaus douz amis' (fol. 42ᵛ)). The *Regle des fins amans* begins with a reference to both sexes, but thereafter has exclusively male references. There may be a Franciscan orientation discernible in this text too, where it associates living without property with the good religious: 'en vainquant le monde par povreté. Ce fait li religieus par vivre sanz propre. Ou par doner aumosnes' (by overcoming the world through poverty. The reli-

[24] Hasenohr, 'Un Enseignement de vie chrétienne du XIIIᵉ siècle et sa postérité', p. 330.

[25] This is number 4 in Meyer's list of contents, beginning: 'Qui en connaissance de son creator et en bone vie vuet porfitier...' Meyer, 'Notice du ms. 535 de la Bibl. Mun. de Metz', p. 46. The version in Paris, Bibliothèque de l'Arsenal, MS 3173 is different, however: see Hasenohr, 'Un Enseignement de vie chrétienne du XIIIᵉ siècle et sa postérité', p. 330. The Arsenal text is published in Hasenohr, 'Un Faux Pierre de Luxembourg'.

[26] Meyer, 'Notice du MS Royal 16 E XII du Musée Britannique', p. 45.

gious do this by living without possessions. Or by giving alms) (fol. 298ᵛ). This manuscript may have been compiled for a group of Franciscan tertiaries. *R* also contains a copy of the same translation of *Introduxit me rex* found in *C*.

To sum up, the evidence from the manuscript context of version α₁ of the *Abbaye* and the textual networks to which it was connected suggests a number of overlapping textual communities in the areas where those manuscripts were produced. There are traces of local communities of women producing and transmitting vernacular religious lyrics, possibly orally. The manuscripts also point to clerical authors engaged in pastoral care of religious women, whether cloistered or lay, who compiled collections and probably composed, adapted, or translated works for them. Finally, the readers for whom the manuscripts were compiled were primarily women who, although in some cases were living in monastic communities and in other cases in formal or informal beguine groups, seemed to have the same spiritual preoccupations and reading tastes. Since the context of the surviving copies of a text is not necessarily the context of its creation, the rest of this chapter examines internal evidence from the *Religion du cuer* to determine whether it is indeed a product of the same milieu in which the earliest manuscripts place it. It first considers indications of the text's intended readership, and then investigates thematic and linguistic links with the texts associated with beguine spirituality among which it circulates.

The World of the Audience

The audience of the *Religion du cuer* lived in a world where poverty was a bar to religious life; this much is evident from the opening words, which speak of those who would enter religious life but cannot: 'Fille, je regarde que mout de gent couvoitent et vauroient entrer en religion, mes il ne pueent, ou c'est par povreté, ou pour ce qui sont retenu par le loien de mariage ou par autre reson' (Daughter, I see that many people would like to be in a religious order, but they cannot, either through poverty or because they are held back by the bonds of marriage, or for some other reason).[27] This of course was true anywhere in Europe in the thirteenth century, especially for women; monasteries required some financial provision from the family of a woman desiring to enter for her upkeep, usually in the form of a dowry. In the region which concerns us it was something that ecclesiastical authorities were aware of; in the 1328 record of an episcopal investigation of the beguinages of the diocese of Tournai, poverty is

---

[27] All quotes from the *Religion du cuer* are from the edition in Part II, unless the wording of a particular manuscript is indicated.

advanced, alongside a shortage of places in existing religious houses, to explain the demand to which the Countesses of Flanders and Hainault, Jeanne and Marguerite, had responded in the preceding century by founding a number of court beguinages.[28] But in the world of the *Religion du cuer* it is not only unmarried women who are seeking a form of religious life, and the inclusion of the married among those to whom the text is addressed indicates an acceptance that holiness was possible within marriage. Indeed, the whole premise of the *Religion du cuer* is that it is possible to live a spiritual life outside the institutional frame to which both marriage and poverty were a bar. Furthermore, listing marriage as a barrier to voluntary professed religious life suggests a context where the pursuit of spiritual development was a first choice, not, as implied by the Tournai document, a second-best imposed by a lack of suitable marriage partners. For many beguines, from what we know of those whose lives were recorded in the thirteenth century, the pursuit of spiritual development was indeed a first choice, and some refused marriage in order to pursue it while others, like Marie of Oignies, were joined in it by their husbands.[29]

Whether or not the audience of the *Religion du cuer* were beguines themselves, two references in the text point explicitly to a context in which beguines and their practices were familiar and approved. One comes after three examples of timekeeping, which evoke familiar daily activities while giving a schematic picture of medieval society: the cock-crow wakes the peasants in the countryside, the horn and call ('je voi le jour dorenlot') of the town watch wakes the merchants, and the bell wakes the monks to pray in the monastery. We may speculate on the reasons for the absence of the nobility, who presumably had some signal to wake them too, from this picture; it may indicate an environment in which urban commercial activity was more salient than that of the knighthood and aristocracy. The three examples pave the way for the allegorical

---

[28] 'Jeanne and her sister Marguerite [...] had observed that these counties teemed with women who were denied suitable marriage [...] and that daughters of respectable men of noble and ignoble birth, desired to live in chastity but on account of numbers or the poverty of their parents were unable to do so easily.' Ghent Memorial in Paul Fredericq, *Corpus documentorum Inquisitionis haereticae pravitatis Neerlandicae*, 1. 176, quoted in Galloway, '"Discreet and Devout Maidens"', p. 101. Simons (*Cities of Ladies*, p. x) gives a slightly different translation, referring directly to the archive source. This document was used as evidence by scholars who saw the origins of the beguine movement in a surplus of marriageable women; for a good summary of the historiography of this question, see Simons, *Cities of Ladies*, pp. x–xii.

[29] Simons, *Cities of Ladies*, pp. 62–71. Reynaert makes an explicit connection between the prologue passage of the *Abbaye* in Metz MS 535 and the early beguines, 'religious women' trying to lead a spiritual life 'in the world'. Reynaert, 'Hadewijch', p. 221.

point that the soul should be woken by 'jalosie et amors de perfeccion', which is, most tellingly, the 'ologe de contemplation et de saint beguinage'. In other words, this is the timekeeper of the abbey built in the soul, and the activity of that abbey (or perhaps the institution itself) is referred to as *saint beguinage*. The term *beguinage* here carries no trace of negative connotations.

Practices that have been described as characteristic of beguines are evoked in another example, the description of holy people who are caught up in mystical contemplation and fall insensible where they sit. One manuscript, *R*, adds that they fall dropping their spindle and distaff, or their book or their psalter, presenting spinning or reading as a typical scenario for ecstatic prayer. *R* is the only surviving witness to give this passage in its entirety, but traces in other witnesses suggest that the full version goes back to the earliest tradition.[30]

> Si puet bien estre avenu que aucunes ont esté si ravies la ou eles se seoient que li fuisiaus leur cheoit d'une part et la quenoille d'autre, u livre, u sautier, et cheoient pasmés ausi comme l'alöese pasme en chantant.
>
> [It can happen that some have been so rapt that they dropped their spindle to one side and their distaff to the other, or their book, or their psalter, and they fell in a swoon just as the lark swoons when it sings.] (*R* fols 135ᵛ–136ʳ)[31]

Many beguines earned their living through textile work, performed at home, and the uniting of this work with prayer and study seems to be a characteristic of beguine spirituality. Simons notes that the reading of religious texts and perhaps parts of the Psalter while spinning or weaving is attested in the rules of beguine communities.[32] James of Vitry reports that Marie of Oignies read her psalter while spinning.[33] The same association is made in a poem by Nicholas of Bibera, writing in the thirteenth century, describing the habits of 'good' beguines:

[30] *A*, which often leaves parts out, has the beginning of the passage: 'S'en puet estre auennu que teilz ou telle ierent sosprise et s'oblioit et ierent rauie' (fol. 51ʳᵃ). The exemplar used by the compiler of *S* must have had the whole passage, since it has 'Il est aucunes fois advenu que ame qui a este ravye se paulme ainsi comme la liache qui se paulme en chantant' (fol. 234ʳᵃ). That exemplar cannot have been *R*, because the extracts from the *Abbaye* in *S* are often textually closer to *Y* than to *R*. There is no independent witness to the detail of the distaff, spindle, and psalter, but the scribe of *R* does not add circumstantial detail like this in any other place.

[31] *R* is the only witness to this reference from the α₁ manucripts (*S* contains the reference to the lark, but not to the spindle and distaff). There is no transcription from this part of the text for *M* and *L*, so we do not know whether they contained it or not.

[32] Simons, '"Staining the Speech of Things Divine"', p. 109.

[33] Bolton, 'Some Thirteenth-Century Women in the Low Countries', p. 24.

> Jejunant, vigilant et lanea stamina filant [...]
> Quamvis sit rarum, tamen accidit hoc, quod earum
> quaedam ducuntur extra se vel rapiuntur,
> ut videant Christum; vulgus jubilum vocat istum.

> [Fasting, keeping vigils and spinning wool [...]. However rare it may be, yet it happens, that one of them is lifted up in rapture, that she may see Christ; in the vulgar tongue this is called *jubilum*.][34]

Although Nicholas of Bibera qualifies the phenomenon of rapture in these circumstances as rare, the very fact that he includes it in this description, even giving it a vernacular name, suggests that it was commonly associated with beguine prayer. The *Religion du cuer* thus presents contemplative rapture as a legitimate culmination of prayer for ordinary Christians, and does so in a similar way to other texts that refer specifically to the practice of beguines. As was noted in Chapter 1 in relation to the passage on Meditation, the *Religion* reflects the acceptance of frequent ecstatic prayer that Bernard McGinn has identified with the 'new mysticism' of the Franciscans and beguines, in addition to the monastic underpinning that it shares with other vernacular texts on contemplation.[35]

The internal evidence from the *Religion du cuer* suggests an audience who, while they might not have been beguines themselves, sympathized with or shared their ideals. The prologue seems to be addressing a wide public of laypeople with religious aspirations: the public from which the beguines, who made temporary vows of chastity, were drawn, but which might include others who attempted to pursue a form of religious life within marriage. Other clues point to a similar social context to that of the beguines of northern France and the Low Countries, and one in which *beguinage* could be seriously regarded as a model for holiness. It remains to be seen whether any more specific affinities with beguine spirituality can be detected in the *Religion du cuer*'s thematic content, to which we now turn.

A Beguine Cloister

In Chapter 1, a number of instances of intertextuality were identified which linked the *Abbaye* as a whole with other works of lay religious instruction. Here

---

[34] Nikolaus von Bibra, *Carmen Satiricum*, ed. by Fischer, 92, quoted in Passenier, '"Women on the Loose"', p. 64.

[35] McGinn notes that rapture was considered a brief and rare phenomenon by the monastic mystical tradition, while extended and frequent experiences of ecstatic contemplation were a hallmark of both beguine and Franciscan mysticism: McGinn, *The Flowering of Mysticism*, p. 152.

I focus on themes, images, and vocabulary the *Religion du cuer* shares with some of the beguine poems and prose texts that accompany it in the networks identified in the first part of this chapter.

One dimension along which the *Religion du cuer* can be measured against what we may call for convenience 'beguine literature' is that of *la mystique courtoise*.[36] The fusion of *fin amor* with love of God in devotional literature of the second half of the thirteenth century is particularly associated with beguines, through the writings of Hadewich, Mechthild of Magdeburg, and Marguerite Porete, and also found in the networks of French vernacular texts described earlier in this chapter.[37] The *Religion du cuer* also shares with those texts an interest in areas of devotion and conduct such as contemplative prayer, Christ's bodily presence in the Eucharist, and the role of poverty associated with humility in religious life. Examining these areas in turn, we will see strong intertextual relations between the *Religion du cuer* and other texts in its shared manuscript networks.

La Mystique Courtoise

At first sight, the *Religion du cuer* is far from the courtly discourse of divine love. In it we see no sign of love as *fin amor*, although love is the virtue chosen to govern the abbey. This conception of love is firmly within the monastic tradition; the abbess is *Charité*, and the authority called upon to justify obedience to her is Paul, *Omnia uestra in caritate fiant* (1 Cor. 16. 14). But the term *Amor* is used in another personification, 'li orloges d'amors' (*A*, fol. 53ᵛ). This is the timepiece that wakes the soul to love of God, and here the word is associated with ideas of desire and bound into a set of images that refer both to the Song of Songs and to a secular love-song. The soul woken by the *orloge* of Love is like the bride in the Song of Songs, who says *Ego dormio et cor meum uigilat* (Cant. 5. 2). This is glossed in French as meaning that when she is physically sleeping to rest her body and mind, her heart is still wakeful, 'en jalousie et en soucist, en amor et en desir' (in zeal and in care, in love and in desire). At this point the secular song is introduced:

---

[36] Here I follow the terminology used by Barbara Newman in *From Virile Woman to WomanChrist*. See the chapter entitled 'La mystique courtoise: Thirteenth-Century Beguines and the Art of Love', pp. 137–81.

[37] Reypens, *Vita Beatricis*; Newman, *From Virile Woman to WomanChrist*, pp. 137–81; Newman, 'The Mirror and the Rose'; Newman, *God and the Goddesses*.

Et tele ame a tousdis le cuer tendu et entendu a Diu, et ainssi puet dire la chansson du siecle: 'J'ai .i. cuer a cloquetes resveillié par amors'.

[Such a soul always has her heart stretched and turned towards God, and she can recite the worldly song: 'I have a heart woken to love with bells'.] (α_1)

In this passage, we can see the mingling of the discourses of the Song of Songs and secular love poetry which Barbara Newman has found to be a characteristic of the literature produced by and for beguines.[38] It is also reminiscent of the way Gerard of Liège incorporates French secular songs into a Latin work that expresses the love between the soul and God in the idiom of courtly poetry and romance. In fact the wording used by the *Abbaye* in its earliest versions — 'et ainssi puet dire la chansson du siecle' — is so similar to Gerard's 'unde hic potest dici quoddam carmen quod uulgo canitur' that it suggests the French author knew his work.[39]

The passage on rapture quoted earlier in this chapter also points to a familiarity with courtly love poetry. When *R* speaks of the enraptured souls who forget where they are and drop their psalters or spindles, it compares them to the lark which swoons as it sings: 'et cheoient pasmés ausi comme l'alöese pasme en chantant' (and they fell in a swoon, just as the lark swoons when it sings) (fol. 136ra).[40] While most medieval encyclopaedists identify the lark's soaring flight with prayer and ascension to God, the description of its sudden plunges as swooning with delight comes only in the troubadour Bernard de Ventador's famous *Can vei la lauzeta mover* and in works that derive from it.[41]

One other aspect of the idiom of courtly love which is reflected in the *Religion du cuer* is the use of narrative allegory: dramas involving characters who are personifications of courtly vices and virtues, on the model of the *Roman*

---

[38] Newman, *From Virile Woman to WomanChrist*, p. 138.

[39] Gerard of Liège, *Quinque incitamenta ad amandum deum ardenter*, quoted in Newman, *From Virile Woman to WomanChrist*, p. 286, n. 20.

[40] Although the mention of the lark is not present in *A* or *C*, it seems likely to have been a feature of α_1. *A* has a tendency to shorten the text, so it might have been present in its exemplar, and the lark image also occurs in the digest of extracts from the *Abbaye* in *S*, which cannot have been copied directly from *R*: 'Il est aucunes fois advenu que ame qui a este ravye se paulme ainsi comme la liache qui se paulme en chantant' (fols 233vb–234ra).

[41] 'Can vei la lauzeta mover | De joi sas alas contral rai, | Que s'oblid' e.s laissa chazer | Per la doussor c'al cor li vai', Lazar, *Bernard de Ventadour*, no. 31, lines 1–4. Information on the lark in various medieval encyclopaedias is summarized in Bawcutt, 'The Lark in Chaucer and Some Later Poets', pp. 5–6. For the use of Bernard's lark image by Dante, see Smith, 'The Lark Image in Bondie Dietaiuti and Dante'.

de la Rose. A number of the anonymous French texts found in the northern French manuscripts we have been considering have such allegories. One is the short allegory at the end of the *Regle des fins amans*, in which *Conscience* is taken by *Jalousie, Esperance, Charité*, and *Fine Amor* to find her lover, Jesus, who has been locked away by the cloistered religious.[42] A further illustration of the taste for sometimes rudimentary allegorical scenarios with a courtly flavour and religious content is a poem contained in both *M* and *L*, *Quant li mundain sont endormi*.[43] A variant of the Daughter Zion story, it recounts the story of a lady (the 'sainte ame') who longs for her absent lover. A group of virtues set off to Paradise where he is king and bring him back to visit her. Within the plot of the soul as romance heroine seeking and finally being united with God, her *ami*, several episodes allow a set of virtues very similar to the nuns of the *Abbaye* to take centre stage performing domestic tasks, making up beds, bathing the child Jesus when he visits the lady, and serving an allegorical meal.

The narrative allegory in the *Religion du cuer* and subsequent versions of the *Abbaye* is not a romance of union with the divine lover, but a *psychomachia*, a struggle between personified vices and virtues, recounting the divinely assisted victory of the virtuous sisters as the Holy Ghost comes to their aid and casts out the daughters of the Devil. However, in the representation of the nuns in the *Religion du cuer* there are a number of parallels with the figures in the beguine narratives. Some of the same personifications occur, often playing similar roles. There is a close parallel between *Devotion* in *Quant li mundain sont endormi* and the cellar-mistress of the *Religion du cuer*, both of whose roles are based on the association of wine with tears (in *Quant li mundain* Devotion serves wine at dinner that is tears of compunction). Two of the guides of *Conscience* in the *Regle des fins amans*, *Charité* and *Jalousie*, personify the same virtues, respectively, as the abbess and sacristan of the *Religion du cuer*. Among the personifications in the *Religion*, we find not only the monastic virtues of the Latin cloister tradition; many are ones that also occur in courtly literature.[44] *Courtoisie* (the mistress of the guesthouse), *Loyauté* (the infirmarer), and *Largesse* (her assistant) certainly belong to this category. These virtues appear in writings by beguines, and most notably they are among the virtues that for Marguerite Porete characterize the nobility of the ascending soul in *Mirror of Simple Souls*.[45]

[42] This allegory is analysed by Newman, *From Virile Woman to WomanChrist*, p. 143.

[43] Hilka, 'Altfranzösische Mystik und Beginentum', pp. 132–42. There is a prose version of the narrative in BnF, MS fr. 1802, fols 89rb–91va.

[44] As noted by Whitehead, 'Making a Cloister of the Soul in Medieval Religious Treatises', p. 39.

[45] Kocher, *Allegories of Love in Marguerite Porete's Mirror of Simple Souls*, p. 107.

The name of the sacristan, *Jalousie*, is also suggestive of a courtly personifica-tion (one of the characters in the *Roman de la Rose* is called *Jalousie*). While *jalousie* can in courtly literature carry its modern connotations of negative, pos-sessive love, it is also the pure desire that underpins *fin amor*. This is the way it is used in the *Religion du cuer* and some of the French beguine texts, where it refers to zeal in loving God, with strong connotations of desire, as will be seen below.

Contemplation

Beguine mystics like Mechthild and Hadewich used the idiom of courtly love to describe their experience of contemplative prayer. Their writings, and the hagiography of James of Vitry and Thomas of Cantimpré, take for granted the experience of frequent and prolonged ecstatic states.[46] This is also the form of contemplative prayer evoked in French texts for and by beguines. When we place the *Religion du cuer* alongside those texts, we find parallels that align its conception of contemplative prayer quite closely with theirs.

In Chapter 1 we saw the importance of the theme to the *Abbaye* throughout its history in the teachings that were assembled in the loci of *Meditation*, the keeper of the granary, and *Jubilation*, the assistant to the choir-mistress. In con-sidering it here I focus on the elements its treatment in the *Religion du cuer* has in common with other texts in its manuscript network, where such states are usually evoked in terms of desire for God (*jelosie*), the experience of *ravissement* with the failure of the bodily senses, burning love, and the inarticulate joy, often expressed in song, that comes with union with God (*jubilation*).

In the *Religion du cuer*, *Jalousie* is the sacristan who calls the nuns to prayer, and it is desire for the love of God that keeps their hearts awake 'en jalousie et en soucist, en amor et en desir' (in zeal and in care, in love and in desire). Desire for God's love is presented as a step or essential component of contemplation in two texts in an early fourteenth-century Picard collection, where *jalous* is used as a synonym for 'desiring'.[47] In *Quinse degres sont par quoy ame conuertie puet aler en paradis*, the fourteenth step is to be 'jalous de dieu amer' (fol. 10ᵛ). The tree allegory in same manuscript (*Boins coers desirans iestre arbres gratieux fruit de vie portans*) has green leaves 'de jalousie et d'emulation' because the soul must be 'jalouse et desirans de croistre en l'amour de Dieu' (fols 106ᵛ–107ʳ).

---

[46] For Barbara Newman, this is one of the features of 'la mystique courtoise'. Newman, *From Virile Woman to WomanChrist*, p. 138.

[47] Lund, UB, MS Medeltidhanskrift 53.

Ravissement is mentioned in the *Religion du cuer* in the context of jubilation: 'Si puet bien estre avenu que aucunes ont esté si ravies la ou eles se seoient'
in *R*, and 'S'en puet estre avennu que teilz ou telle ierent sosprise et s'oblioit et
ierent ravie' in *A*.[48] *Ravissement* is also mentioned in the *Regle des fins amans*,
where it is essential to the definition of contemplation. The *Regle* names contemplation as the fourth kind of prayer, following from meditation, and by
implication the culmination of the four kinds. When the soul meditates on the
mysteries of Jesus's divine and human nature, and of the Trinity, its senses cease
to operate 'et ce apele on ravisement'. When the soul is in this state, the *Regle*
author says, it is said to be in contemplation.[49]

The inflammation of the soul with burning love is a common element of the
experience of contemplation evoked in many beguine texts. It is found in the
Religion du cuer's summary of the progression of prayer from devotion to the
experience of divine consolation in the allegory of the wine (*devotion*), wheat
(*meditation*), and oil (*consolation*), where the oil of consolation illuminates and
inflames the soul:

> c'est l'oile qui donne savor en afection, et enlumine en connaissance et en revela-
> cion, et art en ferveur.
>
> [[it] is the oil that gives flavour in affection and illuminates in knowledge, in revela-
> tion, and burns with fervour.] (α_1)

There is a striking similarity of language and structure here to descriptions of
the soul's entry into contemplation in two beguine poems, one of which was
copied in *M*.

> Celle est vraiement beguine [...]
> Qui plore en orison,
> Sospire par devocion,
> Languit par meditacion,
> Remet et art ou feu d'amours.
>
> [She is truly a beguine [...]
> Who weeps in prayer,

---

[48] The term is omitted in *C*, which often abbreviates. It does occur in *S*, the digest of
extracts from the *Abbaye* copied in one of the anthologies of religious texts compiled for
Margaret of York. The extracts recompiled in that text are entirely consistent with α_1. It also
has the comparison, otherwise only found in *R*, with the swooning of the lark: 'Il est aucunes
fois advenu que ame qui a este ravye se paulme ainsi comme la liache qui se paulme en chantant'
(fols 233vb–234ra).

[49] Christ, 'La Regle des fins amans', p. 201.

> Sighs through devotion,
> Languishes through meditation,
> Recovers and burns in the fire of love.][50]

The other poem, which also concerns itself with the characteristics of *beguinage*, *Savés que j'apiel Beghinage?*, similarly associates burning love with visitation by God in the midst of tearful meditation on the Crucifixion:

> Il embrase affection
> et donne jubilation;
> c'est joie qui le coer comprent.
> Quant l'a trait en la vision
> de li par contemplation,
> la le saveure douchement.
>
> [He kindles affection
> and gives jubilation;
> that is joy which encompasses the heart.
> When the soul has drawn him to itself
> in a vision through contemplation,
> there it savours him sweetly.][51]

This poem unites the idea of burning love with another, jubilation, a term with a specific meaning in the vocabulary of mysticism. Although, as we saw in Chapter 1, the term is also present in vernacular works of spiritual instruction not associated with beguines, the phenomenon it describes was regarded as characteristic of beguine spirituality.[52] While the poem just quoted simply names jubilation, another text in the same manuscript describes it more fully, referring to the expression of such joy through song:

Aprés nos arbres doibt jetter florettes et boutons de jubilation, car quant li ame sent en li le bonté Dieu et les grasces des douls sentements que Dieux li a fait elle est si au coer ferue et navree que recryer li couvient et joie mener et canter amoureusement.

[Next our tree should put out flowers and buds of jubilation, for when the soul perceives the goodness of God within her and the graces and sweet feelings that

---

[50] *Je di que c'est folie pure*, lines 21, 25–28, Hilka, 'Altfranzösische Mystik und Beginentum', p. 154.

[51] Bechmann, 'Drei Dits de l'ame', p. 77.

[52] See the poem by Nicholas of Bibera quoted above.

God has given her she is struck to the heart and wounded, so that she must rejoice and sing like a lover.][53]

The *Religion du cuer* associates the term with song too, by making *Jubilation* the assistant to *Oroison*, the choir-mistress. The association is strongest in the *Religion du cuer*, where the passage goes on to describe the involuntary dancing and singing of those who experience the joy of mystical union:

> Si comme il avient aucune fois en aucune gent esperituel aprés oroison, que si sont si lié et si joiant et si fervent que lor cuers va cantant et murmurant une chanson parmi la sale ou parmi le chambre, et aucune fois la langue ne se puet tenir qu'ele ne chant ne les dois qui ne se muevent, et li orteil qu'il ne dansent et s'envoisent.

> [And thus it happens sometimes to spiritual people after prayer, that they are so happy, joyful, and fervent that they go about through the hall or chamber, singing and murmuring a song in their heart, and sometimes their tongue cannot refrain from singing, nor their fingers from moving, nor their toes from dancing and making merry.] (α_1)

The conception of contemplative prayer which reflects so closely that found in French beguine literature finds its fullest expression in the *Religion du cuer*, although it remains in some form in the other versions. While the passages on *jelosie* as desire for God and oil representing burning love are found in all but γ, the treatment of jubilation and rapture is less consistent. Jubilation receives less attention, with no reference to involuntary singing and dancing, in γ and β, and there are no references to rapture in γ, α_2, or β, suggesting that these concepts resonated less with the audiences for which the *Religion du cuer* was subsequently adapted, or perhaps were considered less suitable for them by their spiritual advisers.

The Eucharist

Eucharistic devotion is particularly associated with beguines, and a number of them worked actively to promote recognition of the feast of Corpus Christi, initiated in the diocese of Liège and mandated by papal decree in 1264.[54] The

---

[53] *Boins coers desirans iestre arbres gratieux fruit de vie portans*, Lund, UB, MS Medeltidhanskrift 53, fol. 106ʳ.

[54] For the history of the feast, see Rubin, *Corpus Christi* and Walters, Corrigan, and Ricketts, *The Feast of Corpus Christi*. Eucharistic devotion among beguines is discussed by Amy Hollywood in *The Soul as Virgin Wife*, pp. 50–52.

Eucharist does not occupy a very large place in the *Religion du cuer*, nor indeed in subsequent versions of the *Abbaye*, but what is there has some telling similarities with a vernacular text on the Eucharist that appeared around the time Juliana of Cornillon and her supporters were working to have the feast recognized. The French adaptation of a sermon preached by Guiard of Laon to the canons of Saint-Martin in Laon in the early decades of the thirteenth century was probably made during Guiard's time as Bishop of Cambrai (1238–47), at the height of his reputation as a preacher on the Eucharist and supporter of the Corpus Christi feast.[55] It had considerable success: there are nine known copies from the last quarter of the thirteenth century and the early part of the fourteenth, including *M* and *Z* as well as a psalter thought to have been made for a beguine from Huy.[56]

Teaching on the Eucharist is gathered in the *Religion du cuer* and subsequent versions of the *Abbaye* under the sign of *Meditation*, the keeper of the granary. It supplies only a small part of the content of that section, most of which is devoted to establishing the place of meditation in the soul's ascent to union with God. What is there, however, corresponds closely to the fifth benefit of the Eucharist in the French sermon, according to which the Eucharist is a food with which one can provision the soul against tribulation, just as a lord will provision his castle with bread, wine, and salt meat when he fears attack by an enemy. The sermon's development of this theme is long and complex, but the *Religion du cuer*'s short passage is closely aligned with it. The *Religion du cuer* places its consideration of the Eucharist in the context of provisioning against hard times: the granary is where the nuns' food supply is kept, and the sense of protection against want is conveyed in the *Religion du cuer* by 'pour avoir soustenance a plenté'. In both the *Religion* and the sermon, the wheat in the granary is identified with Christ's body and explicated with the symbolism of red and white drawn from the Song of Songs (5. 10), 'Dilectus meus candidus et rubicundus'.[57] In the two passages below, the common base of the image is clear, even though the sermon's shorter expression of it identifies whiteness with divinity, rather than innocence:

[55] The primary reference for Guiard's biography is Boeren, *La Vie et les oeuvres de Guiard de Laon*.

[56] Pinder, 'Food for the Journey' has an updated list of manuscripts and a discussion of the relation between the Latin and the French versions of the sermon. The beguine psalter was identified by Judith Oliver, 'Je pecherise renc grasces a vos', pp. 251, 254.

[57] The Latin sermon on which the French one is based makes the connection with the Song of Songs explicit.

Li froumens qui est rouges par defors senefie l'umanite nostre signeur qui fu rouiges en la crois. La blanceurs par dedans senefie la deuinite qui fu douce et soes.

[The wheat which is red outside signifies the humanity of our Lord who was red on the cross. The whiteness inside signifies the divinity which was sweet and gentle.][58]

le grain de fourment [...] est rouges par dehors et fendu u coste et en fait on le bon pain. C'est Jhesucrist qui fu rouge de son sanc en pacience (*A* passion) blanc en s'ame par dedens par innocence, et fenduz u coste en sa mort par le fer de la lance.

[the grain of wheat [...] is red on the outside, and white inside, and split along the side, and from it the good bread is made. This is Jesus Christ, who was red from his blood in patience (*A* passion), and white within his soul from innocence, and split in the side in his death by the tip of the lance.] (*R*, 137vb)[59]

While the brief evocation of the Eucharist in the *Religion du cuer* is completely in harmony with Guiard's sermon, it only takes up a small part of it. It may be significant that the aspect that it focuses on unites the idea of Christ's body as the bread of the Eucharist with his sufferings on the cross. Meditation on the Passion is not a strong theme in the *Abbaye*, but the two places where the Passion is evoked are the granary and the cellar, which immediately associate it with the two elements of the Eucharist, bread and wine. Although in the *Abbaye* wine is given a broader allegorical association with remembering (the pains of hell and the joys of heaven, as well as the Passion), the link with the memorial function of the Eucharist is clear.

The Religion du cuer and the Regle des fins amans

The comparison of the *Religion du cuer* with texts from its manuscript context that have explicit connections with beguines has revealed many similarities in religious sensibility and expression. Indeed, some of the examples discussed here suggest a network of intertextual connections which, if not always cases of borrowing per se, point to a shared stock of language and images. To further illustrate its embedding in this network, there is at least one example of what looks like a direct reference to the *Religion du cuer* in another text. In the rule of life in manuscript *A*, which begins 'Fille, qui en cognoissance de son createur vuelt proufiter' (Daughter, whoever wants to benefit from knowledge of her

---

[58] Boeren, *La Vie et les oeuvres de Guiard de Laon*, p. 314. This edition is based on an early fourteenth-century manuscript; older manuscripts have 'la passion' instead of 'la crois'.

[59] *C* omits the sentence explaining the meaning of the colours.

creator), comes the instruction: 'Amie, quant vous vous levés au matin et li orloges de Dieu vous avroit esvillie, si getés les iex de vostre cuer a vostre Dieu' (Friend, when you rise in the morning and the timepiece of God has woken you, cast the eyes of your heart towards your God). This evocation of the 'orloge de comtemplation et de sainte beguinage' is not confined to the copy in *A* either; an earlier variant of the text in a manuscript from Saint-Quentin also has it.[60]

To conclude this investigation of the context of the *Religion du cuer*, I want to turn again to the *Regle des fins amans*, the beguine rule mentioned in Chapter 1, with which the *Religion* has many affinities. Although the *Religion du cuer* is not a rule in the same sense as the *Regle*, both texts convey a vision of religious life outside traditional monastic structures which is governed by love and marked by the practice of poverty and contemplative prayer, a way of life they both call *beguinage*. It has been suggested that the *Regle* was one of the *Abbaye*'s sources, but the parallels between them point more to a shared ethos than to direct borrowing.[61] In any case, although both texts date from the late thirteenth century, it is impossible to say which was composed first. The shared ethos of the two texts is particularly evident in some of their allegorical figures, and in the structure of the idealized religious institution each text evokes.

The first element the *Regle* and the *Religion* share aligns them closely with the very particular way the mendicant orders expressed the value of poverty. Both texts assign a joint foundational role to poverty and humility. The pairing of humility and poverty is characteristic of mendicant teaching: both Francis and Dominic elevated poverty and humility among the virtues their followers should practise, and Francis did so with frequent reference to the poverty and humility of Christ.[62] The *Regle* and the *Religion* clearly share this way of seeing the two virtues. *Povreté* and *Humilité* are the two maidens who dig the foundations of the abbey:

> Si convenra fere les fondemens larges et parfons, et ce feront .ii. damoisieles. L'une a a non Humilités et l'autre Povretés. Humilités les fera bas et parfons. Et Povretés les fera grant et larges et jetera la terre de sa et de la, en largement donner quant qu'ele porra avoir et tenir.

[60] See the edition in Hasenohr, 'Un Faux Pierre de Luxembourg', p. 182.

[61] The suggestion was made, on the basis of some of the parallels outlined above, in Rice, 'Spiritual Ambition and the Translation of the Cloister', p. 235.

[62] For the pairing of humility and poverty in Franciscan and Dominican sources, see Mews, 'Apostolic Ideals in the Mendicant Transformation of the Thirteenth Century'.

[It is necessary to make the foundations wide and deep, and this will be done by two ladies. One is called Humility and the other, Poverty. Humility will make them low and deep, and Poverty will make them great and broad, and will cast earth this way and that by giving generously whatever she might possess.] (α_1)

Humility is often associated with the lower parts of the building in architectural allegories, but it is only in the *Religion* and the *Regle des fins amans* that Humility is paired with Poverty in this role.[63] For the author of the *Regle*, poverty and humility are two of the four pillars on which the order of *fins amans*, elsewhere equated with *beguinage*, reposes (the remaining two are purity and charity). Those in the order should love poverty because God loves the poor and chose to be poor on earth, and because all 'religions' are founded on poverty, growing and prospering while they love it, and being destroyed temporally and spiritually if they abandon it.[64] The implicit criticism of established religious orders which is conveyed in the *Regle*'s warning of what happens when an order abandons poverty is echoed by the *Religion*:

> Hé, benoite soit relegions qui est fondee en humilité et en povreté. Et c'est encontre aucuns mauvais relegieus orguelleus et couvoiteus.

> [Ah, blessed be an order of religion that is founded in humility and poverty; this is against certain bad religious who are proud and covetous.]

For the *Religion du cuer* and the *Regle* then, poverty is an essential criterion for judging the authenticity of any religious order and is fundamental to the order they are describing, which both call *beguinage*. Beguines and their male counterparts regarded poverty as central to their endeavour, as is illustrated by the poem *Qui veut droit beguignage avoir*: 'Car povreteis et beguignages | Doit estre ensi con mariages' (For poverty and beguinage | Should be like a marriage).[65] In this poem, the virtues of poverty and humility are once again closely associated and are used to judge existing religious orders. While neither the *Religion du cuer* nor the *Regle des fins amans* names the Franciscans as models of pov-

---

[63] In the *Droite forme pour vivre qui doit mener l'ame qui s'est donnee a Dieu en gardant sa virginité, sa veueté, son pucellage a tousiours au monde* (see Chapter 3) and the fourteenth-century spiritual allegory, the *Chastel perilleux* (see Brisson, *A Critical Edition and Study of Frere* Robert, Chartreux: 'Le Chastel Perilleux'), the moats are humility and the foundations are faith. In the *Vita* of Alice of Schaerbeck, humility forms the foundation of her edifice: Crassons, *The Claims of Poverty*, p. 73. Guiard of Laon's sermon on the Eucharist, in both its Latin and French forms, associates the humility of the Virgin with the depth of a moat.

[64] Christ, 'La Regle des fins amans', p. 198.

[65] Hilka, 'Altfranzösische Mystik und Beginentum', p. 148.

erty, although elsewhere the *Religion* mentions them favourably, this poem is explicit. The Franciscans' humility in openly showing their poverty makes them 'bon beguin'.[66]

Two of the virtues which constitute the four pillars of the order of *fins amans* also have parallels in the nuns who govern the *Abbaye du saint Esprit*. Humility, as well as being one of the ladies who digs the abbey's foundations, is its sub-prioress, and Charity is its abbess. The fourth pillar, Purity, corresponds to one of the servants of the Holy Spirit who is sent to clear the site for the abbey to be built.

When we come to the direction and spiritual oversight of the two orders, the similarities are striking: God is the visitor of both (the *Regle* does not differentiate between the members of the Trinity and assign them different roles as the *Religion* does; for the *Regle*, 'Deus' is both custodian and visitor of the order). The abbess of the *Religion* is Charity, and while the abbot of the *fins amans* is said to be Jesus, the rules of the order itself are to be carried out 'in obedience to holy charity'.[67] The admonition to the reader of the *Religion* not to come or go without the leave of the abbess, 'Et tout aussi c'on ne doit riens fere sans le congié de s'abesse' (And just as one should do nothing without the leave of one's abbess), echoes the stipulation of the *Regle* that the beguine should not go out without the leave of her superior, 'nule religieuse n'i ise sanz le congié de sa souvrainne' (no sister should go out without the leave of her superior). Apart from the fact that the *Religion* uses *abbesse*, in keeping with its allegorical framework of a traditional monastic institution, rather than *souverainne*, the common French term for the superior of a beguine community, the wording of the two texts at this point is similar enough to suggest borrowing. However, both texts may simply be echoing similarly worded prescriptions from beguine statutes.[68]

The vision of *beguinage*, a form of religious life existing outside traditional monastic structures, governed by love and marked by the practice of poverty and contemplative prayer, which the *Religion du cuer* shares with the *Regle des fins amans*, fits into the social and religious world the *Religion du cuer* reflects.

[66] Hilka, 'Altfranzösische Mystik und Beginentum', p. 147.

[67] 'Nos ordenons et establissons de par Jhesucrist, l'abé des fins amans, en l'obedience de sainte charité, par la vertu d'amors que li cuer soient estable et joint ensanble en l'amour de Jhesucrist.' (We ordain and establish through Jesus Christ, the abbot of true lovers, in the obedience of holy charity, by the virtue of love that hearts should be established and joined together in the love of Jesus Christ.) Christ, 'La Regle des fins amans', p. 199, lines 235–38.

[68] Christ, 'La Regle des fins amans', p. 208, n. 264.

They mark the *Religion du cuer* as a product of the conversation about ways of attaining Christian perfection in the world that was continuing to take place between clerics and laypeople throughout the thirteenth century, and particularly of the form it took in northern France and the Low Countries. Together with its dense fabric of intertextual resonances with other texts composed for, and occasionally by, beguines, these features confirm that the audience for whom the *Religion du cuer* was originally composed corresponded closely to that of some of the earliest manuscripts it was transmitted in.

When this is placed alongside the early dates of *M* and *C*, it seems reasonable to conclude that the *Religion du cuer* represents the earliest version of the *Abbaye*, from which the other surviving versions were derived. The *Religion du cuer*, that is, the redaction of the *Abbaye* from the α_1 family of manuscripts, had a wide influence: it was the source of the English translation, the fifteenth-century Picard rewriting for Franciscan nuns, and both the expanded version written in Ghent for Margaret of York and the fragmentary text in another of her manuscripts, *S*. Placing the *Religion du cuer* at the head of the *Abbaye* tradition shifts our view of the *Sainte abbaye*, long accepted, following Chesney, as the original form of the text. It leads us to see the *Sainte abbaye* as a very early reworking for a new audience, moving beyond its bourgeois origins and into the highest circles of the aristocracy, but also into the physical cloister.

Chapter 3

A Royal Cloister: The *Sainte abbaye*

At the end of the thirteenth century, a richly decorated manuscript was produced in Paris, probably for the royal Cistercian abbey of Maubuisson at Saint-Ouen-l'Aumône. It contained a copy of the *Somme le roi*, a compendium of moral advice produced by the Dominican Laurence of Orleans for Philip III, and four shorter works of spiritual advice, also illuminated, with one called *La Sainte abbaye* at their head. This version of the *Abbaye* became a valued text among women close to the crown; all of the surviving copies from this branch of the manuscript tradition are associated either with the royal abbey or with royal or ducal households. Two copies of it (including the one in the *Somme le roi* manuscript) are recorded in the Maubuisson inventory of 1463, and another was made at the end of the fourteenth century for Pierre Basin, confessor of the dowager queen Blanche de Navarre (widow of Philip VI).[1] A modified version, called the *Cloistre de l'ame*, was included in an illuminated book of moral and spiritual advice addressed to women, probably made for Jean, Duke of Berry, but presumably intended to be used by female members of his family, of which four copies are known. These six manuscripts constitute the surviving witnesses to the β redaction of the *Abbaye*.[2]

---

[1] BL, MS Additional 20697 (*N*).

[2] See the list of manuscripts of the β_1 and β_2 groups in Part II, Introduction. *B* passed at Jean de Berry's death into the library of his younger daughter, Marie, as part of the property she selected to make up her unpaid dowry; see Beaune and Lequain, 'Marie de Berry et les livres', pp. 49–50. *B* later became part of the library of Margaret of Austria; see Debae, *La Bibliothèque de Marguerite d'Autriche*, p. 37.

Because of the elite milieu in which most of these manuscripts were produced, much more information is available about their ownership and production than there is for the α_1 group. They can with one exception be placed in aristocratic households or convents and in some cases be linked to individuals, thus providing a precious window into the circulation of vernacular moral and spiritual advice among elite women in France in the thirteenth and fourteenth centuries.

Recent textual and manuscript studies suggest a concern for the moral formation of women in the aristocratic milieu for which these manuscripts were made, on the part of the women themselves and also of the dynastic interests they represented. Women were not mere passive recipients of moral writing; research on the book ownership of women of the same aristocratic milieu shows that they actively collected books and exchanged them as gifts or bequests, using them to cement relationships and maintain friendship and patronage networks.[3] The thirteenth and fourteenth centuries saw the composition of moral treatises, in both Latin and the vernacular, addressing royal women. Before the *Somme le roi* was created for the king, a treatise was written for Blanche of Castile, mother of Louis IX, called the *Speculum animarum* and translated into French. Later, at the beginning of the fourteenth century, Durand de Champagne wrote the *Speculum dominarum* for Jeanne de Navarre, wife of Philip IV. The French versions of both texts were copied for other noblewomen.[4] Recent research on these two treatises suggests an interesting development over the two generations that separate them; while the *Speculum animarum* concentrated on the queen's personal salvation and advised her to resist the worldly temptations of her role, the *Speculum dominarum* addressed the possibility that carrying out her public role in an ethical fashion would contribute to the queen's salvation.[5] Concern to shape the queen's fulfilment

---

[3] Much of this work has centred on the libraries of Jeanne d'Evreux and Blanche de Navarre, whose long widowhoods allowed them to manage their own affairs and occupy an important place within court networks. See Buettner, 'Le Système des objets dans le testament de Blanche de Navarre'; Holladay, 'Fourteenth-Century French Queens as Collectors and Readers of Books'; Green, 'What Were the Ladies in the City of Ladies Reading?'. For an individual case, see Field, 'Marie of Saint-Pol and her Books'.

[4] Copies of the *Miroir de l'ame* were made for Marie de Saint-Pol, an otherwise unidentified Madame de Macy, and possibly for Jeanne de Navarre: Field, 'From *Speculum anime* to *Miroir de l'âme*', pp. 83, 85–86. The *Miroir des dames* was copied for Jeanne d'Evreux, and copies were owned by Blanche de Navarre, Marie de Berry, Valentina Visconti, and Louise of Savoy: Mews, 'The *Speculum dominarum* (*Miroir des dames*)', p. 23. See also Mews and others, 'Introducing the *Miroir des dames*'.

[5] Mews, 'The *Speculum dominarum* (*Miroir des dames*)', p. 20.

of her role as king's consort and remind her of her position in the Capetian dynasty is at work in the book of hours produced for Jeanne d'Evreux, third wife of Charles IV.[6] It has been suggested that a book made for Marie de Berry, which included both spiritual and political texts, was part of an effort by Jean de Berry's entourage to create an image for her as an ideal lady — educated, virtuous, and devout — at a time when the queen, under attack, did not provide a female role model for the kingdom.[7]

It is clear that spiritual advisors to the court, who were often also confessors, played a role in the production and circulation of moral literature for royal women. Both the *Miroir de l'ame* and the *Miroir des dames* were written, at least in their original Latin versions, by such a person. Durand was the confessor of Jeanne de Navarre, while the author of the *Miroir de l'ame* is likely to have been a spiritual adviser in Blanche's circle.[8] Simon de Courcy, the confessor of Marie, daughter of Jean de Berry, compiled a book of spiritual advice for her, and presents his translation of the *Stimulus amoris* in that book as being made in response to her request, thus indicating that the composition of such works was not a one-way process. Similarly, the manuscript made for Pierre Basin, which will be discussed later in this chapter, shows him taking an interest in vernacular works of spiritual and moral advice, presumably for use in preaching and conversation with his royal patron and probably shaped by her interests.

Book production for aristocratic women did not only involve the composition of new texts. Sylvia Huot has drawn attention to manuscripts for aristocratic female readers which bring together pre-existing works but are shaped for a particular reader through their decoration and minor modifications to the texts.[9] The examples she studies are Paris, Bibliothèque de l'Arsenal, MS 3142, made for Marie de Brabant (widow of Philip III), and BnF, MS fonds français 24429, which may have been made for the same person. The patron can sometimes be identified by armorial decorations (Marie de Brabant) or explicit textual references, as in the case of Simon de Courcy's compilation for Marie de Berry, but sometimes only 'details and intermittent reminders' point to the shaping of a collection for a specific reader.[10]

---

[6] Holladay, 'The Education of Jeanne d'Evreux'; Caviness, 'Patron or Matron?'.

[7] Beaune and Lequain, 'Marie de Berry et les livres', p. 59. See also Walters, 'Le Thème du livre comme don de sagesse'.

[8] Sean Field suggests William of Auvergne or Vincent of Beauvais: 'Reflecting the Royal Soul', pp. 5–13.

[9] Huot, 'A Book Made for a Queen'.

[10] Huot, 'A Book Made for a Queen', p. 138.

Within these anthologies there are indications that the spiritual direction and moral formation of women was moving from the oral mediation of written Latin texts (reading aloud by a clerk or confessor who translated and explained as he went) to written mediation through vernacular translations. In these translations the monastic practice of private, meditative reading was sometimes scaffolded by written instructions. The examples provided by Huot are complemented by Simon de Courcy's instructions to Marie de Berry in his translation of the *Stimulus amoris*.[11] Not all the texts in anthologies were translations, of course, but it seems that texts composed in the vernacular were considered to be more straightforward than those based on Latin works, and not in need of explicit instructions for reading. Indeed, in most cases the very production of the text constituted a radical mediation of content drawn from a variety of sources and packaged in a form considered to be accessible to a lay reader.[12]

The two anthology manuscripts that are the main subject of this and the following chapter are further examples of such production. Both the Maubuisson and *Miroir* anthologies bear signs that they, like the examples mentioned above, were conceived as a curated programme of reading. Unlike the surviving α_1 manuscripts C and R, which bring together a wide selection of religious texts dealing with similar themes, the Maubuisson and *Miroir* anthologies present a small selection seemingly chosen to complement a major vernacular text of moral advice with royal associations — in the case of the Maubuisson manuscript, the *Somme le roi*, and in the later collection, the *Miroir des dames*. In these anthologies, the transmission of the *Abbaye* intersects with the project of moral formation of aristocratic women, within the context of textual circulation in the long fourteenth century. This chapter examines the Maubuisson manuscript and its version of the *Abbaye*, while the following chapter deals with the *Miroir* anthology.

The Maubuisson Manuscript

The uniform layout and decoration of this manuscript anthology, now split into two, makes it clear that it was conceived as a whole. It has attracted scholarly attention as one of the luxury illuminated copies of the *Somme le roi* produced during the reign of Philip IV. It is unusual among those copies in that the *Somme*

[11] Discussed by Beaune and Lequain, 'Marie de Berry et les livres', p. 57.

[12] Beaune and Lequain note in relation to *Bonne doctrine*, a vernacular text in Simon de Courcy's manuscript to which he did not add instructions, that it is lively and easy to memorize. 'Marie de Berry et les livres', p. 54.

forms part of a collection of texts, rather than being copied alone. Its association with Maubuisson rests on its identification by Richard and Mary Rouse with an item in the 1463 inventory of the books owned by the abbey. They argue on the basis of the miniatures that show nuns wearing what is arguably a Cistercian habit that it was probably made for the abbey, rather than being a later gift.[13] The making of this luxurious book was the product of a number of deliberate choices — of content, arrangement, and illustration — which, while they cannot be recovered with certainty, are hinted at by the history of Maubuisson and its relations with the crown, and by the evidence of the book itself.

The abbey of Notre Dame-la-royale was founded by Blanche of Castile, mother of Louis IX, in 1241. Blanche specified in the charter of foundation that the abbey should follow the Cistercian rule.[14] The abbey remained closely connected to the royal family; Blanche had a royal residence constructed in the abbey gardens, and a succession of kings made frequent visits there. It served as a retreat for royal women throughout the fourteenth century, and several queens and princesses endowed chapels in the abbey church.[15]

One clue to the circumstances of the manuscript's production may be provided by its central text, the *Somme le roi*. Although the *Somme* was written during the reign of Philip III, it is only in the 1290s, when Philip IV was on the throne, that copies with full-page illuminations begin to appear, the earliest ones belonging to the king and queen themselves.[16] The Rouses suggest that the making of illuminated copies may have been an initiative of Philip IV himself, to put his own mark on something that belonged to his father.[17] It certainly seems that a number of people in the king's entourage subsequently ordered

---

[13] Rouse and Rouse, *Manuscripts and their Makers*, pp. 155–56.

[14] Lemoine, *Inventaire sommaire des Archives Départementales*, 72 H. 115. The story of the foundation and building of Maubuisson is summarized in Kinder, 'Blanche of Castile and the Cistercians'.

[15] Marguerite de Provence; Mahaut, countess of Artois; Marguerite de Beaufort, princess of Antioch; Jeanne d'Evreux, widow of Charles IV; Philippe de Montmorency, widow of Jean. See Lemoine, *Inventaire sommaire des Archives Départementales*, 72 H. 81, 72 H. 82. Jeanne d'Evreux commissioned the altarpiece for the main altar of the abbey church: Baron, 'Le Maître-autel de l'abbaye de Maubuisson', p. 538.

[16] BL, MS Additional 54180, and Paris, Bibliothèque Mazarine, MS 870. The former has been identified as Philip the Fair's 'well illuminated copy', mentioned in Blanche de Navarre's will, and the latter, which also contains a copy of the *Miroir de l'ame*, was probably made for Jeanne de Navarre. Rouse and Rouse, *Manuscripts and their Makers*, pp. 148–54. Sean Field also makes the case for Mazarine MS 870 being made for Jeanne: 'From *Speculum anime* to *Miroir de l'âme*', p. 83.

[17] Rouse and Rouse, *Manuscripts and their Makers*, p. 147.

copies for themselves; there are a further five known illuminated versions of the text dating from the 1290s to the early 1300s, many of which can be connected to relatives of the king.[18]

The abbess of Maubuisson at this time, Blanche d'Eu, fitted the profile of women for whom copies of the illustrated *Somme* were made; indeed, one of the early illuminated copies was made for her nephew's wife, Jeanne, Countess of Eu and Guines.[19] Daughter of Alphonse de Brienne (Count of Eu) and Marie de Lusignan, Blanche was closely related to the royal family, and Blanche of Castile is reported to have overseen her education and been responsible for her taking the veil at Maubuisson.[20] At the time the manuscript was made she had been abbess for twenty years, and during that time had worked tirelessly to strengthen the economic base of the abbey and bolster its prestige. She must have been a woman of some means, since at her death, she endowed a chapel to the Holy Trinity in the abbey church.[21] It fits with what we know of her actions that she would, as the Rouses argue, seek a copy for the abbey of a prestigious new illuminated book that was closely associated with the king.[22] A recent study of the Maubuisson manuscript notes that it was 'the most copiously illuminated *Somme le roi* volume of its day' and 'a book that even a King might envy', arguing that this indicates an awareness on the part of the owner of (and access to) 'the latest thing in regal patronage'.[23] Blanche, as head of a royal foundation to which the royal family made frequent visits, and relative of the king, was well placed to have access to such patronage and to seek to acquire an object that would add to the prestige of her abbey. Those same characteristics, of course, also made her a possible recipient of such an object as a gift.

Such is the circumstantial evidence that points to the manuscript's production for the abbey of Maubuisson. This identification has been recently questioned by Aden Kumler, who has studied the relation between the programme of illumination and the content of the texts. She argues that the texts are directed at laywomen and that the miniatures represent an idealized way of thinking of the soul as a cloister rather than representing actual nuns, conclud-

---

[18] They are listed in Laurent d'Orléans, *La Somme le roi par Frère Laurent*, ed. by Brayer and Leurquin, pp. 34–35. Royal connections are listed on p. 24.

[19] Paris, Bibliothèque de l'Arsenal, MS 6329: Laurent d'Orléans, *La Somme le roi par Frère Laurent*, ed. by Brayer and Leurquin, p. 24.

[20] De Marsy, *Les Abbesses de Maubuisson*, p. 2.

[21] Lemoine, *Inventaire sommaire des Archives Départementales*, 72 H. 81.

[22] Rouse and Rouse, *Manuscripts and their Makers*, p. 156.

[23] Kumler, *Translating Truth*, p. 165.

ing that the manuscript was made for a high-born laywoman and only later given to the abbey.[24] We should not assume, however, that texts written for laywomen would not be considered suitable for nuns, since there was little composed in French specifically for nuns before the mid-fifteenth century.[25] Nor should we assume that a book owned by a women's community such as Maubuisson would be for the exclusive use of nuns. The continuing close contact between the abbey and women of the extended royal family, which included their residence there for periods of varying length, makes it quite probable that they too had access to some of the books owned by the abbey. The fifteenth-century inventory contains similar books of a spiritual nature to those listed in the wills of aristocratic women. There is no reason why the manuscript could not have been commissioned to be at the same time a showpiece for visitors to the abbey and a precious book in which the nuns could take pride and find spiritual nourishment, and the examination of the *Sainte abbaye* below will show that some features of that text could be interpreted as modifications made for an audience of nuns.

The argument that the miniatures represent an idealized way of thinking of the soul as cloister, as does the *Sainte abbaye* text, does not exclude the possibility of reading them as a symbolic representation of Maubuisson itself. Seen in the context of a desire to promote the abbey's close connections with the crown, the daring extension of the programme of illumination beyond the end of the *Somme le roi* could represent a type of corporate spiritual and political ambition. Just as Paris, Bibliothèque Mazarine, MS 870 customizes the queen's copy of the king's *Somme* by linking it to a work of moral and spiritual advice written for an earlier queen, the Maubuisson manuscript associates the king's favoured, richly illuminated text with a collection of works for women that is headed and framed by textual and pictorial representations of a women's abbey.

The Maubuisson manuscript, in its original form, was dominated by the illuminated *Somme le roi*. The rest of the manuscript consisted of a small library of spiritual advice with the *Sainte abbaye* at its head. The three texts following the *Sainte abbaye* are a treatise on the love of God, another on the three states of the soul, and a treatise on the twelve spiritual benefits of suffering, called in other manuscripts the *Livre des tribulations*. These texts complement the *Somme*; while it concentrates on moral teaching and the proper observance of practices such as confession, the others, with the exception of the *Livre des tribulations*, are more concerned with spiritual progress. Aden Kumler's perceptive study shows how the interplay between the full-page miniatures and the first three of

---

[24] Kumler, *Translating Truth*, p. 167.

[25] Hasenohr, 'Aspects de la littérature de spiritualité en langue française', p. 30.

the additional texts, in concert with the *Somme le roi*, constructs a 'program of interior edification' framed within the imagined architecture of the cloister.[26]

None of the additional texts are unique to this manuscript. The treatise on the love of God is known from one earlier manuscript, Paris, Bibliothèque Mazarine, MS 788, which is dated to the thirteenth century.[27] The treatise on three states of the soul is also found in two earlier thirteenth-century manuscripts, Paris, Bibliothèque de l'Arsenal, MS 2058 and Poitiers, Bibliothèque municipale, MS 83 (187).[28] The Mazarine and Arsenal manuscripts also contain copies of the third text, the *Livre des tribulations*. Both from the Walloon linguistic region, the two manuscripts have a considerable amount of content in common, including a collection of sermons in French. It is likely that they both reflect an earlier anthology of sermons and religious treatises which Michel Zink, in his study of medieval French vernacular sermons, suggests was of Cistercian origin, and possibly written for beguines.[29]

Zink's Cistercian identification was based on the content of the sermons, but the treatises on love and on the three states of the soul also show strong Cistercian influences. The treatise on love takes up the Bernardine theme of the ordering of love (divine and human) but focuses on human love. It begins by considering love of others, dividing it into three kinds, carnal, natural, and common, the latter being a general desire for the good and salvation of all. The author considers these three categories quite easy to grasp, but singles out for special attention a fourth kind, spiritual love — 'especiaus amours entre religieuse gent' — which is more complex. This is divided in turn into four types, which closely match Bernard's four degrees of love for God: love of the friend for one's own sake, love for the friend's sake, love of God in the friend, and love of the friend in God. In the next part of the text, which uses the three heavens of St Paul's vision as an allegorical frame, there is a further Bernardine echo. The gloss on the third heaven, saying that the soul cannot reach it by itself, just as Paul did not ascend by his own efforts but was lifted up, is the same as that used by Bernard in *On Humility and Pride*, VIII. 22.

---

[26] Kumler, *Translating Truth*, p. 163. Kumler analyses the spiritual texts (except the *Livre des tribulations*) in some detail but does not discuss their relation to copies in other manuscripts.

[27] There are also copies, some incomplete, in later manuscripts: BL, MS Royal 20 B III (complete), and the *Abbaye* manuscripts *C* and *DPBQ* (two differently abridged versions).

[28] Section romane, notice for 'Trois états de l'âme chrétienne, anonyme', Jonas-IRHT/CNRS, <http://jonas.irht.cnrs.fr/oeuvre/13732> [accessed 9 July 2016]. There is also a later copy in *C*.

[29] Zink, *La Prédication en langue romane*, pp. 52–53, 56, 135. See also Friesen, 'The Seven Gifts of the Holy Spirit'.

The treatise on the three states of the good soul also owes a great deal to Bernard's fourth sermon on the Song of Songs. The three states, ruled respectively by fear, hope, and charity, are equated with three stages of spiritual progress: 'des commencanz', 'des profitanz', and 'des parfaiz' (*Y*, fol. 28vb). As in Bernard's sermon, the three kisses of the feet, hand, and mouth correspond to the three states. In the three states treatise the appropriate behaviour at each stage is respectively contrition, prayer, and contemplation, which echoes what Bernard says in Sermon 4 about the movements of the soul that correspond to each kiss.[30] The treatise also draws on other sermons of Bernard's, sometimes citing him by name.[31]

The final text in the manuscript, the *Livre des tribulations*, was probably part of the original anthology, since it is present in the Arsenal and Mazarine manuscripts, and the copy in *Y* belongs to the same manuscript family.[32] Nonetheless, it is much more widely copied than the other texts and thematically somewhat different. It is also the only text in the collection to be a translation of a known Latin work, rather than an independent composition in French. Its source, the *Tractatus de Tribulatione*, has been erroneously attributed to Peter of Blois, but it is likely that it dates from the third quarter of the thirteenth century.[33] The work addresses the same broad, non-gendered audience as the *Somme le roi* — it is associated with the *Somme* in another manuscript of the same period, Paris, Bibliothèque Sainte-Geneviève, MS 2899 — and may have been included simply because it was widely regarded as a useful source of religious advice. However, a number of the benefits of suffering that it lists (purging, leading to knowledge of God and self, guarding and nourishing the heart, and prepar-

---

[30] 'Invenit profecto apud Deum et verecunda confessio, quo se humiliando deiciat, et prompta devotio, ubi se innovando reficiat, et iucunda contemplatio, ubi excedendo quiescat.' ('The heartfelt desire to admit one's guilt brings a man down in lowliness before God, as it were to his feet; the heartfelt devotion of a worshiper finds in God renewal and refreshment, the touch, as it were, of his hand, and the delights of contemplation lead on to that ecstatic repose that is the fruit of the kiss of his mouth.') Bernard of Clairvaux, 'Sermones super Cantica Canticorum', ed. by Leclercq, Talbot, and Rochais, Sermon 4. 4. Subsequent citations are from this edition. Translation from Bernard of Clairvaux, *On the Song of Songs I*, trans. by Walsh. See also McGinn, *The Growth of Mysticism*, p. 184.

[31] For example: 'Et de ce dist saintz bernarz. Touz li mondes tramble et les montaignes remetent devant lui, et ceste est si hardie que ele le requiert pour baisier. Est ele yvre? Oil voir' (And of this Saint Bernard said: the world trembles and the mountains melt before him, and she is so bold that she asks him for a kiss. Is she drunk? Yes, indeed) (*Y*, fol. 40^{ra-b}), translating 'Respicit terram, et facit eam tremere, et ista se ab eo postulat osculari? Ebria ne est? Ebria prorsus' (Sermon 7. 3).

[32] Barratt, *The Book of Tribulation*, p. 20.

[33] Barratt, *The Book of Tribulation*, p. 28.

ing it to receive grace) can be applied to the quest for spiritual perfection that characterizes the *Sainte abbaye* and the treatises on love and the three states of the soul.

The evidence points to the possibility of an existing collection of spiritual reading, itself produced in a Cistercian milieu and possibly originally intended for laywomen pursuing a religious life at home, being the source for the additional texts in the Maubuisson *Somme le roi* volume. The compiler of the Maubuisson manuscript must have had access to a copy that combined the texts now represented in Arsenal MS 2058 and Mazarine MS 788. Was the *Abbaye* also part of that collection? There is no trace of it in the transmission history of the sermon and treatise collection, but in the early fourteenth-century manuscript *C*, the *Religion du cuer* (α_1) occurs together with the treatises on the love of God and the three states of the soul as well as two other texts from Arsenal MS 2058, the *Sermon du palmier* and the *Garde du coeur*. Therefore, the existence of another manuscript containing all those texts is certainly a possibility. On the other hand, the exemplar for the *Sainte abbaye* may have been the other copy mentioned in the 1463 inventory, which was in a manuscript containing stories of the Passion and the Meditations of St Bernard in French, and some stories in Latin. The origins and subsequent fate of that manuscript are unknown.

The Sainte abbaye

The *Sainte abbaye* (β_1) has been regarded by most scholars (following Chesney) as the original from which the others are derived. I have argued in the preceding chapter that there is a strong case for considering the *Religion du cuer* (α_1) as the original, as it had a far wider distribution and influence than β_1. If we accept α_1 as the original, the *Sainte abbaye* appears in a different light: as a text reshaped for a new audience. As I have argued in the earlier parts of this chapter, that audience would have been cloistered nuns and possible also laywomen, drawn from the ranks of the nobility.

The first difference that strikes a reader familiar with the other *Abbaye* versions is that the *Sainte abbaye* begins directly with the location of the abbey in the conscience. The *Religion du cuer* is directed towards people living outside the cloister in a context of urban lay piety, but while there are points where this original context shows through in the *Sainte abbaye*, such as the use of the word *beguinage*, many of the other markers of that context are absent. The first-person prologue which alludes to the situation of those who would like to belong to a religious order but cannot, because they are married or too poor, is

absent. The audience is thus widened; it may include those who are already in a religious order, as well as those who are not.

Another difference is the positioning of the *Sainte abbaye* in relation to traditional monasticism. The *Religion du cuer*, while using the construct of the abbey for its model of lay spiritual interiority, at times adopts a critical stance in relation to organized religious life and privileges the mendicant orders over the monastic ones. In two places it criticizes unworthy members of religious orders. One is where Poverty and Humility dig the foundations, and their work is presented as an antidote to pride and covetousness among 'mauvés religieus': 'Hé, benoite soit religions qui est fondee en humilité et en povreté. Et c'est encontre aucuns mauvais relegieus orguelleus et couvoiteus' (Ah, blessed be an order of religion that is founded in humility and poverty; this is against certain bad religious who are proud and covetous) (α_1). The other comes in a passage on the importance of charity, criticizing those religious whose actions are not governed by charity:

> Je voi moult de gens en relegion qui moult sont relgions petis. Et mout de choses font et dient et en mout de lieus vont, qui moult de choses prendent et donent encontre le commandement de Madame Carité. Si est tout perdu devant Dieu.

> [I see many in religion who do not hold it in high regard, and who act and speak, and go to many places, and take and give many things against the commandment of my lady Charity, and all of it is lost before God.] (α_1)

The *Sainte abbaye* is less critical, only reproducing the first of the two passages. It also omits references to the mendicants. Speaking of the benefits of establishing an abbey in the conscience, all the surviving α_1 and α_2 witnesses specifically credit the Friars Minor and the Preachers with improving desolate and barren sites. The *Sainte abbaye*, on the other hand, simply says: 'Souvent est avenu que li lieu qui suelent estre mout lait et gaste, la sunt les religions fondees, s'en sunt li lieu plus bel et plus delitable' (It has often happened that religious communities are set up in places that used to be ugly and laid waste, making those places fairer and more delightful).[34] While not the only explanation for these changes, adaptation for an audience of enclosed monastic women following the Cistercian rule could account for the softening of the criticism of unworthy religious and the specific reference to other orders.

Some differences between the *Sainte abbaye* and α_1 reflect a change in orientation away from mystical prayer and a strengthening of the penitential

---

[34] All quotes from the *Sainte abbaye* are from the edition in Part II, unless the wording of a particular manuscript is indicated.

aspect of the *Abbaye*'s teachings. The references to people praying and falling into rapture while spinning or reading the psalms are missing from the treatment of ecstatic prayer in the *Sainte abbaye*. This passage is reduced to a translation of Gregory's definition of *jubilatio*, with the brief comment 'si comme il avient aus genz esperituels' (as happens to spiritual people). At the very least, we can say that the author of the *Sainte abbaye* had little sympathy with this kind of prayer, but it may also be that he found the descriptions in his model to be, like the introductory passage, too marked as belonging to a particular lay religious milieu.[35]

There are also two passages in the *Sainte abbaye* which do not appear anywhere in α_1. One is the short musical allegory that comes at the end of the passage on the sacristan's timepiece:

> Cest auloge doit chanter par trois manieres de chanz: par nature, par bequarré, par bemol. C'est a dire qu'ele doit chanter par nature, que ele doit (5rb) penser et regarder la nature dont ele est, qui est vilz et abhominable, par bequarré a la mort d'enfer, qui est fort et pardurable, par bemol qui est uns chanz plus douz, a la joie de paradis qui est douce et delitable. Pour la premiere chose se doit on humiliier, pour la seconde tout pechié fuir et eschiver, pour la tierce bien faire, pour gaaignier et desservir si grant loyer.

> [This clock should sing in three ways: natural, sharp, and flat. That is to say, she should sing natural by thinking and looking at the nature she partakes of, which is vile and abominable, sharp by thinking of death in hell, which is powerful and everlasting, flat, which is a sweeter music, by thinking of the joy of paradise which is sweet and delightful. For the first of these one should humble oneself, for the second all sin flee and shun, for the third do good, to earn and deserve such great reward.]

The passage develops an extended metaphor of singing and wakefulness, present in α_1 and α_2, which begins with the soul singing like the bride in the Song of Songs, remaining wakeful while the body sleeps and thus able to sing a secular song about a heart woken by bells to love. The doctrinal content introduced by the allegory is penitential in tone, in contrast to the rest of the passage, which is concerned with love and desire for God. Seen beside the paring-back of the material on ecstatic prayer in the *jubilatio* passage, this looks like another example of downplaying the tendency towards mysticism of the *Religion du cuer*.

---

[35] Another removal of a reference to a lay context comes in the passage on the sacristan, *Jalousie*, where the heart woken to prayer by the desire for God evokes the words of a secular song. The words of the song are retained in the *Sainte abbaye*, but the reference to its secular nature is not.

This passage represents a very early use of the musical terms *bemol* and *bequarre* in French.[36] Although they were being used in everyday expressions in the early fifteenth century, they may at this time still have been specialist technical terms, familiar only to those working with music, such as choir nuns. The large number of liturgical books in the Maubuisson library attests to the importance of sung prayer in the nuns' lives, and the activity of liturgical singing is depicted in the miniature on folio 6ᵛ of *Y*.[37] The allegorical use of musical terms would seem particularly appropriate to them.

The other added passage strengthens and clarifies the didactic import of the narrative of the four daughters of the Devil, the *locus* where the *Abbaye*, in all versions except γ, dramatizes the struggle between virtue and vice. The introduction to this episode in α₁ is quite brief, saying that when the abbey is established, a great usurer (the Devil) uses his wealth to gain entry for his daughters. In the *Sainte abbaye*, this is much expanded. The incursion is attributed to the negligence of the portress, Fear of God, and presented as habitual, rather than an isolated occurrence. The Devil's operation as a usurer is explained; he lends souls a little honour and pleasure in this life and exacts payment from his debtors in the form of endless torment in the next. This framing of the episode strengthens its admonitory nature and reinforces the penitential aspect of the *Abbaye*'s message.

In the subtle refashioning of the *Sainte abbaye* two trends can be observed. One is the move away from obvious markers of a lay audience. The other is a tendency to attenuate the material on contemplative prayer or counterbalance it with more penitential teachings. Behind these trends there was probably an interplay between the writer's own preoccupations and his perception of the needs and tastes of his audience.

The readers of the Maubuisson manuscript did not encounter the *Sainte abbaye* in isolation, however. The texts of the collection provided rich content for meditative reading, from which the reader could construct spiritual meanings in many ways. If she was left wanting more about contemplative prayer after reading the *Sainte abbaye* she could find an ample development of the subject in the *Trois etats*. The reader of the *Somme le roi* would find in the other

---

[36] The *Dictionnaire étymologique de l'ancien français* gives an example of use of *becarré* from the chronicle of Geoffroy de Paris, dated to 1316: DEAF, *becarré*, <https://deaf-server.adw.uni-heidelberg.de/lemme/cadre#bécarre> [accessed 17 November 2018].

[37] Liturgical books account for three quarters of the Maubuisson manuscripts in the fifteenth-century inventories. Bondéelle-Souchier, 'Les Moniales cisterciennes et leurs livres manuscrits', p. 212.

texts a number of themes which resonate with or extend its material. There is extensive use of building metaphors to represent the construction of the interior self in the *Somme* and the *Sainte abbaye*, while spiritual ascent is a strong theme in the *Sainte abbaye*, the four loves treatise, and the *Trois etats*. Teaching about the sacraments, an important element in the *Somme*, has a substantial place in the four loves treatise, where the Eucharist is linked to meditation, as it is in the *Sainte abbaye*.[38] If the first three short treatises following the *Somme le roi* can be seen as extending that text in the direction of spiritual self-fashioning, the final one (the *Livre des tribulations*) might be seen as a counterbalance, affirming the positive role of suffering in Christian life. Suffering is less present elsewhere in the collection, although the three spiritual texts follow convention in presenting purgation through contrition and penitence as the foundation for spiritual ascent.

Finally, the interplay between the text and the miniatures in this richly illuminated manuscript cannot be ignored. The miniatures arguably privilege certain readings, for instance presenting a heightened emphasis on sacramental participation, and portraying an unmediated access to God that goes beyond what is present in the texts.[39] They also present female figures (generally nuns, but in one case a laywoman) with which a female reader can readily identify.[40] Michele Tomasi links the emphasis on the Eucharist in the miniatures with an existing culture of eucharistic devotion at Maubuisson, evidenced in the sculptures of the altarpiece commissioned by Jeanne d'Evreux.[41]

A Chaplain's Copy

In the prestigious collection of moral and spiritual advice that was the Maubuisson manuscript, the *Abbaye* occupies a central role. At the head of the appended texts, it provides the turning point between the moral-theological advice of the *Somme* and the counsels on perfecting the interior life. As Kumler demonstrates, this transition is underlined in the programme of illumination, which moves at this point from a secular architecture to that of the cloister.[42] There

---

[38] These themes are signalled by Kumler, *Translating Truth*, pp. 165, 186–96, 230–35.

[39] Kumler, *Translating Truth*, pp. 222–35.

[40] The figure in the miniature on fol. 29ʳ is often described as a nun, but Kumler points out that her dress suggests she is a lay penitent: *Translating Truth*, pp. 230, 267 n. 163.

[41] Tomasi, 'La pala d'altare di Maubuisson', p. 129.

[42] Kumler, *Translating Truth*, p. 165.

is some evidence that the *Abbaye* occupied a central role for readers, too. The further transmission of this version of the text suggests that it was regarded as an important source for the spiritual edification of aristocratic women.

A manuscript (*N*) made for Pierre Basin, confessor to Blanche de Navarre, widow of Philip VI, contains a faithful (though now incomplete) copy of the *Sainte abbaye* as it occurs in *Y*.[43] *N* is only a fragment of Pierre Basin's original manuscript, since 145 folios, according to the original numbering, are missing. It consists of two whole texts, Jean Ferron's translation of the *Liber moralis de ludo scaccorum* by Jacques de Cessoles, and a verse translation of Bonaventure's *Lignum vitae*, and two incomplete texts, the *Sainte abbaye* and the end of a text on the Last Judgement. These two fragments occupy the end of the final quire of the *Liber moralis* translation and the beginning of the initial quire of the *Lignum vitae* translation respectively. Whether this is the result of deliberate breaking up of the manuscript by a collector or of damage to the original is impossible to tell, although the fact that the two main texts have recognizable authors could indicate a deliberate choice. It seems, however, that damage also played a part: the first thirteen folios of the *Liber moralis* translation come from a different copy of the text.[44] Extensive marginal notations in Latin throughout the original part of the manuscript suggest that it was used by a priest who wanted to be able to quickly identify exempla, material on the virtues, and other useful supports for preaching or spiritual direction in the vernacular.

This fits well with the little we know about Pierre Basin. He was Blanche's confessor at the time of her death in 1398, when he had been in her service for over thirty years, and like most of the confessors of French queens in the fourteenth century, was a Franciscan.[45] She valued him highly enough to make

---

[43] A note in a fifteenth-century hand at the end of the last text reads: 'Iste liber pertinet fratri Petro Basin, quem fecit scribi Neauphe dum erat ibi residens cum domina regina Blancha, cujus deus habeat animam.' See Meyer, 'Notice sur le manuscrit du Musée britannique Add. 20697'.

[44] Although the format is almost identical (double columns of thirty-seven lines), there is a slight overlap in the text at the join: fol. 13vb ends with: 'Valere raconte quil estoit vn trop bon aduocat qui auoit nom anthoine qui en iuge', while fol. 14ra begins: 'antoine qui en iugement fu accuse'. It is on fol. 14 that the original numbering starts, and the marginal notes which continue through the manuscript. The original folios seem to have been trimmed at the time when the slightly narrower quires were added, since many of the notes in the outer margins have been cut off.

[45] A document concerning the carrying out of one of Blanche's bequests names him as 'Petrus Basin ordinis fratrum minorum'. Printed in Félibien, *Histoire de la ville de Paris*, III, 226. Marguerite Keane provides evidence for the length of his service in Keane, *Material Culture and Queenship in 14th-Century France*, p. 6. On the Franciscans as confessors to French queens, see de la Selle, *Le Service des âmes à la cour*.

him a very generous bequest and trust him to be her executor. As well as money, vestments and altar vessels, a religious painting, a reliquary, and a set of room hangings, she left him two books. One of them was the missal 'he and his brothers' used when saying Mass in her chapel.[46] The other was a book from her library, containing a copy of Gregory the Great's sermons and dialogues and the *Vies des Peres*, a collection of exempla.[47] Blanche's other bequests indicate that she gave some thought to choosing appropriate books to give people, so this one may indicate a recognition that Pierre was interested in preaching and would appreciate the sermon-making resource that such a book represented.

The volume he had made at Neauphe, when he was in attendance there on Blanche, looks to have been another such resource, and it is likely that its content was chosen to inform his preaching to and conversation with her. The four texts represented in the surviving manuscript are all eminently suitable for discussion with a lay noblewoman interested in spiritual matters, and two of them, the *Histoire morale et philosophique du Jeu des Echecs* and the *Sainte abbaye*, were already present in Blanche's environment; she may have drawn them to her confessor's attention. The *Histoire morale et philosophique du Jeu des Echecs* was a collection of moralized exempla which used the game of chess as a frame, so like the dialogues of Gregory the Great and the *Vie des Peres*, it was a handy resource for a preacher.[48] But since the frame dealt with the moves of each chess piece in turn, it also considered, in a stylized way, the role of a queen, presenting a particular vision of a queen's virtues.[49] Blanche herself owned a copy of the work, although it was probably a different translation from the one in *N*.[50] The *Jeu des Echecs* was a valuable storehouse of exempla for any preacher, but it might have been particularly useful for the queen's confessor to gather examples from a work she knew herself. Pierre Basin's choice of the translation by Jean Ferron is interesting: based on the longer version of the Latin original, it offers a closer and more readable translation than the one by Jean de

---

[46] Delisle, *Testament de Blanche de Navarre*, art. 263. The gifts to Pierre Basin are listed in Keane, *Material Culture and Queenship in 14th-Century France*, pp. 210, 218–19, 228–29.

[47] Delisle, *Testament de Blanche de Navarre*, art. 259.

[48] *Jacques de Cessoles, 'Le jeu des eschaz moralisé'*, ed. by Collet, p. 93.

[49] Quentel-Touche, 'Charles V's Visual Definition of the Queen's Virtues', pp. 69–70.

[50] Her copy is likely to have been the translation by Jean de Vignay, who had been under the protection of her husband Philip VI and had dedicated the work to Philip's son Jean. The translation in Pierre Basin's manuscript is by Jean Ferron, written in the middle of the fourteenth century, possibly at the court of Pope Clement VI in Avignon. See *Jacques de Cessoles, 'Le jeu des eschaz moralisé'*, ed. by Collet, pp. 85, 90–91.

Vignay.[51] The other surviving text from Pierre's compilation was a translation of the *Lignum vitae*, Bonaventure's meditation on the life and crucifixion of Christ written for his fellow friars. It proposed a practice — imaginative meditation on the Passion — that was widely recommended to women.[52] Such texts also provided a source of information about the life of Christ, which is precisely what the annotations in Pierre Basin's copy focus on.

While she possessed many books of spiritual reading matter, Blanche did not own a copy of the *Sainte abbaye* at the time she made her will, but may have had access to it at Maubuisson, so like the *Jeu des Echecs*, it may have provided examples — in this case of the working of the virtues — in a context familiar to the queen. Given the religious interests reflected in her books, and her closeness to and esteem for Pierre Basin, it is reasonable to see his manuscript as an element in a dialogue on spiritual matters between the dowager queen and her confessor, and its contents, including the *Abbaye*, as reflecting her interests.[53]

Pierre Basin's manuscript, as well as providing an insight into the involvement of confessors, particularly Franciscans, in the circulation of spiritual advice for women, attests the presence of the Maubuisson collection within the ambit of the court at the end of the fourteenth century. Not long after his manuscript was made, there was further interest in the *Abbaye* within court circles.

---

[51] Evdokimova, 'Deux types de traduction au milieu du xivᵉ siècle'. Evdokimova sees early signs of humanist interests in Jean Ferron's translation (pp. 56–57, 61). The translations were first compared by Jean Rychner, who noted Ferron's superior ability to render the Latin into readable French: Rychner, 'Les Traductions françaises de la Moralisatio super Ludum scaccorum de Jacques de Cessoles'.

[52] The translation reproduced in Pierre Basin's manuscript exists also in a manuscript from Nevers, dated 1376, BnF, MS nouvelles acquisitions françaises 4276.

[53] Keane suggests that Pierre Basin's inscription in the manuscript he had made indicates 'that he wanted to make reference to a book community in Blanche's household': *Material Culture and Queenship in 14th-Century France*, p. 114.

Chapter 4

THE *MIROIR DES DAMES* COMPILATION

During the first decade of the fifteenth century, a reworked version of the *Sainte abbaye* was included in a collection of moral and spiritual advice for aristocratic women.[1] The *Miroir des dames* anthology targets an aristocratic female reader and presents her with resources to nourish a programme of virtuous self-fashioning. Its layout and decoration provide a visual unity that positions the additional texts as a continuation of the *Miroir*. Like the Maubuisson manuscript, this collection of texts is built around a major work on the cultivation of virtue addressed to a member of the royal family. Its centrepiece is the *Miroir des dames*, the French translation of a treatise on queenship, the *Speculum dominarum*, written for Jeanne de Navarre, wife of Philip IV, by her Franciscan confessor Durand de Champagne. The treatise covers the moral considerations necessary for a queen: the virtues she should cultivate both as a female member of fallen humanity and in her public role in the government of the kingdom. It was the first moral treatise for a queen to deal with this public role.[2] The French version was widely disseminated among women close to the crown.[3] As a group the β_2 manuscripts constitute an impor-

---

[1] There is a preliminary analysis of this collection in Pinder, 'A Lady's Guide to Salvation'. What follows here is amplified and corrected by further research.

[2] For a summary of scholarship on *Speculum dominarum*/*Miroir des dames*, see Mews and others, 'Introducing the *Miroir des dames*'.

[3] See Green, 'Christine de Pizan', pp. 244–45, and Mews and others, 'Introducing the *Miroir des dames*', pp. 321–34.

tant witness to the dissemination of the *Miroir*, representing just under a third of the surviving examples.[4]

Most collections of devotional texts made for women were one-off productions, like the Maubuisson manuscript. The multiple copies of this collection make it unusual and indicate that it was valued as a whole and not just as a copy of the *Miroir des dames*. Three illuminated copies (*D*, *B*, and *Q*) survive, along with a later copy on paper, without illuminations (*P*). Of the illuminated copies, two have miniatures (*D* and *B*) and were made in one of the commercial manuscript workshops in Paris — the workshop of the Virgil Master — soon afterwards entering the library of the Duke of Berry.[5] The third illuminated copy (*Q*) is less richly decorated and may be later.[6] It was given to Thomine de Villequier, Countess of Villars, by Charles, Count of Nevers, in 1454.[7] Charles de Nevers was the grandson of Marie de Berry, who owned one of the copies that had been in her father's library, so it is possible that manuscript was the model for the copy he presented to Thomine de Villequier.

There is no evidence of how the two copies of the *Miroir des dames* collection came to be in Jean de Berry's library, but it seems likely that he commissioned them. The two manuscripts are not identical. Meiss dates *D* to 1407–10 and *B* to 1410, which makes it possible that *D* is the earlier copy. *B* is more richly illuminated, with a double-column miniature at the beginning of the *Miroir des dames* showing Durand presenting his book to the queen (*D* only has a single quarter-column miniature), and an extra miniature at the start of the poem *Je vois morir* showing three richly dressed men on horseback beside a cross, fac-

[4] Mews and others, 'Introducing the *Miroir des dames*', p. 321.

[5] Meiss, *French Painting in the Time of Jean de Berry: The Limbourgs*, I, 408–09. In the earlier volume of this series, Meiss did not list BL, MS Additional 29986 among the manuscripts associated with the Virgil Master: Meiss, *French Painting in the Time of Jean de Berry: The Late Fourteenth Century*.

[6] The manuscript is described in Laborde, *Les Principaux Manuscrits à peintures conservés dans l'ancienne Bibliothèque publique de Saint-Petersbourg*, p. 69, with a more recent summary of information in Sylvie Lefevre, 'SANKT-PETERBURG, National Library of Russia, fr. 4° v. III. 0001', Jonas-IRHT/CNRS, <http://jonas.irht.cnrs.fr/manuscrit/80982> [accessed 30 June 2017]. Laborde states that there are no miniatures, but the notes taken by S. Lefevre and made available by the IRHT indicate that there was once a presentation miniature, which has been cut out of the manuscript. 'SPfrqvIII1', *IDeAL*, <http://ideal.irht.cnrs.fr/document/819696> [accessed 5 July 2017].

[7] Thomine de Villequier was the daughter of a powerful Norman family close to the crown, and both her brother, André de Villequier, and her husband, Jean de Lévis, were members of Charles VII's inner circle. Beaucourt, *Histoire de Charles VII*, v, 59–76.

ing three cadavers. This is a representation of the legend of the Three Living and Three Dead, a medieval form of memento mori closely related to the poem that follows it.[8] This miniature, and perhaps also the poem that it accompanies, may provide another link with the Duke of Berry, since three other representations of the subject are associated with him. Two are miniatures in books of hours that he commissioned: one in the *Tres riches heures*, where the three living are pictured on horseback, and one in the *Petites heures*, where they are on foot. The other is a sculpture that was on the south porch of the Church of the Holy Innocents in Paris, the same church that was well known for the Dance of Death represented on the walls of its cemetery. According to a poem accompanying the sculpture, it was put up in 1408, very close to the time manuscript *B* was produced.[9]

If Jean de Berry did commission the manuscripts, it was not for his own use, since it is clear from the contents and the illustrations that the collection was intended for a lady of noble birth. He had two adult daughters at that time, and a young second wife, Jeanne de Boulogne, whom he had married in 1389, all of whom are possible recipients. One of the miniatures shows three ladies in ermine-trimmed robes listening to the teaching of a seated figure (in one manuscript it is a man in clerical dress, but in the other the figure is a haloed woman in a blue robe with ermine trimming), so perhaps one was made with the three of them in mind, and then a second copy was ordered. One copy (*B*) seems to have passed out of his possession by the time of his death; there is no trace of it in the 1416 inventory, and no clue to its subsequent location before its appearance among the books of Margaret of Austria in 1523–24.[10] The other (*D*) was among the books Jean's younger daughter, Marie, chose from his library after his death. It did not pass into the library of the dukes of Bourbon with her other books at her death; she may have given it to her daughter Bonne d'Artois, since it was Bonne's son Charles who presented a copy to Thomine de Villequier.[11]

Marie also owned an earlier, incomplete copy of the *Miroir des dames*.[12] She evidently had an interest in devotional literature; she was also the recipient,

---

[8] See below, note 16.

[9] These images are discussed in detail in Kinch, *Imago mortis*, pp. 131–38.

[10] See Debae, *La Bibliothèque de Marguerite d'Autriche*, p. 38.

[11] On the other hand, the copy given to Thomine de Villequier may have been made for Bonne, and *D* given to someone else. In the early sixteenth century it was in the possession of a Jehan Sala, probably the brother of the Lyonnais humanist Pierre Sala.

[12] BRB, MS 11203–04. For the identification with Marie, see Bousmanne, Johan, and Van

in 1406, of a collection mixing spiritual reading and Jean Gerson's proposals for reform of the kingdom, compiled by her confessor, Simon de Courcy.[13] In content and execution, this book has many similarities with the *Miroir* collection. It contains works attributed to known spiritual masters (Bonaventure and Suso), as well as an anonymous work, *Bonne doctrine*, a 'rule of life' for a woman living in the world, like two of the texts in the *Miroir* collection, the *Cloistre de l'ame* and the *Droite forme pour vivre*. It came from another of the prestigious Parisian workshops patronized by the Duke of Berry, that of the Luçon master. It provides a programme of instruction the lady reading it can follow for herself; Simon de Courcy's introduction to his translation of the *Stimulus amoris* indicates that the book can stand in his stead, and when Marie reads it she will be her own teacher. To help her do this, in the tables of contents of the two longer works he indicates how she can use each chapter.[14] Finally, the combination of devotional texts with one advocating political reform in Simon de Courcy's compilation to a certain extent has a parallel in the combination of devotional texts with a mirror for princesses which, although largely concerned with spiritual and moral well-being, is also concerned with the public role of women who wield political power.

Shaping into a Collection

Whether made for Marie de Berry or some other lady, the *Miroir* anthology is certainly a similar type of creation to the book put together by Simon de Courcy. It too is an instrument of instruction, bringing together a library of moral and spiritual works the lady can read for herself. A variety of iconographic, formatting, and textual features are combined to weld its parts together. Its consistent programme of decoration and formatting makes it clear that the collection is conceived of as a whole. The miniatures underline the didactic mission of the compilation: in the opening miniature, the queen is receiving Durand's educative mirror treatise, and in the miniature at the head of Anselm's meditation three ladies are being taught by a figure of religious authority. The running

Hoorebeeck, *La Librairie des ducs de Bourgogne*, p. 244. That copy must have been in Bonne's possession when she married Philip the Good, since it passed into the ducal library of Burgundy.

[13] Beaune and Lequain, 'Marie de Berry et les livres'. The manuscript is BnF, MS fonds français 926, now available online through Gallica at <http://gallica.bnf.fr/ark:/12148/btv1b9059107q/f.1.item>.

[14] The textual scaffolding Simon provides is discussed in Beaune and Lequain, 'Marie de Berry et les livres', pp. 54–57.

chapter titles that are a feature of many copies of the *Miroir des dames* are here extended to the additional texts, as though they were further chapters of the *Miroir*. This impression is reinforced at the end of the final text, with 'Explicit le livre du mirouer de dames'.[15] There are also two short introductory passages, presumably composed by the compiler, which attempt to increase coherence and, while not giving such explicit guidance on how to read the works as Simon de Courcy does in his book for Marie de Berry, to orient the reader. The first forms a bridge between the *Miroir des dames* and the poem on death that follows it, the *Miroir de mortel vie*. In it, the writer positions himself as though he is accompanying the reader, deftly using the *Miroir*'s organizing motif of the three houses the wise woman should build to justify the inclusion of the poem that follows and underline the theme of the transitoriness of human life. In that way it turns the poem into a pendant to the *Miroir des dames*:

> Et pour ce que derrainement auons fait mencion de la maison de paradis de laquelle parle le sage en ecclesiastique, *Ad domum convivii in illa finis est cunctorum*. En la maison du conuit la est la fin de tous. Afin que chascun s'auise que en ce monde n'a nulle habitacion pardurable ains est chascune transitoire. *Et fugit velud umbra*. Pour ce s'ensuit le traitte qui demoustre de chascun estat la finable conclusion humainne. *Vt quisque de se ipso loquatur*. Selon son estat en disant [...].

> [And since we have just made reference to the house of paradise, of which the wise man in Ecclesiastes speaks, *Ad domum convivii in illa finis est cunctorum* (Ecclesiastes 7. 3). In the house of [feasting] is the end of all. So that each may realize that in this world there is no lasting dwelling; rather, each is transitory — *Et fugit velud umbra*. For this reason, there follows here a treatise which shows the final conclusion of every human estate. *Vt quisque de se ipso loquatur*. According to his estate, saying [...].] (*D*, fol. 147ʳᵃ)

The second passage is at the beginning of the text that follows the *Cloistre de l'ame*, the *Meditation* of St Anselm. Like the tables of contents in Simon de Courcy's book, it indicates how the text it introduces can be used by the reader: 'Cy commencent les meditacions St Anseaume et ore parle sa raison a s'ame. Et donne exemple a pecheur comment il doit son peche congnoistre en grant douleur et soy convertir et dit ainsi [...]' (Here begin the meditations of Saint Anselm and now his reason speaks to his soul, and gives an example to the sinner of how he should recognize his sin in great sorrow and turn back to God, and says this [...]) (*D*, fol. 152ᵛᵇ).

---

[15] *D*, fol. 167ʳᵃ and *Q*, fol. 222ᵛᵃ; *B*, fol. 179ʳ adds 'et autres livres'.

There is an echo here of the ascetic tone of the bridging passage that pre-
cedes the *Miroir du monde*. Naming the author of the meditation may be
another attempt to tie the collection together. In the other manuscripts in
which translations of this meditation survive, its author is not identified, so
perhaps the compiler is simply showing off his familiarity with the text. But
being able to attribute a text to a named author seems to be important for the
compiler of the *Miroir* collection. The *Cloistre de l'ame* is also attached to a
well-known spiritual master, Hugh of St Victor, although in this case the attribution is incorrect. Perhaps these attributions are intended to demonstrate that
the additional texts that have been chosen are worthy companions to the work
of Durand, named as author in the *Miroir des dames* and shown in the opening
miniatures presenting his work to the queen.

The care that has been taken in crafting this spiritual guidebook is reflected
in the choice and treatment of the texts to accompany and complement the
Miroir des dames. Some of them show signs of having been modified (in ways
that will be explored in detail below) in the light of their aristocratic reader's circumstances, sometimes criticizing aspects of the world in which she
lived, and sometimes changing details in ways appropriate to her standing.
The grouping of shorter, carefully chosen treatises with a major, well-known
work also recalls the Maubuisson manuscript, and it is possible that it provided
inspiration for the *Miroir* collection through its form, as well as contributing
one of the texts.

The texts that accompany the *Miroir des dames* follow it in the same order
in all four manuscripts:

1.   *Le miroeur de mortel vie*, which begins 'je vois morir, venez avant'. It is a
        set of verses in which people from different stations in life lament their
        impending death and is one of the many vernacular versions of a text
        also found in Latin, whose first words, *vado mori*, give the name to the
        genre, which is one of the sources of the *danse macabre*.[16]

2.   *Le livre du cloistre de l'ame que fist Hue de Saint Victor*, which is a modi-
        fied copy of the *Sainte abbaye*.

3.   *Les Meditacions saint Anseaume*, a translation of Anselm's first medi-
        tation, designed to move the soul to fear of God and dependence on
        God's mercy.

---

[16] Hammond, 'Latin Texts of the Dance of Death'. *B* has a miniature at the beginning of this
text showing the Three Living and the Three Dead (fol. 148rb).

4. *La droite forme pour vivre qui doit mener l'ame qui s'est donnee a Dieu en gardant sa virginité, sa veueté, son pucellage a tousiours au monde.* Like the *Cloistre de l'ame*, this text is addressed to a woman and proposes the construction of an edifice of virtues in her heart — in this case a castle — and deals with guarding the senses, which are the entrances to the allegorical castle. It also gives instructions on integrating a routine of prayer and meditation on the Passion into the reader's daily round of activities in a noble or bourgeois household.[17]

5 & 6. Two extracts from the *Somme le roi*, here called *De repentence et vraye confession* and *Pour bien mourir.*[18]

7. *De vraie amour.* This is a truncated version of the treatise on the four kinds of love found in *Y*. It omits most of the prologue and the final developments on ardent love, providing only the parts about the four kinds of love, the three heavens, and the sacraments.

Like the additional texts in *Y*, all of these also appear in other sources anterior to the *Miroir* collection. Indeed, four of the items are also present in some form in *Y* itself. The *Cloistre de l'ame* is a modified version of the *Sainte abbaye*, and the Maubuisson copy may have been the model on which the revised version was based.[19] The two short treatises, *De repentence et vraye confession* and *Pour bien mourir*, are excerpts from the *Somme le roi*. *De vraie amour* is a shortened version of the treatise on love found in *Y*. It is tempting to conclude that *Y* had served as the model for these texts as well as for the *Abbaye*, but for *De vraie amour*, at least, the picture is more complicated. This version has some readings that are closer to the copy in Mazarine MS 788 than to *Y*. The Mazarine copy cannot be its source, however, since it is much shorter, and the *Miroir* version also reproduces parts of the text that are in *Y* but not in Mazarine MS 788. This suggests an intermediary version, longer than that reproduced in Mazarine MS 788, used by both the Maubuisson and the *Miroir* compilers.

---

[17] See Hasenohr, 'La Vie quotidienne de la femme vue par l'Eglise', pp. 79–80. Reprinted in Hasenohr, *Textes de dévotion et lectures spirituelles en langue romane*, pp. 682–83.

[18] *De repentence et vraye confession* corresponds to Chapter 56, 179–366, while *Pour bien mourir* corresponds to Chapter 40, in the edition by Brayer and Leurquin, *La Somme le roi par Frère Laurent*. The short sections on the seven deadly sins and seven virtues that follow *De repentence et vraye confession* are not from the same source.

[19] Pierre Basin's copy cannot be the exemplar: the revised version in the *Miroir* collection does not reproduce the small errors it makes. It is of course possible that the exemplar was the other copy of the *Sainte abbaye* listed in the Maubuisson inventory of 1463.

A second possible source for parts of this compilation is the anthology found
in the early fourteenth-century manuscript BnF, MS fonds français 1802.[20] Like
the *Miroir* collection, this manuscript brings together a number of works of
spiritual advice with a longer treatise written for a queen by her confessor and
appears to have been compiled for a noblewoman. The treatise in question is the
Miroir de l'ame, written for Blanche of Castile.[21] In BnF, MS fr. 1802 the letter
of dedication has been altered to present the work to a certain 'Marie, dame de
Macy', who has not been identified. The two texts this manuscript shares with the
Miroir collection are the *Droite forme de vivre* and the *Meditation St Anseaume*.[22]
This translation of Anselm's meditation seems to have been written with a female
reader in mind. Where Anselm addresses himself as *peccator*, the translation has
pecheresse, so the female reader can speak the meditation to herself as though it
were her own words.[23] The two texts occur close together in BnF, MS fr. 1802,
separated by two other short pieces that are not identified in the catalogue. The
copies in the *Miroir* compilation are closely related to the BnF, MS fr. 1802 versions but are not exact copies. There is also a copy of the meditation in *R*, incorporated without title into the Meditations of St Bernard.[24]

The collection thus draws on earlier sources for all of its content. There is
no sign of newly created works of spiritual advice, such as the vernacular pastoral works of Jean Gerson, which were beginning to circulate at the time it was
made; indeed, two of them are found in the almost-contemporary manuscript
containing the *Abbaye* made for Franciscan nuns, discussed in the next chapter.
The evidence suggests a deliberate selection of texts among existing collections
of spiritual works for aristocratic women known to the compiler or his patron.

As mentioned above, three of the texts have been modified in ways that
attune them more closely to the circumstances of a woman of high social standing, whether in criticizing aspects of the world with which she had to engage or
in evoking situations with which she would be familiar. The *Cloistre de l'ame*,
the *Droite forme de vivre*, and *De vraie amour* each differ in some way from
the versions identified in other earlier or contemporary manuscripts. I will deal
with the last two before turning to the features that distinguish the *Cloistre de
l'ame* from the *Sainte abbaye*.

---

[20] Described in Field, 'From *Speculum anime* to *Miroir de l'âme*', p. 83.

[21] Field, 'Reflecting the Royal Soul'; Mews, 'The *Speculum dominarum* (*Miroir des dames*)'.

[22] There is a different translation of Anslem's first meditation in *R*, fol. 329.

[23] This is true of both the BnF, MS fr. 1802 copy and the *Miroir* version.

[24] Warner and Gilson, *Catalogue of Western Manuscripts in the Old Royal and King's
Collections*, II, 197.

In the case of *De vraie amour*, the significant alteration is the cutting out
of text from the beginning and the end. The way the text has been truncated
works with its new title to present it as a treatise on love, even though its contents are wider ranging. The new start and end points of the text frame it as a
criticism of worldly love; it begins with the author deploring the prevalence
of self-interested love in the world and ends with a reflection on false forms of
love that lead us astray.[25] It is perhaps also significant that the major part that
is cut from the text is the final section, on the ardent love experienced in contemplation, since reticence towards this form of prayer is also a feature of the
modifications to the *Cloistre de l'ame*.

The *Miroir* version of the *Droite forme pour vivre* agrees closely in substance
with the earlier version of this text found it BnF, MS fr. 1802, but modernizes
the language and removes some of the details present in the earlier version that
appear to reflect the circumstances of the composition of the text.[26] The earlier
version addresses a young single woman living in her parents' house. The author
speaks of acceding to the recipient's request to provide her with guidance in living in the world as a virgin out of love for God, despite his own unworthiness.
He seems to know her circumstances well, enjoining her to serve her brothers
and sisters and especially her mother (there is no mention of her father), and
suggesting that when she is alone in her room, as well as praying or reading, she
make something useful for the household. He also makes frequent references to
the book of hours she will have with her ('que tu aura') as she follows his instructions, which also contains the text of the grace after meals she should recite.

Most of this detail identifying a young unmarried woman is absent from
the *Miroir* version. The prologue addresses a woman more generally, a spiritual
daughter who lives in the world ('fille en dieu [...] demourant es perilz de ce
monde'), addressed throughout the text as 'fille', 'fille en dieu', or 'fille espouse

---

[25] 'Se ie pouoie trouuer vraie amour voulentiers my reposeraye. mais ne la say ou trouuer,
car ie ne sent nul bien en moy. En autrui voy ie trop de defaux car les amours qui orent vont pres
que toutes par marchandise' (If I could find true love I would gladly rest in it, but I do not know
where to find it, for I find no good in myself. In others I see too many faults for their loves are
almost all bought and sold) (*D*, fol. 167vb); 'les foles et fausses amours que nous auons. Car nous
suiuons si noz propres volentez et noz propres sens [...] par quoy nous encombrons noz cuers des
choses vainnes qui esloingnent de dieu' (the foolish and false loves we have. For we follow our
own wills and our own senses [...] by which we weigh down our hearts will vanities that take us
away from God) (*D*, fol. 175ra).

[26] This is subject to the caution that prologues which seem to refer to the original creation of a text can be added later to fit new circumstances, as demonstrated in Hasenohr, 'Les
Prologues des textes de dévotion en langue française'.

et amie dieu', and the rubric refers to widowhood as well as virginity. There is
no mention of the reader's book of hours, or the details of her family life. There
are some small additions of content in the *Miroir* version. In one, the author
advises his reader to welcome the gift of tears and prolong her devotions if she
is fortunate enough to receive it: 'Et selon ce que tu trouueras plus deuocion si
pourras illec demorer et t'ame recreer plus longuement vne foiz que autre, mais
pour dieu ne refuse pas la deuocion de lermes quant elle venra et habondera'
(And as you enter into a state of greater devotion you might remain longer in it
at one time than another, refreshing your soul, but for God's sake do not refuse
the devotion of tears when it comes abundantly) (*D*, fol. 159ᵛᵃ). Here it seems
that the adaptor is adding some advice in line with his own spiritual prefer-
ences. Another addition is perhaps more of a reflection of the events in the
outside world. It expands the simple list of people to pray for found in BnF, MS
fr. 1802 with details that resonate with the conditions prevailing at the time of
the *Miroir* compilation's creation:

> Aprés si prie pour toute sainte eglise pour paix que diex la mecte en terre. Et puis
> pour les biens de terre que diex les vueille sauuer. Et pour les princes crestiens que
> dieux leur doint paix ensemble, et pour tous prelas qui ont cures d'ames, especial-
> ment pour le pape que diex le face tel come il appartient a son estat.

> [Then pray for all the holy Church that God may bring peace on earth. And for
> the goods of the earth, that God may save them. And for the Christian princes,
> that God may give them peace together, and for all prelates who have care of souls,
> especially for the pope, that God may make him such as befits his estate.] (*D*,
> fol. 157ᵛᵇ)

Peace among Christian princes was a pressing need, in the context of the civil
war in France and the war with England. The prayer for the pope, to make him
'such as befits his estate', could be understood as a veiled criticism and is perhaps to be understood as a reference to the situation, which many saw as scan-
dalous, of two popes, one in Rome and one in Avignon.

The Cloistre de l'ame

The text called the *Cloistre de l'ame* in this collection, which is clearly derived
from the *Sainte abbaye* of *Y*, has been modified by modernizing language and
making some additions. Many of the changes are small, but when taken together
some patterns emerge, playing down the mystical elements of contemplative
prayer and strengthening the penitential aspect of the doctrinal content. Some

changes also serve to adapt the *Cloistre de l'ame* to the social status of its audience, in the same way that we have just seen in *De vraie amour* and the *Droite forme pour vivre*.

The *Cloistre de l'ame* seems to be greatly concerned with control of behaviour, and its tone is more ascetic and penitential than that of the *Sainte abbaye*. Many of the added details concern sin and its avoidance. The vices represented by the daughters of the Devil (Envy, Presumption, Detraction, and Suspicion) are described more graphically and at far greater length. Correspondingly, the theme of the custody of the senses is more fully developed and linked to the narrative of the invasion of the abbey by the daughters of the Devil. Four senses, or rather, faculties (sight, hearing, thought, and speech), are the entrances to the cloister. All versions of the *Abbaye du saint Esprit* tell the reader to guard these if she would be a perfect *religieuse*, but this one adds some subsidiary vices associated with each faculty. Elsewhere, when noting that the entrances of the senses must be guarded by the gatekeeper, *Paour de Dieu* (Fear of God), this version adds that it was her failure which allowed the Devil's daughters to enter and corrupt the abbey. Her responsibility is invoked again at the end of the text, in a prayer to the Holy Ghost to command her to guard the entrances and to expel any undesirable elements. The role of the sacraments in protecting the soul is underscored in this version by giving the gatekeeper an assistant, *Confession*. Following the expulsion of the vices, and concluding the text, is an added definition of *religion* which reinforces the message of control and containment of this version: 'Religion est dicte de relier, car la conscience si est le tonnel de vin de graces du saint Esperit, qui doit estre si forment relié que il n'espande pour nulle achoison' ('Religion' is from 'bind', since the conscience is the barrel that holds the wine of graces of the Holy Ghost, which must be so strongly bound that it will not burst on any account).[27] Conversely, contemplative prayer receives less emphasis. In the passage on *Jubilation*, the description of rapture is absent. The passage on *Meditation* leaves out the reference to pseudo-Dionysius, and its approach to prayer has more of an emphasis on praying for one's needs.

There is also some increase in emphasis on the cultivation of virtues for the active life, particularly charitable giving. As one might expect in a text written for a wealthy laywoman who was also the custodian of family wealth, giving generously to the poor is strongly urged, but in a measured way. The network of references to poverty and almsgiving in the *Sainte abbaye* stress the need to

---

[27] All quotes from the *Cloistre de l'ame* are from the edition in Part II, unless the wording of a particular manuscript is indicated.

give unstintingly: *Povreté* digs the abbey's foundations and makes them broad, 'en largement doner quanque ele ara' (generously giving whatever she has). The almoner, *Misericorde*, gives without holding anything back: 'Misericorde [...] sera aumosniere, qui tant donra que riens ne retenra' (Mercy [...] will be almoner, giving so much that nothing is held back).

The *Sainte abbaye*, written towards the end of the thirteenth century, reflects the milieu of imitation of apostolic poverty of the *Religion du cuer* (itself probably composed in the last quarter of the thirteenth century) even though its audience is aristocratic; this may be another indication that its primary audience was cloistered nuns, who were expected to subscribe to the ideal of poverty, even if they lived within a wealthy institution. But the *Cloistre de l'ame* was written over a century later, outside that milieu, and it reflects the realities of the life of its lay aristocratic audience and changing attitudes to poverty. In the corresponding passages, the *Cloistre* takes care to note the voluntary nature of poverty and the proper recipients of alms: 'Povreté Volentive qui les fera larges quant elle gettera la terre ça et la en donant largement les biens terriens aux povres' (Voluntary Poverty, who will make them broad as she casts the soil to one side and the other, by generously giving earthly goods to the poor). The almoner's giving without holding back is tempered, described as giving what is left after necessity has been catered for: 'Misericorde sa suer sera aumosniere, qui tout donra aprés sa necessité prise' (Mercy her sister will be almoner, who will give all, once necessities have been provided for). Instruction on the virtues to cultivate is also provided with additional detail: the cardinal and theological virtues associated with the seven pillars of Wisdom's house are named individually, where the *Sainte abbaye* only names the groups.

In addition to these adjustments of pastoral emphasis, there seems to be a concern to establish respectable ecclesiastical credentials, hinted at by the association of the work with Hugh of St Victor and the bolstering of the Latin authorities in the text. A number of extra ones are added, including one from Gregory the Great (added to Humility, sub-prioress) and two from St Bernard (on Discretion and on the side wound of Christ 'et vulnere latis'). This perhaps also reflects the shift in audience from the thirteenth-century context, where naming authors beyond the patristic *auctores* was less important. There is also an extra-biblical reference for tears of contrition associated with the Magdalene:

> Telle fu l'abbaye a la Magdalene. *Cuius oculi et cetera. Et fluminis impetus.* C'est a dire que l'oeil de la Magdalene decouroit en l'amour de Dieu en lermes aussi come le ruissel d'une fontaine.

[Such was the abbey of the Magdalene. *Cuius oculi et cetera. Et fluminis impetus.* That is to say, the Magdalene's eye ran like the spout of a fountain with tears of love for God.][28]

Some citations have the author's name added, where it is absent in the other versions: for example, the more explicit 'saint Pol' is preferred to 'Apostolus', and 'la glose' is replaced by 'saint Augustin'. This extra information, the added authorities, the expanded listings of vices and virtues, and the closing etymology, all suggest an adapter who wished to display his learning, but perhaps also a changing sense of what was necessary in a work written for a literate, aristocratic audience.

Reflecting the Miroir

The aristocratic female reader targeted by the *Miroir* anthology was presented with a comprehensive set of resources for her moral and spiritual nourishment, which at the same time reminded her of her social status, the *Miroir des dames* positioning her as the reader of a text written for a queen. While it is impossible to know how any individual reader of the anthology would have used it, it is interesting to consider some of the ways she could encounter themes present in the *Miroir* reflected and reinforced in the other texts.

The Metaphor of Construction

As in the Maubuisson manuscript, constructing a building is a central metaphor for the ordering of the interior life in the *Miroir des dames*, the *Cloistre*, and the *Droite forme de vivre*. While the queen to whom the *Miroir* is addressed is advised to imitate the wise woman of scripture in building her house, the reader of the *Cloistre* is advised to build an abbey, and of the *Droite forme* to build a castle, in each case in her conscience. In all three texts the constructions offer a set of variations on the theme of building with virtues: faith and good works are combined in some way in all three in the building of the foundations or the walls, the building is protected by a moat or watered by a river of tears of

---

[28] Although the abbreviation 'cujus oculi' makes it appear that the citation refers to Jeremiah 32. 19 'cujus oculi aperti sunt super omnes vias filiorum Adam', the translation makes it clear that the reference is to Psalm 118. 135, 'exitus aquarum deduxerunt oculi mei'. A sermon by William of Auvergne associates this verse with the one that follows in the *Abbaye*, 'Et fluminis impetus letificat ciuitatem Dei' (Psalm 46. 5 [45. 5])) in a passage on cleansing tears. The pairing was probably common in sermons for the feast of Mary Magdalene.

contrition, strong walls or pillars protect those inside from winds of tribulation or temptation, the construction site (*Cloistre*) or the rooms (*Miroir* and *Droite forme*) must be cleaned, by combinations of love of purity, contrition, and confession. The house of conscience in the *Miroir* and the castle in the *Droite forme* are both intended to be places where God will be received as a guest and want to remain.[29]

The buildings of the *Miroir* and the *Droite forme de vivre* 'mirror' the noble reader's own surroundings, and the activities they place within the buildings are those household activities particular to aristocratic hospitality: preparing a guest room, making the guest comfortable, serving a meal. Other secular imagery in the *Droite forme* includes hunting, women putting on make-up, siege warfare, domestic cleaning. The passage on cleaning, where the castle of the soul is kept clean through confession, echoes a passage in the *Miroir*, which speaks of cleaning the interior house.[30] The *Droite forme* also echoes courtly romance in the way it speaks of receiving the divine guest; the lady is to prepare a bedchamber for Jesus, her beloved, who was wounded for her love at the tournament of the Cross. The *Cloistre*, on the other hand, evokes a less immediately familiar set of surroundings and activities in its description of the functional spaces and the office holders of the abbey. This provides a different kind of positioning in relation to the text, inviting the reader to situate herself imaginatively within the world of the cloister, held up as the ideal of religious life for those outside as well as those within it.

Guarding the Senses

The construction aspect of the building metaphor provides a framework for self-fashioning, but the metaphor also functions as a symbol of enclosure. All three texts that employ it (the *Miroir des dames*, the *Cloistre*, and the *Droite forme de vivre*) make use of the ideas of defensive walls and entrances that must be guarded. The *Cloistre* is the only one where the defences of the edifice are actually breached, but the other two make the danger of such an incursion clear with references to keeping the walls strong and guarding the entrances lest thieves break in. All three texts link the theme of enclosure and its breaching to the guarding of the senses. These are described as the entrances to the soul, as in this passage on the house of conscience from the *Miroir*: 'Or devroient donc

---

[29] The theme of building also runs through the Maubuisson collection: it is discussed at length in Kumler, *Translating Truth*, pp. 186–96.

[30] In *D*, the passages are located at fols 156[ra–b] (*Droite forme*) and 124[ra–b] (*Miroir des dames*).

toutes les fenestres de ceste maison estre closes. Par les fenestres nous enten-
dons les senz lesquelz nous deuons soingneusement garder' (Now all the windows of this house should be closed. By windows we mean the senses, which we
must guard carefully) (*D*, fol. 124va). The *Droite forme* also provides extensive
advice to the reader on regulating her behaviour both inside and outside her
house, giving instructions on integrating a routine of prayer and meditation
on the Passion into the reader's daily round of activities in a noble or bourgeois
household, and on decorum (behaviour on the way to and from, and during
Mass, and behaviour at meals, which turns briefly into instructions on table
manners).[31]

The link between guarding the senses and prescriptions of behaviour is
clearly seen in the short text on the examination of conscience (an extract from
the *Somme le roi*), where the sins of the senses are listed in a way that recalls
both the *Droite forme de vivre* and the *Cloistre*:

> Aprés si doit l'en corre aux .v. sens du corps ou l'en peche mult souuent, par les yeux
> en folement regarder, par les oreilles en folement escouter et oir volentiers medis-
> ans menteurs et autres folies, ou par la bouche en folement parler ou trop boire ou
> trop menger, ou par les narines en soy deliter en bonnes odeurs, ou par folement
> touchier et deshonnestement.

> [After that one should proceed to the five bodily senses by which one sins very
> often, with the eyes by unruly looking about, with the ears by foolishly listening
> and willingly hearing slandering liars and other vain words, or with the mouth by
> foolish talk or excessive drinking or eating, or with the nostrils by indulging in
> sweet perfumes, or through unruly and shameful touching.] (*D*, fol. 165ra)

The *Cloistre* is less explicit and less prescriptive than any of the other texts.
Guarding the senses is equated with a nun's keeping to her cloister. The eyes, ears,
and mouth are the entrances, which are to be guarded by Fear of God. As we have
seen, the *Cloistre* adds some more details to this struggle between virtue and vice
that are not present in other versions of the *Abbaye*. The role given to confession
in helping to guard the entrances makes the same connection between the senses
as occasions for sin and the remedy of confession as the text on examination of
conscience. The *Cloistre* makes it clear that the failure of cultivating fear of God
and practising confession lets in the vices that are the daughters of the Devil, and

---

[31] This text falls into the pattern remarked on by Hasenohr, of grafting the monastic prayer
schedule onto lay activities. See Hasenohr, 'La Vie quotidienne de la femme vue par l'Eglise',
pp. 40–41. Reprinted and updated in Hasenohr, *Textes de dévotion et lectures spirituelles en
langue romane*, pp. 631–711.

that vigilant observance of these precepts will allow the abbey of the conscience to continue better than before, when the vices have been expelled.

Death, Judgement, Penitence

Wherever she dipped into the collection, the reader would encounter reminders of the inevitability of death and judgement, with the urgent need that this brings for repentance and proper dealing with sins. This is dealt with in the *Miroir des dames* in the first part, where the queen is instructed to reflect on her own mortality. But its strength in the rest of the collection may indicate that this was a theme the compiler felt needed reinforcing. The two texts that reflect it most strongly are the *Miroir du monde* verses and the translation of Anselm's meditation, which are also the only two to receive added introductions. Both introductory passages have a message of turning away from worldly concerns: the first with its reminder of the transitoriness of earthly life, and the second with its call to repentance and conversion. The reader of *B* would receive an additional reminder from the *Three Living and Three Dead* miniature.

Meanwhile practical advice on carrying out the action that should accompany repentance is provided by the set of short texts on confession and preparing for death. Many of the modifications made to the *Cloistre* also fit in with this penitential theme. Along with the development of the theme of containment through the custody of the senses, there is more attention paid to vice and its description than in other versions of this text. In the description of the four senses, or rather, faculties (sight, hearing, thought, and speech), that are the entrances to the cloister, some subsidiary vices associated with each faculty are added. The vices represented by the daughters of the Devil are described more graphically and at far greater length than in other versions.

Love

Beside the reminders of death and judgement, however, the reader would frequently encounter the theme of love. In the *Miroir*, it appears twice. The first treatment is in the section on the passions, where the focus is on love of the common good, singled out as a necessary kind of love for a ruler to practise. The second occurs in the section on the theological virtues, where under the heading of Charity there is a more conventionally religious treatment of love that draws on Augustine, Gregory the Great, Hugh of St Victor, and others.[32]

---

[32] Durand de Champagne, *Speculum dominarum*, ed. by Flottès-Dubrulle, I. 3. d4. 10–15, pp. 200–10.

Charity of course plays an important role in the *Cloistre de l'âme*, where it is personified as the abbess, and therefore presented as the governing virtue in the spiritual cloister.[33] The final text in the collection, *De vraie amour*, is presented as a treatise entirely devoted to love, although the developments of some of the types of love include material on the sacraments and an allegory based on St Paul's ascent through the three levels of heaven. As noted above, the way the text has been trimmed places emphasis on the unworthiness of worldly forms of love. In this way it might be seen as a counterbalance to worldly or courtly love ideals that the aristocratic female reader could be expected to have encountered elsewhere.

Although the tone is anti-worldly, there are plenty of reminders to the reader of this collection that she is participating in a prestigious activity, shared with other women of wealth and power. As she reads the *Miroir des dames*, she is being addressed as though she were a queen, and both the presentation miniature at its head and the text itself tell her that she is reading the words addressed to the queen by her confessor, Durand. The rubrics of the *Cloistre de l'âme* and the *Meditacions saint Anseaume* also inform her that the words of prestigious spiritual masters have been gathered in this book for her. The miniature at the head of the *Meditacions saint Anseaume* invites her to identify with the three richly dressed ladies receiving teaching from the seated figure. This miniature may reflect the illuminations of a number of the Latin manuscripts of Anselm's *Meditationes* which preserve the memory of their presentation to Countess Matilda of Tuscany.[34] The *Cloistre* may also have had royal associations through its presence as the *Sainte abbaye* in manuscripts at Maubuisson and in the entourage of Blanche de Navarre. The *Droite forme de vivre* addresses a woman who is familiar with the conventions of courtly love and aristocratic hospitality.

* * *

The construction of the anthology is consistent with the project suggested by Beaune and Lequain to construct an image of Marie de Berry as a model of female virtue, and a credible successor to her father, in a time of political tension.[35] Its main text is one that constructs a princely woman as having a public role to fulfil virtuously. Its emphasis on justice is congruent with the reformist concerns of one of the texts copied for Marie, Gerson's *Vivat rex*.

---

[33] I discuss hierarchies of virtues in cloister allegories in Pinder, 'Love and Reason from Hugh of Fouilloy to the *Abbaye du Saint Esprit*'.

[34] Pächt, 'The Illustrations of St Anselm's Prayers and Meditations'.

[35] Beaune and Lequain, 'Marie de Berry et les livres', p. 59.

I have suggested elsewhere that the overall tone of the texts combined with the *Miroir* suggests that in this collection, the latter is being read less as a mirror for princes than as a work concerning personal morality and salvation.[36] However, although the aspects of the *Miroir des dames* that are complemented and amplified by the other texts in the collection are not the public virtues, but the private, penitential ones, this emphasis on pious behaviour also had its place in the construction of public female virtue, particularly in the climate of criticism of the queen.[37] It certainly attests to an interest in the moral and spiritual formation of women in the Duke of Berry's entourage, and the history of its transmission suggests that interest continued in his daughter Marie's family.

The manuscript anthologies into which the β_1 and β_2 redactions of the *Abbaye* were copied reflect the project of spiritual and moral formation of noble women. The expense lavished on the Maubuisson manuscript and the illuminated *Miroir* manuscripts establish their readers as women who enjoy privileged access to a prestigious object. It may have been the status of the enormously ambitious Maubuisson manuscript that sealed the prestige of the *Abbaye* among the women of the court over the next century. While the *Sainte abbaye* occupied an ambiguous space between the cloister and the world, its programme of spiritual self-fashioning both proposing the cloister as a model and evoking an interior life not dependent on external regulation, the *Cloistre de l'ame* moved with the *Miroir* collection more explicitly into the world of the aristocratic laywoman. In the other fifteenth-century adaptations of the *Abbaye*, discussed in the next chapters, its continuing attractions for both the cloister and the court are evident. While the earlier of the two (γ) returns to the cloister in a collection for Franciscan nuns, the later one (α_2) once again shows the *Abbaye* being refashioned for a princess, this time Margaret of York, Duchess of Burgundy.

---

[36] Pinder, 'A Lady's Guide to Salvation', p. 51.

[37] Beaune and Lequain, 'Marie de Berry et les livres', p. 59.

A Franciscan Version:
La Religion du benoit saint Esprit

The *Abbaye* was reworked twice more during the fifteenth century, in both cases using α_1 as a base. Neither of these reworkings, made completely independently of each other in Picardy and in Ghent, can be linked to any of the surviving manuscripts, but their existence testifies to the continued circulation of α_1 in the fifteenth century. The earlier one, which will be treated in this chapter, is found in a manuscript associated with a convent founded by Colette of Corbie, the reformer of the Clarissan Order, in Amiens at the end of the first half of the fifteenth century. Colette's reform was supported by the dukes and duchesses of Burgundy, and Amiens was the last of her foundations in the duchy. The second, treated in Chapter 6, is part of a compilation manuscript produced for Margaret of York, wife of the Duke of Burgundy Charles the Bold. Coincidentally, Margaret of York was a supporter of the Clarissan nuns who followed Colette's reform, but there is no connection between the two versions of the *Abbaye*.

The Amiens Manuscript

At around the same time as the *Miroir des dames* compilation was being made, another reworking of the *Abbaye* was produced in a different context, for quite a different audience. Instead of noble ladies of the royal court in Paris, its intended readers were Franciscan sisters in one of the prosperous towns of Picardy. It appears in a compendium of doctrinal and spiritual instruction

that clearly proclaims a Franciscan identity, with Franciscan hagiography and prayers.[1] This version of the *Abbaye*, like the one made over a century earlier for another group of nuns (as I have argued in Chapter 3), is based on α_1; however, as this chapter will show, it departs much more radically from its model.

This collection of prose and verse texts belonged, at least during the sixteenth century, to the convent of St Clare in Amiens. Originally a single manuscript, the collection was split and rebound in the seventeenth century and now exists as BnF, MSS fonds français 2093 and 2095 (X).[2] It was a small book (measuring 195 by 134 mm), which would have sat comfortably in the hand and been suited to individual reading. The two parts bear witness to a well-made but not sumptuous manuscript, with a number of miniatures and some gilded decoration, written in a clear book-hand by at least two scribes.[3] Apart from some Latin prayers, the collection contains only works in French. There is a life of St Francis in verse, illustrated by miniatures (now BnF, MS fr. 2093), a prose life of St Clare, some prayers, and a number of other French prose and verse works on aspects of religious life and duty. The language suggests that it was written in Picardy.[4]

An inscription in an early sixteenth-century hand at the bottom of folio 28^v of X indicates that the book belonged to the convent of St Clare in Amiens. However, it seems unlikely that that was its original home. The manuscript has been dated on palaeographic grounds to the very early years of the fifteenth century, but the Amiens convent, part of the fifteenth-century reform of the Franciscan movement by Colette of Corbie, was not founded until 1442–45.[5] There is no evidence of when the manuscript came into the nuns' possession. There is strong evidence, though, that the manuscript was made for a community of nuns following the rule of St Clare. The miniature which decorates the first folio of the life of St Clare shows the saint handing a book to a nun in the

---

[1] This was not the first time the *Abbaye* appeared in a Franciscan context; R contains a prose life of St Francis and may have been made for a group of Franciscan male tertiaries (see Chapter 2).

[2] The BnF, MS fr. 2095 (X) version was unknown to Kathleen Chesney. There is another copy of this version of the *Abbaye* in BnF, MS fonds français 19397 (Z), a fifteenth-century paper manuscript; it ends immediately after an expanded treatment of the cloister passage.

[3] Thomas, 'Recherches sur les légendes françaises de Saint François d'Assise', pp. 54–55.

[4] The two manuscripts are described in Charles-Gaffiot and Rigaux, *Beauté et Pauvreté*, pp. 62–63. See also Pinder, 'Un recueil picard de lectures spirituelles pour des sœurs franciscaines'.

[5] Charles-Gaffiot and Rigaux, *Beauté et Pauvreté*, p. 63. For the details of the Amiens foundation, see Richards, 'Franciscan Women', pp. 100–104, and Desobry, *Un aspect peu connu de la Révolution française de 1789 à Amiens*, p. 8.

Clarissan habit. Clare is holding an abbess's crosier, and in association with this the book is almost certainly her Rule.[6] The miniature at the beginning of the life of St Francis shows the saint blessing a female figure in the Clarissan habit which is very similar to the one that accompanies the life of St Clare. The contents have a strong Franciscan flavour: as well as the lives of St Francis and Life of St Clare, there is a small collection of Latin prayers from the offices for the feasts of Clare and Francis, which link the reader of the manuscript to a communal liturgy. In addition, one of the texts it contains draws on Bonaventure's *Itinerarium mentis in Deum*. And as we will see below, the reworking of the *Abbaye* includes Francis among the authorities quoted. The identity of the community for which the manuscript was made remains a mystery. The only Clarissan convent in the region at the beginning of the fifteenth century was the royal abbey of Le Moncel (founded 1309) in the diocese of Beauvais, and the earliest Colettine foundation was at Hesdin in 1437. However, as Bert Roest suggests, there were probably more Poor Clare houses than are visible in the sources, and official foundations were often preceded by less formal groups.[7] The Amiens manuscript may be a trace of one such group.

A closer look at the contents, while not disclosing the identity of the original owner or owners, does offer some more clues to the manuscript's place of origin. Two texts in the collection link it to the city of Douai. The life of St Francis in verse (already a rather old-fashioned form for saints' lives by the time it was copied) is known from only one other manuscript, BnF, MS fonds français 19531, a collection of verse saints' lives thought to have been produced in the thirteenth century in Arras, probably for beguines, which by the fourteenth century was in the possession of a Douai family.[8] The Amiens life of St Francis was most probably copied directly from that manuscript; not only does it follow the text very closely apart from some interpolations and modernizing of the language, it adds a prologue copied directly from a life of St Elizabeth of Hungary that is unique to BnF, MS fr. 19531.[9] The second text with a Douai

[6] Rigaux, 'Claire et le livre, parcours iconographique', p. 42.

[7] Roest, *Order and Disorder*, pp. 76, 105. Boriosi suggests that the manuscript may have been brought to the convent by a new member who had been a beguine in Amiens: Boriosi, 'Saint François en vers', p. 246.

[8] Hasenohr, 'D'une "poésie de béguine" à une "poétique des béguines"', pp. 928–29.

[9] The source of the new prologue was noted by Thomas, 'Recherches sur les légendes françaises de Saint François d'Assise', p. 58. A recent study casts some doubt on the status of BnF, MS fr. 19531 as the direct exemplar of BnF, MS fr. 2093, but the two variants advanced to support the argument are not conclusive: Boriosi, 'Saint François en vers', pp. 242–45.

connection is the first of the three poems that close the volume. It is a copy of the *serventois de Nostre Dame* by Jean le Court, dit Brisebarre, of Douai.[10] Jean Brisebarre is not named as the author, but as no authors are named in this manuscript, including Jean Gerson, this is not an indication that the origin of the poem was unknown.

It is possible then, that the manuscript was made in Douai. In its combination of locally sourced texts with others that were more widely circulated (such as the Gerson treatises and the Life of St Clare), it fits Keith Busby's observation on manuscripts produced in regional centres for local patrons: 'What is particularly noticeable about this kind of manuscript [...] is the manner in which they combine texts from a pool of works copied in all regions [...] with others typical of the region in which they were produced'.[11] The intended recipient may have been a woman from a merchant family of the city (perhaps the owners of BnF, MS fr. 19531) who belonged to a Clarissan convent or one that aspired to Clarissan status. Although there is no record of a Franciscan women's community in Douai at the beginning of the fifteenth century, there may have been either an unrecorded one or an informal group, one or more of whose members later joined the Amiens foundation.

The Amiens manuscript is a heterogeneous collection, which bears no trace of the thirteenth-century network of texts the *Abbaye* is associated with in other manuscripts, and contains a number of unique texts, which may even have been composed especially for the occasion. The first part of the original manuscript seems to have been devoted to the memorialization and veneration of the nuns' two founding figures, Clare and Francis. It is not certain which of the lives came first in the original arrangement of the texts, but the life of St Francis is by far the longer text; it occupies twenty-three quires, while the life of St Clare and the other texts together only take up nine. Its first page is also the most richly decorated one in the manuscript, suggesting that it was the opening page of the codex. Prayers from the offices of St Clare and St Francis are copied in the leftover space at the end of the final quire of the life of St Clare. Their presence in the manuscript would have allowed the reader to incorporate liturgical prayer into her meditation on the lives of the two founding saints.[12]

---

[10] *X*, fol. 80ᵛ. This is one of only three known manuscript copies of the poem. For the career of Jean Brisebarre, see Lefèvre, 'Jean le Court, dit Brisebarre', pp. 801–02.

[11] Busby, *Codex and Context*, p. 564.

[12] I have discussed the Franciscan content of this manuscript in greater detail in Pinder, 'Un recueil picard de lectures spirituelles pour des sœurs franciscaines'.

The life of St Clare is a translation of the Latin *Vita* attributed to Thomas of Celano. This is an unsurprising choice, as that *Vita* was the main Latin source for the saint's life, and the French translation must itself have been readily available, since it survives in a number of copies.[13] The life of St Francis is more unexpected, both in its form and in the stage of the Franciscan hagiographic tradition it represents. As mentioned above, it is written in verse, no longer the literary form of choice for vernacular saints' lives by the beginning of the fifteenth century. Furthermore, it is based on the *Vita Prima* by Thomas of Celano, which had been officially superseded by Bonaventure's *Legenda Maior* in 1260, although Thomas is not named in this copy of the poem.[14] For these reasons, it is likely that its inclusion represented some kind of personal choice. The fact that it was not simply recopied, but recreated through modernizing archaic language, extending the programme of miniatures, and adding episodes from more recent sources, makes it tempting to see a desire to modernize and embellish a prized family possession playing a role in the composition of this manuscript.

The remaining texts fall into two groups: doctrine and spiritual advice. Works related to doctrine include a series of mnemonic verses on the twelve articles of faith, the ten commandments, the seven sacraments, the seven gifts of the Holy Ghost, the seven works of mercy, the Beatitudes, and the five senses. Similar, though not identical, verses are found in other manuscripts; designed to be learnt by heart, they no doubt circulated orally.[15] In this manuscript, however, the way they are set out maximizes their usefulness to a reader, rather than a hearer. Each set of verses is accompanied by key words in the margin which make it easy for the reader to locate the relevant couplet (for example, the names of the apostles for the articles of faith, the number of each commandment, the sin for which each virtue is a remedy). Another text in the same category of mnemonic schemas is the *Tour de sapience* on folio 76ᵛ. This schema of virtues, which uses a very rudimentary architectural framework, has its origin in one of the didactic diagrams created by John of Metz; it was widely copied

---

[13] A recent study lists eight manuscripts, including BnF, MS fr. 2095. See Pagan, 'Les Légendes françaises de Claire d'Assise', pp. 24–25.

[14] As Boriosi has pointed out, the passage from the life of St Elizabeth interpolated in the prologue replaces the part of the original poem which referred to its source, naming Thomas: 'Saint François en vers', p. 243.

[15] An example is Lille, Bibliothèque municipale, MS 452 (795), a vernacular legendary from the fifteenth century, where the topics are the same, but the wording is different. See Section romane, notice de 'LILLE, Bibliothèque municipale, 452 (795)', Jonas-IRHT/CNRS, <http://jonas.irht.cnrs.fr/manuscrit/28955> [accessed 30 October 2014].

in that form, but here only the text of the labels is reproduced.[16] A much more extended treatment is given to temptation and how to avoid it, and the nature of mortal and venial sin, with the inclusion of two treatises by Jean Gerson (anonymous in this manuscript).[17] The sin of ingratitude is treated separately, in a short text organized around the gifts of nature, grace, and fortune.

Three texts give advice on the spiritual life. The first, and longest, is a version of the *Abbaye*, here called *La Religion du benoit saint Esprit*, which will be discussed in detail below. The second, shorter text of spiritual advice begins: 'Tres chiere espouse de l'espous tres hault' (Most dear bride of the most high bridegroom) (*X*, fol. 35ʳ). Taking Psalm 45. 11 (44. 11) as its basis, it addresses the reader as the bride of Christ, betrothed to him at the baptismal font, and invites her to leave her father's house behind: 'Doncques oubliés vostre peuple et la maison de vostre pere et enclines vos oreilles et vees la bonté de Dieu' (Therefore forget your people and the house of your father and incline your ears and see the goodness of God) (*X*, fol. 35ʳ). The people of her father are interpreted as the sins, bad thoughts, and bad desires that hold the soul back from spiritual sweetness, the 'people of confusion' that want to enslave the daughter of God. Her father's house is equated with the present world, and forgetting it amounts to holding worldly things in contempt and loving the spiritual instead. This interpretation is grounded firmly in the tradition of advice to virgins — close, although in simplified form, to that given in the twelfth-century Latin book of advice for nuns, the *Speculum virginum*.[18] Like the *Speculum*, it weaves a quote from the Song of Songs (1. 3) into the exegesis of the psalm, commenting that the bride of Christ will run towards eternal life saying with the holy virgins: 'A Diew, nous courrons en douceur de ces oinguemens'.[19] It uses another commonplace of advice to virgins (also used in the *Speculum* passage), the image of the fidelity of the turtle dove, and ends with a call to perseverance in her chosen path, as the reader is advised to pray tearfully to see her bridegroom face to face.[20]

---

[16] See Sandler, 'John of Metz, the Tower of Wisdom'.

[17] *Traité des diverses tentations de l'ennemi* and *Le profit de savoir quel est péché mortel et véniel*, numbers 324 and 328 in Glorieux, *Jean Gerson, Œuvres complètes*, VII.

[18] *Speculum virginum*, ed. by Seyfarth. All quotations are from this edition. The passage which corresponds to our text is *Speculum virginum* III. 1–45, pp. 58–59. See also the discussion of this passage in Pinder, 'The Cloister and the Garden', p. 163.

[19] The *Speculum* uses only the first part of this verse: 'Trahe me post te' in the passage on Psalm 44, but quotes it in full elsewhere, *Speculum virginum* II. 185, p. 47.

[20] 'Item resamblés la tourterelle qui n'a que faire du second mari mais soiés morte au monde

The final text giving advice on the spiritual life, which begins 'Devote creature vos devés scavoir' (Devout creature you should know), is a simplified digest
of material on contemplation from several sources. Parts of it seem to be based
on Bonaventure's *Itinerarium mentis in Deum* and other parts on Richard of
St Victor's *Benjamin major*, but there may be other sources that have not yet
been identified. It begins by listing and elaborating five powers of the soul
(senses, imagination, reason, understanding, and intelligence) and explains
how the soul should use these powers to separate itself from corporal sensuality
so that it can be raised by contemplation and meditation on the divinity and
humanity of Jesus. The treatise is followed by a short exposition of three kinds
of prudence: of the heart, of the tongue, and of good works. Neither this work
nor *Tres chiere espouse* has been identified in any other manuscript. They may
have been composed for the women the Amiens manuscript was made for.

The manuscript closes with three verse texts. Two are devotional poems: the
sirventois by Jean Brisebarre mentioned earlier, and an anonymous allegorical
poem in which Christ is presented as the crossbow used by the soul to hunt the
jay, a symbol of the Devil.[21] A final series of quatrains gives advice to a nun on
religious conduct, praising humility and especially discretion in speech.[22]

La Religion du benoit saint Esprit

La Religion du benoit saint Esprit is based on α_1, but it is a far more radical
reworking, in terms of adding and removing content, than any other version of
the *Abbaye*. While the allegorical frame of building and nuns remains the same,
this version shifts the balance of content away from populating the abbey and

---

avoeucques vostre espous, et ne querés aultre, et souvent parlés a ly et vostre voys sera oÿe u chiel
et la voys de la tourterelle se ainssy vous le faites' (Resemble the dove who will not have a second
husband but be dead to the world with your spouse, and do not seek another, and speak to him
often and your voice will be heard in heaven and be the voice of the dove, if you do this) (*X*,
fol. 35ᵛ). Cf. *Speculum virginum* III. 14–17, p. 58: 'Cuius filia? Vis nosse? Filia regus regum, filia
rectoris creaturarum, immortalis sponsi per fidem sponsa, singularitate dilectionis unica, gratia
simplicitatis colomba, castitatis dono formosa' ('Do you want to know whose daughter? The
daughter of the king of kings, daughter of the ruler of creation, bride by faith of the immortal
bridegroom, unique by the singularity of love, dove by the grace of simplicity, beautiful by the
gift of chastity'); trans. by Barbara Newman, in Mews, *Listen, Daughter*, p. 281.

[21] This poem has the same form and uses the same analogy between Christ and the crossbow shaft as 'L'arbalestiere reale' published by Langlois, *Recueil d'arts de seconde rhéorique*,
pp. 82–83.

[22] Edited by Morawski, 'Deux poèmes en quatrains monorimes', p. 35.

back to its construction, amplifying the material gathered under each building or room while reducing most of the obedientiaries to a simple matching of office with virtue. It entirely omits the narrative allegory of the daughters of Satan, along with the shorter exempla, such as the house of Wisdom with its seven pillars, the three bailiffs of Nebuchadnezzar, and the three sorts of timekeeper.[23] In this way it returns the vernacular *Abbaye* to the architectural allegory form of the earliest Latin models, and as in the Latin, the virtues correspond to the buildings themselves, not to those who construct them. It is possible that the person who composed the *Religion du benoit saint Esprit* was familiar with one or more of the Latin cloister allegories, and that the revisions contain an element of deliberate realignment with their model.

This version of the *Abbaye* returns in another way to the spirit of the early Latin cloister allegories, in that it is directed to the end of purifying the interior life of those already following a formal religious rule. Like its model the *Religion du cuer*, it positions itself explicitly as a letter of spiritual direction, but the prologue is reworked to make it relevant to a woman in professed religious life. The woman it addresses is not attempting to follow a rule of life in her own home; rather, she has decided to withdraw from the world:

> Par moy considerant vostre tres boin desir et parfait, qui est que volentiers seriés en religion a che que plus parfaitement puissiés Dieu amer et servir tant de nuit comme de jour et a che aussy que vous fussiés hors de la solicitude mondaine et des empeschemens qui sont en chu monde.

> [Bearing in mind your good and perfect desire, which is that you would willingly be in religious life so you could love God more perfectly and serve him night and day, and would be removed from worldly solicitude and the obstacles that are in this world.][24]

The prologue opens with an added passage, citing and expounding Psalm 45. 11 (44. 11), a verse that was widely used to introduce texts of advice for professed

---

[23] There are also some minor modifications of the distribution of roles among the virtues. The second 'demoiselle' who is to clean the site is 'Creanche et Doubtanche de Dieu' instead of 'Amors de Purté'. Fear is still the gatekeeper as well, but the scriptural quotation 'timor domini expellit peccatum' (Ecclesiasticus 1. 27) that is found in the other versions has been transferred from the gatekeeper passage to the site-cleaning passage. The roles of 'Orison' and 'Devotion' are reversed: in α_1 for example, 'Orisons' builds the chapel and is the chantress, accompanied by 'Jubilations', while 'Devocions' makes the cellar and is cellar-mistress. In *X* 'Jubilacion' is choir-mistress, 'Devocion' builds the chapel, and 'Orison' builds and keeps the cellar.

[24] All quotes from the *Religion du benoit saint Esprit* are from the edition in Part II, unless the wording of a particular manuscript is indicated.

religious women: 'Audi, filia mea et vide et inclina aurem tuam'.[25] Unlike the other adaptation for nuns, the *Sainte abbaye*, the *Religion du benoit saint Esprit* keeps in its prologue the reference to those who are prevented by marriage or poverty from pursuing the path of corporal religion — that is, joining a religious order. However, it transforms the passage into a reminder that spiritual religion should be practised by all, changing the purpose of the advice that follows from sanctifying a life in the secular world to deepening the spiritual life in the cloister.[26]

The model of religious life that the *Religion du benoit saint Esprit* presents to its reader is an ascetic one, marked by penitence and discipline. This emphasis is created by filling the allegorical framework of the abbey buildings with new explanatory content and a wide range of new authorities.[27] One of these new authorities marks the text's Franciscan orientation: among the biblical and patristic authors quoted, this version alone includes St Francis, in the passage where poverty is named as one of the foundations of the allegorical monastery.[28] The tone of these expanded passages is ascetic rather than mystical. The passage on contemplation, for example, expands the original connection of contemplation with the dormitory because of that room's elevation in the upper story of the abbey buildings with a citation from Gregory the Great and an exhortation to the reader to lift her thoughts above earthly things and contemplate the heavenly rewards God has promised. The shift of emphasis away from spiritual ascent is also reflected in omissions. Moving the weight of content towards the

---

[25] For instance, Aelred of Rievaulx, *De institutione inclusarum*, ed. by Talbot, lines 464–68, p. 650, and the *Speculum virginum* III. 1–2, p. 58. It was also occasionally used in texts for laywomen such as the *Speculum dominarum*, discussed in Chapter 4. The text which follows the *Religion du benoit saint Esprit* in X, *Tres chiere espouse*, uses the next part of the same verse: 'et obliviscere populum tuum, et domum patris tui'.

[26] 'Toute foys en la secunde religion qui est espirituelle devons nous tous estre. Si vous fault savoir doulce fille comment de cheste religion serés et qui plus est comment en vous ferés un glorieux couvent' (Nevertheless, we must all be in the second religion, which is spiritual. Gentle daughter, you need to know how to be in this religion, and what is more, how to make a glorious convent within you).

[27] There are many more scriptural and patristic quotations in this version compared to the others (thirty against eighteen in α_1 and α_2).

[28] 'Éllas doulce fille, pourtant disoit saint Franchois preschant a ses freres eulx enortant d'estre fondés sus chu fondement de povreté, *Fratres mei noverint paupetatem esse specialem viam salutis*. Mes freres sachiés que povreté si est l'especialle voye de salut' (Ah, gentle daughter, *Saint Francis said, preaching to his brothers and exhorting them to base themselves on the foundation of poverty: Fratres mei noverint paupetatem esse specialem viam salutis*. My brothers, know that poverty is the special way of salvation).

construction of the abbey and away from the nuns who inhabit it means that the major passage on contemplation associated with Meditation, the keeper of the granary, is drastically shortened. The passage on the nature of meditation is omitted, as is the explanation of the significance of the abundance of wheat, wine, and oil following, 'A fructu frumenti uini et olei sui multiplicati sunt', which describes the progression through meditation and devotion to the experience of divine consolation.[29] The authorities from Augustine and pseudo-Dionysius relating to desire and mystical ascent are also omitted, as is the description in the passage on Jubilation of the way 'gens espirituelz' sometimes manifest the joy of mystical experience.

In contrast to the reduced emphasis on spiritual ascent, the disciplinary advice of the cloister passage is greatly amplified. In the other manuscripts of the *Abbaye* the four corners of the cloister are equated with the control of the four faculties of sight, hearing, speech, and thought. In the *Religion du benoit saint Esprit* this passage is expanded to many times its original length by the addition of authorities and elaboration of the need to restrain each faculty. The faculty of thought is replaced by 'alees et venues' (comings and goings), and the reader is warned at length against keeping bad company and participating in singing and dancing. She is advised rather to keep to her oratory, meditating on the joys of eternal life, the Passion of Jesus, and the pains of hell.[30] The penitential tone is also strengthened in the passage that recommends that the convent be built alongside a river of flowing tears. All of the other manuscripts quote Psalm 1. 3, 'Tanquam lignum quod plantatum est secus decursus aquarum' (Like a tree which is planted near the running waters) and Psalm 46. 5 (45. 5), 'Et fluminis impetus letificat ciuitatem Dei' (The stream of the river maketh the city of God joyful). The *Religion du benoit saint Esprit* refers instead to the contrition of St Peter, with 'Quia fleuit amare' (for he wept bitterly) (X, fol. 30ʳ).[31]

---

[29] 'in tempore frumentum et vinum eorum multiplicata sunt' (Psalm 4. 8).

[30] This passage is given even greater expansion in Z, and in that manuscript the text concludes immediately afterwards, with 'Et se ainsi faictes vous serez parfaicte religiouse. Et serez du nombre des oueilles qui seront mises es pastures tres plantureuses de paraïs. Que nous vueille octroyer le pere le filz et le benoist saint esprit. Amen' (And if you do this you will be a perfect nun. And you will be numbered among the sheep placed in the rich pastures of paradise. May the Father, the Son, and the blessed Holy Spirit grant us this. Amen) (fols 100ᵛ–101ʳ).

[31] This is clearly a reference, probably from memory, to Luke 22. 61–62: 'et conversus Dominus respexit Petrum et recordatus est Petrus verbi Domini sicut dixit "quia priusquam gallus cantet ter me negabis" et egressus foras Petrus flevit amare' (And the Lord turning looked on Peter, and Peter remembered the word of the Lord, as he had said: 'Before the cock crow, thou shalt deny thrice', and Peter going out, wept bitterly).

It is tempting to see in the penitential and ascetic emphasis of the *Religion* and its accompanying downplaying of contemplative prayer and spiritual union a reflection of anxieties about women's mysticism. If that is the case, however, those anxieties do not seem to extend to the rest of the collection, since *Tres chiere espouse* (which comes immediately after the *Religion*) is replete with the language of bridal mysticism, and *Devote creature* theorizes the ascent of the soul. If the decision to include those texts was made by the same person who created the *Religion*, then hostility to the practice by women of contemplative prayer aiming at mystical union cannot have been the motive for the reshaping of the *Religion*. It may instead indicate a perception that the explicit framing of the *Religion* as a rule required more focus on the disciplinary and penitential aspects of its source, perhaps allied with a desire to treat the subject of mystical ascent more systematically than in the scattered references of the *Abbaye*. The placement of the *Religion du benoit saint Esprit* and *Tres chiere espouse* within a single quire, and the thematic resonance provided by their shared use of Psalm 45. 11 (44. 11) further suggests that the compiler saw the two texts as complementary.

* * *

The version of the *Abbaye* presented in the Amiens manuscript is situated in a compendium of texts covering the basics of faith, penitential practice, and spiritual development, as well as essential support for its readers' identity as followers of Francis and Clare. This collection combines basic catechetic material expressed in mnemonic verse with devotional lyrics, hagiography and liturgical prayer, and abstract teaching on contemplation that requires a sophisticated understanding. The juxtaposition of simpler and more sophisticated teaching raises the possibility of two different audiences — those in need of basic doctrinal knowledge and the more spiritually advanced. Perhaps the intended audience was the community the owner was joining, which may have included members at different stages of spiritual development. Alternatively, the compiler may have set out to make a compendium that would be of value to its receiver at different stages of her religious life.

The *Religion du benoit saint Esprit* is clearly situated, by both its content and its enhanced clerical apparatus of authorities, within the group of more advanced teaching. Much less connected to lay culture than its source, this version of the *Abbaye* emphasizes the penitential, ascetic aspects of its model in its transformation into a spiritual guide for women who were living their daily lives in the physical version of its allegorical frame.

Chapter 6

A Devotional Text for Margaret of York: The *Abbaye du saint Esprit*

The final adaptation of the *Abbaye* is the only one created for an identifiable individual — one, moreover, who is relatively well documented. She was the much-studied consumer of religious texts, Margaret of York, Duchess of Burgundy and sister of the King of England, Edward IV, and her version of the *Abbaye* is found in Oxford, Bodleian Library, MS Douce 365 (*O*), one of the volumes prepared for her by David Aubert, scribe to the Burgundian court.[1] The scholarly attention that Margaret of York has attracted means that much more can be recovered of the context of this reworking of the *Abbaye*, although some remains frustratingly hidden. In turn, the investigation of this context offers some insights into the processes of text choice and adaptation involved in the making of her books.

Margaret of York: Book Ownership and Commissioning

Margaret's role in the choice of content for her books is unclear, but most scholars see her taking an active interest in spiritual matters and artistic patronage,

---

[1] For details of Margaret's life, see Weightman, *Margaret of York*. For Aubert's life and work, see Straub, *David Aubert*, and the essays collected in Quéruel, *Les Manuscrits de David Aubert 'escripvain' bourguignon*.

allied to political strategy.[2] Given her independence and determination in both political matters and artistic and religious patronage, it seems unlikely that she would have been a passive recipient of texts. If others were making selections on her behalf, they were surely doing so with a shrewd sense of what would interest her. An exception to this might be the two manuscripts that were compiled for her by Nicolas Finet, a clerical functionary of the Burgundian court who refers to himself as her almoner.[3] Although neither manuscript is dated, it is likely that they were both made soon after her marriage to Charles the Bold, possibly under the guidance of Charles's mother, Isabella of Portugal, to instruct Margaret on the duties of her role.[4] One of them, *Le dialogue de la duchesse de Bourgogne a Jesus Christ*, is closely modelled on a dialogue written in Latin for Isabella by Denis the Carthusian, to aid her in the same role.[5] Isabella was noted for her piety and, as the preceding Duchess of Burgundy, served as a strong role model for her daughter-in-law, particularly in the patronage of religious orders. Margaret's interest in religious works may have been stimulated earlier, by the activities of her mother, Cecily Neville, Duchess of York, who amassed an impressive library of pious texts.[6] She seems to have followed her own path, however; none of her titles correspond to those in her mother's library.

The texts in the manuscripts she commissioned for her own use are a mixture: there are recent compositions by known spiritual masters, such as Jean

---

[2] Anne-Marie Legaré attributes agency to Margaret in her disscussion of the books she commissioned herself in Legaré, 'Les Bibliothèques de deux princesses', while Nancy Warren speaks of 'crafting political legacy through pious practices' in Warren, *Women of God and Arms*, p. 53. Sharon Michalove notes Margaret's active role in political affairs and numbers her with Isabella of Portugal and Elizabeth Woodville as a disseminator of culture for political ends through book ownership, in Michalove, 'Women as Book Collectors and Disseminators of Culture', pp. 68–74. Andrea Pearson and Andrew Taylor both caution against overemphasis on Margaret's agency, pointing to other forces shaping her image and behaviour, in Pearson, 'Gendered Subject, Gendered Spectator', and Taylor, 'Displaying Privacy'.

[3] For a biographical summary, with details of his court offices, see Van Hoorebeeck, *Livres et lectures des fonctionnaires des ducs de Bourgogne*, p. 349.

[4] Pearson, 'Gendered Subject, Gendered Spectator', pp. 49–50. On Isabella of Portugal's role, see also Blockmans, 'The Devotion of a Lonely Duchess', p. 30.

[5] Normore, *A Feast for the Eyes*, p. 190. Finet claims authorship of the *Dyalogue*, but he can only have been responsible for translating it and changing the details that applied to Isabella into those specific to Margaret. Denis's text, 'De vita et regimine principissae Dialogus', can be found in Denis the Carthusian, *Opera Omnia*, xxxvii (1909), 502–18.

[6] Pearson, 'Gendered Subject, Gendered Spectator', p. 50. Spedding, '"At the King's Pleasure"'. See also the account of Cecily's reading in Taylor, 'Displaying Privacy', pp. 275–76.

Gerson, works falsely attributed to authorities such as Seneca, Gerson, and Pierre de Luxembourg, recent anonymous works, and older classics by authors both anonymous and named, such as Boethius. In 1475–76 David Aubert produced five illuminated manuscripts for Margaret. Aubert had worked for Margaret's father-in-law, Philip the Good, and Philip's illegitimate son Antoine. Margaret may have been first exposed to his work when a manuscript he had been working on for Philip at the time of his death came into her possession.[7] It is likely that he had a role selecting the content of the volumes he produced for her, probably subject to her approval.

Three are single-text manuscripts: the first two are visions of the otherworld, and the last is a French translation of Boethius's *De consolatione philosophiae*. The other two are collections of shorter texts. The earlier of the two is entitled *Somme de Perfection* and consists of the last three books of the *Somme le roi* and a heterogeneous collection of shorter, anonymous works, including one which is mostly composed of phrases from the *Abbaye*.[8] The second collection is the one which contains the *Abbaye* proper. It is in these two volumes that several works familiar to us from earlier manuscripts of the *Abbaye* are found, such as the *Sermon du palmier*, the *Livre des tribulations*, the *Garde du coeur*, and a version of the *Règle des coeurs ordonnés*. There is also a text which incorporates the first part of the sermon on the twelve fruits of the Eucharist; like the *Abbaye* pastiche, it combines part of the sermon with material from other sources. Since the earlier volume ambitiously announces itself as a *Somme de Perfection*, while the second simply refers to 'moult devots traitties moralz', it is possible that, like the compiler of the Maubuisson manuscript, David Aubert set out to put together a collection of texts that would complement the *Somme*, but found enough to warrant the creation of a second volume. The final creation, however, is far more than just a collection of leftovers: there are no short, place-filler texts like the 'biaux enseignemens' of the *Somme de Perfection*, and with four miniatures rather than one, it is a more sumptuous manuscript.

The process by which these texts were brought together is, as in the case of most compilations, shrouded in mystery. Aristocratic book owners often lent texts to be copied, and this was no doubt how Margaret acquired many works. Her personal networks, among both her family in England and those attached to the Burgundian court, gave her contact with many owners of books, such as her husband's half brother, Antoine de Bourgogne, and her brother's brother-

---

[7] Wijsman, *Luxury Bound*, p. 198.

[8] This pastiche is based on a different version of the *Abbaye* from *VO*, so must have been copied from elsewhere, not created by David Aubert.

in-law, Anthony Woodville, like her a patron of William Caxton.[9] She had access to the ducal library and seems to have kept a small collection of its books with her in later years, probably for the education Marie de Bourgogne's children, Philip and Margaret, when they were in her care.[10] In the case of the *Abbaye* manuscript, at least one text appears to have been copied from a volume belonging to Antoine, and two others from a book from the ducal library (see below).

The Abbaye Manuscript

The *Abbaye* manuscript is dated March 1475, though by modern reckoning it was probably finished in 1476.[11] It was finished later than the *Somme*. The *Abbaye*, here attributed to Jean Gerson, opens the collection and is prefaced by a miniature showing four women, two of whom are dressed as nuns, against an architectural background. Labels above their heads designate them as *Verité* (Truth), *Amor de Purté* (Love of Purity), *Povreté* (Poverty), and *Humilité* (Humility) — the four ladies who clear the site and dig the foundations of the *Abbaye du saint Esprit*.[12]

The collection contains nine works of spiritual and moral advice, listed below, and has a detailed table of contents at the beginning.[13]

1.   *L'abbaye du saint Esperit*, here falsely attributed to Jean Gerson, fols 1r–16v

2.   *Comment l'on doibt tout son temps ordonner a dieu servir et ferventement amer*, here falsely attributed to Pierre de Luxembourg, fols 17r–22r

3.   *Livret*, falsely attributed to Pierre de Luxembourg, fols 23r–62r[14]

---

[9] Weightman, *Margaret of York*, p. 138.

[10] Wijsman, 'Femmes, livres et éducation dans la dynastie burgondo-habsbourgeoise', pp. 183–85.

[11] In that year Easter, which started the new year in the Burgundian Low Countries, fell late in March; see Cockshaw, 'Some Remarks on the Character and Content of the Library of Margaret of York', p. 58. But see Straub's reservations on this dating: Straub, *David Aubert*, p. 74.

[12] *O*, fol. 1r. The Bodleian Library has a digitized image of this miniature at <https://digital.bodleian.ox.ac.uk/inquire/p/47448262-84a0-4fee-974d-1c6e26937ebf>.

[13] The contents of this manuscript were described, giving the rubric for each text in full, in Chesney, 'Notes on Some Treatises of Devotion'. This description is complemented, with particular reference to text 2, by Hasenohr, 'Un Faux Pierre de Luxembourg'.

[14] Likely to be a fifteenth-century forgery created to advance Pierre de Luxembourg's canonization. See Hasenohr, *Textes de dévotion et lectures spirituelles en langue romane*, pp. 99–100 (Fiche 19940).

4.   *Comment l'on se doibt gouverner en cœur et en pensee*, fols 63^r–114^r

5.   *Les douze fleurs de tribulation*, fols 115^r–138^r

6.   *La garde du cœur et de l'ame*, fols 139^r–154^r

7.   *Des remedes de fortune*, falsely attributed to Seneca, fols 155^r–170^r

8.   *Des quatre vertus cardinalz*, falsely attributed to Seneca, fols 171^r–192^r

9.   *Le miroir des pecheurs*, here falsely attributed to Bernard of Clairvaux, fols 193^r–267^v.

Three of the texts in this collection — the *Abbaye*, *Comment l'on doibt tout son temps ordonner a dieu servir et ferventement amer* (2), and *Des remedes de fortune* (7) — form the contents of *V*, an unfinished manuscript which also appears to come from David Aubert's workshop, and to be slightly earlier in date than *O*.[15] The *Abbaye* occupies an important position in both manuscripts, being the opening text, but its centrality to *V* is particularly clear: the table of rubrics positions it as the principal text, and the leather binding, which appears to be contemporary with the manuscript, has 'L'abbaye du saint esprit' in a title window.[16] There is no indication of the intended recipient of *V*, although a later hand records on folio i that it had belonged to the Benedictine monastery of Saint-Servule de La-Roche-Morey, in Franche Comté.[17] The wording

[15] Hasenohr notes the similarity of the hands of the two manuscripts, and identifies modifications to the text of *O* which indicate that it is later than *V*: 'Un Faux Pierre de Luxembourg', pp. 175, 179. The pages of *V* are ruled with spaces for miniatures and illuminated initials, which are left blank. There is a table of contents, however, which indicates that the manuscript was finished off for someone's use without the illuminations.

[16] The opening of the table of rubrics reads: 'Cy commence la table des rubrics de ce present traittie intitule labbaye du saint esperit. Item apres trouuerez vng petit traittie que saint pierre de Luxembourg compila et enuoia a sa suer. Item encoires trouuerez vng traittie iadiz compile par seneque le venerable orateur intitule De seneque Des remedes contre les maulz de fortune'. *V*, fol. i.

[17] Five leaves have been cut from the last quire, removing the end of the concluding sentence of *Des remedes de fortune* and any colophon that may have followed it: Chesney, 'Notes on Some Treatises of Devotion', p. 30. Saint-Servule cannot have been its original home, as it was only founded in the seventeenth century. Wijsman (*Luxury Bound*, pp. 190, 274) refers to an unverified report that Vesoul, Bibliothèque municipale, MS 91 bore the owner's marks of Margaret of York and Antoine de Bourgogne; I have examined the manuscript and found no trace of such marks. It is possible the end of the third text was excised to remove a dedication to Margaret of York when the decision was made to expand it, so that the manuscript could be sold or given to someone else.

of the rubrics and the layout of the manuscript pages (spaces are ruled up for miniatures and capitals, which have not been filled in) are very similar to *O*, which suggests that *V* was a prototype, or even a false start on a new manuscript for Margaret of York. Was Margaret dissatisfied with the breadth of the selection that was being proposed? Did new material suddenly become available? Did she want something grander? The manuscript David Aubert finally presented to her was larger in format, allowing more space for the miniatures and more lines per page. Aubert had added six more texts: two more from the fund of thirteenth-century moral-spiritual advice (5 and 6), two more that were present in the ducal library (8 and 9), one more recent, well-known work (3). The other addition was also a relatively recent text, though apparently not so well known as the one attributed to Pierre de Luxembourg; *Comment l'on se doibt gouverner en cœur et en pensee* (4) is a complete guide to spiritual life drawing on the *Miroir des simples âmes* of Marguerite Porete, identified by Geneviève Hasenohr as having been produced in the mid-fifteenth century by a Celestine from Ambert, near Orleans.[18] The only other known copy is in a manuscript from Ambert itself. What circumstances brought a copy into the orbit of Margaret of York is unclear, but its appearance in her collection may indicate that through either David Aubert or other contacts, she had people on the lookout for interesting new religious texts. There is evidence of contact between Ambert and Picardy, so in this case they might not have had to go too far afield.[19]

In the case of Margaret's copy of the *Abbaye*, the source may have come through family networks. None of the existing manuscripts can be identified as its source, but Kathryn Hall noticed that the conclusion of Margaret's version (in both *V* and *O*) matched that of the English translation, and concluded that the adapter had access to a copy of the translation, which could have come from Margaret's family.[20] She did not notice, however, that the conclusion is not the only textual parallel between the two versions. None of the others is as long as the concluding passage; in two cases, it is simply a wording that they share that is not found in any of the other French manuscripts, but the other two represent additional content. The way they are scattered through the text makes it difficult to see them as the work of a compiler scouring the English text for

---

[18] Hasenohr, *Textes de dévotion et lectures spirituelles en langue romane*, p. 82. See also Hasenohr, 'La Seconde vie du Miroir des simples âmes en France', p. 280.

[19] Hasenohr, 'La Seconde vie du Miroir des simples âmes en France', p. 280.

[20] Hall, 'The Abbey of the Holy Ghost', p. 108.

additional content, particularly since none of the English translator's own new content is represented. All of this points to *VO* having been based on a copy of the French *Abbaye* which was very close to that used by the English translator, if not that manuscript itself. The manuscript containing the French source of the English translation has never been identified, although scholarship about it tends to suggest that *R* comes closest. In fact the translation shares more readings with *A*, although the resemblances are somewhat obscured by the poor quality of *A*'s copy. More strikingly, it shares a number of readings with *VO* that are not found in any other copy of the *Abbaye*.[21] The absence of these readings anywhere else in the continental manuscript tradition of the *Abbaye* makes it likely that they were unique to the manuscript which travelled to England and was subsequently translated there. It is most probable, therefore, that the source of Margaret's version of the *Abbaye* was a manuscript obtained through Margaret's English contacts, which may have been either the one from which the English translation was made or a copy of it.

The exceptional quality of *O*, qualified by Kren as the 'the most splendid of the various collections of spiritual writings that entered the library of Margaret of York', suggests that it was special.[22] It contains four miniatures, formerly thought to be the work of the Master of Mary of Burgundy, but now tentatively attributed to the Master of the First Prayerbook of Maximilian.[23] Two are presentation miniatures, those accompanying (2) and (7) in *O*. The miniatures have been studied in their own right, as part of the considerable body of manuscript painting commissioned by Margaret, in particular the portrait on folio 155^r, which is one of nine in books that she owned.[24] The illuminations in *O* are an integral part of its conception, however; they need to be considered in relation to the texts they illustrate. Already in *V* there were spaces left for two miniatures, at the head of the first two texts. In *O*, all three texts copied from *V* have miniatures, and in addition the *Douze fleurs de tribulation* has the celebrated portrait of Margaret of York at prayer. While it is highly probable that the image of her that is presented in the two early manuscripts by Nicholas Finet was constructed according to a court agenda of portraying her as a Burgundian princess (they show her performing works of mercy and praying — one striking image shows Jesus appearing to her as she prays), she is more likely to have had

---

[21] These are presented in the Introduction to Part II.

[22] Kren and McKendrick, *Illuminating the Renaissance*, p. 197.

[23] Kren and McKendrick, *Illuminating the Renaissance*, pp. 197–98. Kren's attribution is followed by Legaré, 'Les Bibliothèques de deux princesses', p. 257.

[24] Smith, 'Margaret of York and the Burgundian Portrait Tradition', p. 49.

some personal control over her portrayal in the manuscripts commissioned at the height of her authority as duchess, and therefore the form and placement of the portrait of *O* may to some extent reflect her choices.[25] There are two portraits in the manuscripts she commissioned from David Aubert: this one, and a conventional presentation miniature in the Boethius volume. Presentation miniatures are the exception in works commissioned by and for Margaret: the only other one is in Caxton's printed translation of the *Histoire de Troie*. The other portraits mostly show her at prayer or performing charitable works. Smith points out that the 'image of the devout noblewoman' is a staple of female portraiture in the Low Countries during this period, and he and Andrew Taylor both argue that Margaret saw her commissioned religious manuscripts and the portraits they contained as part of her self-presentation in the duchess's role as exemplar and leader of religious behaviour.[26] In the *Abbaye* manuscript, it is surely significant that the portrait accompanies the *Douze fleurs de la tribulation*. Its placement may be meant to underline her stoic and pious endurance of the tribulations besetting her at the time, which included the recent invasion of Burgundian lands by France, her husband's absence and military setbacks, and no doubt her failure to conceive an heir.

There is another aspect of the image Margaret needed to project, also identified by Taylor, which is magnificence: the conspicuous display of wealth which signified political power and authority.[27] The luxury of the illumination and format of this manuscript certainly does that. The two presentation miniatures (Pierre de Luxembourg presenting his book to his sister, and Seneca handing his work to the translator, who then presents it to the duke in the background) also underline the prestige of the volume, reinforcing the effort in the rubrics to identify the works it contains with well-known authors.[28] Further, there seems to be an attempt in this manuscript to align Margaret with Philip the Good, perhaps to strengthen her position in promoting Burgundian interests in Flanders. The portrait echoes the composition of a depiction of Philip the Good at prayer, investing the conventional image of noble female devotion

[25] The major work on the portraits of Margaret of York is Smith, 'Margaret of York and the Burgundian Portrait Tradition'. See also Pearson, 'Productions of Meaning in Portraits of Margaret of York'; Taylor, 'Displaying Privacy'.

[26] Smith, 'Margaret of York and the Burgundian Portrait Tradition', p. 49; Taylor, 'Displaying Privacy', pp. 278–79.

[27] Taylor, 'Displaying Privacy', p. 279.

[28] This interpretation of the Seneca miniature is Kren's. Kren and McKendrick, *Illuminating the Renaissance*, p. 197.

with a layer of ducal authority.[29] Philip's own image is shown in the presentation miniature mentioned above, at the beginning of the copy made from his own copy of the translation of *Des remedes de fortune* (which, like the *Douze fleurs de la tribulation*, offers advice on dealing with misfortune). Both *Des remedes de fortune* and *Des quatre vertus cardinalz*, a translation made by Jean Courtecuisse for Jean de Berry, are reproduced with the prologues that name their dedicatees, placing Margaret in princely company. All of this suggests that *O* was a production of particular importance, and raises the question of whether it was responding to specific circumstances in Margaret's life. If it was completed in early March 1476, it came at the end of a period during which she had needed to be very active on behalf of her husband, whom she had last seen in July of the preceding year (and would not see again).[30] As well as dealing with diplomatic negotiations for military aid against the French and organizing transport for her brother's army from England, her role in 'soft diplomacy' to keep the towns of the Low Countries loyal to Burgundy meant that she had to shore up her authority against challenge from anti-Burgundian factions.[31] She may have been sorely in need of both the reinforcement of her prestige and authority her new book provided and the sources of fortitude offered by the texts it contained. That the book was designed for use and not simply for display is indicated by the very detailed table of contents, giving folio numbers for beginnings and ends of texts and in some cases for their subdivisions, and descriptive rubrics, all of which makes it easy for a reader to choose and locate material on particular subjects.

The Abbaye du saint Esperit

The *Abbaye* might be considered within this context as merely providing spiritual nourishment and consolation, but its position at the head of the collection of texts suggests that it also had a role to play in projecting Margaret's image. The choice of illumination foregrounds the notion of virtue: the opening miniature shows four young women representing the virtues who clear and dig the foundations of the abbey: *Verité*, *Amor de Purté*, *Povreté*, and *Humilité*. So that there can be no mistaking who the figures are, each bears a label above her head. While Margaret herself is not represented in this miniature, its pres-

[29] Smith, 'Margaret of York and the Burgundian Portrait Tradition', p. 51.

[30] Weightman, *Margaret of York*, p. 84.

[31] Weightman, *Margaret of York*, pp. 74, 83.

ence at the opening of her book associates them with her and positions her as an exemplary cultivator of virtue. Although a less explicit association, it could play a similar role to the depiction of Charles the Bold as an ideal ruler with the labelled virtues Justice, Truth, Wisdom, Chastity, and Sobriety in his ordinance book.[32]

Apart from some modernizing of the language, and some further revisions of the wording of *V* in *O*, Margaret's version of the *Abbaye* closely follows the text of α_1. The modifications are mostly stylistic, consistent with David Aubert's treatment of other texts. There are no theological additions, and few changes or additions to the authorities — another indication that the adapter was a secular writer and not a spiritual adviser. A major difference in presentation is that the text is divided into twenty-one chapters, each with a heading summarizing the content. These headings create an outline of the *Abbaye*, framing it as a treatise ('ung beau traittié') which in this version is attributed to Jean Gerson. However, while the content gathered in each locus is the same as in α_1 some new content is introduced by way of a substantial interpolation. This is in line with David Aubert's modus operandi as a compiler, which he demonstrated in his earlier work for Philip the Good and other patrons, producing 'new and improved' versions of texts, often with additions from other sources.[33]

The interpolation comes at the end of the description of the founding and governance of the spiritual convent. It is presented as an address by Jesus to the reader (whom he calls 'daughter') graphically outlining the sufferings he has endured for mankind, followed by five chapters of response from the nuns of the abbey, in which they recognize and express sorrow for their sins. This response is described in the chapter rubrics as being that of the nuns, but it is written in the first person singular and provides the reader with a prayer script for contrition and supplication. It is impossible to say whether David Aubert was the author of the interpolated chapters or found them somewhere else. The rudimentary dialogue form, with Jesus as one of the speakers, immediately recalls another of the works produced for Margaret, the *Dyalogue de la duchesse de Bourgogne a Jesus Christ*, although that dialogue is clearly not the direct source of the interpolated chapters in the *Abbaye*. The *Dyalogue*, based on a work created for an earlier duchess, is personalized in a way that leaves no doubt that the advice it contains is intended for Margaret of York herself. Some scholars have interpreted the interpolation in the *Abbaye du saint Esperit* in the same way, and indeed have

---

[32] Montpellier, Bibliothèque municipale, MS Fonds C. Cavalier 216. See Smith, 'Margaret of York and the Burgundian Portrait Tradition', p. 50.

[33] Straub, *David Aubert*, pp. 14–16.

suggested that it contains thinly veiled criticism of her behaviour.[34] But there are some differences which caution against this interpretation.

In the *Dyalogue*, Margaret is explicitly made an active participant, asking questions, but that is not the case in the *Abbaye*, where Jesus's interlocutor is named collectively as the nuns of the abbey. The nuns act as proxies for the reader, but as reader Margaret is positioned much more as a generic penitent than as Duchess of Burgundy, and simply responds to Jesus's exhortations to contrition. As a devotional script, the *Abbaye* dialogue functions in much the same way as Anselm's meditation in the *Miroir* compilation, which also provides a penitential prayer script for an aristocratic woman.[35] The *Dyalogue* also has a much wider scope: although introduced by Finet as a guide to the contemplative life, it is more a description of virtuous action in the world. Only the final six of thirteen sections deal with contemplation; the rest are concerned with conduct and the virtues to be cultivated by rulers. One of the final sections is closer to the *Abbaye* dialogue, consisting mostly of a speech from Jesus recalling the events of the Passion and advising the duchess how to meditate on them and translate her meditation into penitence, followed by a very short prayer from the duchess asking for the grace to accomplish what he has asked. But although the *Abbaye* dialogue covers some of the same ground, its elaborations are very different from the measured tone of Denis the Carthusian, as conveyed in Nicholas Finet's French prose. It may nonetheless be that the interpolated chapters are a conscious effort to imitate the *Dyalogue*, which Aubert probably knew to be a book prized by the duchess, and that in his business as compiler of 'improving' texts by embellishing them and incorporating relevant material from other sources, he was attempting to produce something that he knew would be to her taste. If this is the case, it confirms *V* as an attempt to make a manuscript for Margaret, since the interpolation is already present in *V*'s copy of the *Abbaye*.

David Aubert's effort to refashion the *Abbaye* for the duchess is evident also in smaller modifications, and there is evidence that the process continued in the recopying of the text from *V* (generally closer to the source, α_1) into *O*. Many of them are of minor stylistic changes to wording and word order, but some serve

---

[34] This is the interpretation of Kathryn Hall, and Andrew Taylor notes that a number of the works in *O* contain passages that could be considered to be condemning the worldly vanity of Margaret's court, focusing on some of the additions to the *Miroir des pecheurs*, which he attributes to David Aubert: Hall, 'The Abbey of the Holy Ghost', pp. 65–67; Taylor, 'Displaying Privacy', pp. 286–88.

[35] Anselm's meditation is also one of the sources of the third text in *O*, the *livret* of pseudo-Pierre de Luxembourg. See Hasenohr, *Textes de dévotion et lectures spirituelles en langue romane*, p. 99 (Fiche 19940).

to adapt the text more specifically for a noble laywoman such as Margaret of York. For example, the description of Mercy, the almoner, who gives all without holding back ('tout donne et riens ne retient') is modified in *O* so that she gives so much that little remains ('tant donne que gaires ne luy demeure'). Generosity to the extent of complete dispossession may have seemed unsuitable advice for a woman in Margaret's position; indeed, this recalls the similar adjustment made in the *Cloistre de l'ame* (β₂), another version of the *Abbaye* for an aristocratic laywoman, which at the same point in the text has 'tout donra aprés sa nécessité prise' (will give all, once necessities have been provided for). Another small change relates a comment about prayer more closely to Margaret's context. In the passage on members of religious orders who are woken by desire to pray before the bell has rung for Matins, *O* changes the phrase in *V*, 'devant Dieu' (before God), to 'devant la representation de nostre seigneur' (before the representation of Our Lord). This conjures up a much more concrete image, evoking the representation in the same manuscript of Margaret at prayer before a devotional image and a similar picture in another manuscript she owned of a woman praying before an image of the Trinity.[36]

* * *

The final reworking of the *Abbaye* is thus a customized version for a particular reader, Margaret of York, which may have a connection to her through her country of birth. It occupies pride of place in a manuscript book that projects her image as a devout woman while at the same time being full of reminders of her wealth and power. While the first two religious manuscripts produced for Margaret by Nicholas Finet can be seen as part of the project of educating aristocratic women that was alluded to in relation to the *Miroir* collection, her later commissions show her taking up their advice on her role as exemplar of religious practice and shaping its expression in her own way. The penitential and ascetic tone of many of the works in the *Abbaye* collection could be construed as criticism of the luxury of Margaret's court, but they could just as well be understood as the means she chose to shore up her perceived virtue as she carried out the duties of her role as ducal consort. The place of the *Abbaye* in this collection attests to its continuing importance as a vehicle of spiritual and moral advice for women.

---

[36] BRB, MS 9272–76, fol. 182. This collection of moral treatises was owned by Margaret and produced in David Aubert's workshop, but has no colophon stating that it was made for her. The miniature is generally considered to be a portrait of Margaret of York. See Smith, 'Margaret of York and the Burgundian Portrait Tradition', pp. 51–52.

CONCLUSION

The history of the *Abbaye du saint Esprit* and its successive reworkings demonstrates some of the complexity of the production of vernacular theology. For the creator of the *Abbaye*, it was not simply a matter of modifying a given monastic text for a lay audience. The dissemination of the content of the original twelfth- and early thirteenth-century monastic texts of what Whitehead calls 'interiorizing interpretations of an external rule' was already well under way, and the author of the *Abbaye* was able to draw on three separate formulations of the metaphor of monastic life and structures.[1] This multiplicity of vernacular paths of transmission is evident in manuscripts *C* and *R*, which record copies of the more straightforward translation of *Introduxit me rex* as well as the *Abbaye*. The adaptation of monastic spiritual formation literature for the laity was thus not a simple linear process, nor was it accomplished in a single moment with the production of a new vernacular text. The history of the *Abbaye* demonstrates a continuing process of adaptation and reinterpretation, frequently dipping back into the pool of scriptural and patristic authorities to refresh its message.

From its earliest existence, the *Abbaye* is framed as a point in a dialogue between a spiritual adviser and his advisee. It is thus an embodiment of the conversation alluded to by Bernard McGinn, between clerics and laypeople, about the ways of pursuing spiritual perfection in the world. To be sure, those opening words are a literary convention, but the conventional form of the letter of spiritual direction itself grows out of such conversations. And the frame is preserved in all the versions except β, whether the addressee is a beguine, a male tertiary, a Franciscan nun, or the Duchess of Burgundy. Two of the *Abbaye*

---

[1] Whitehead, *Castles of the Mind*, p. 78.

manuscripts illustrate one form the conversation could take: in *L* and *N*, the *Abbaye* figures among texts chosen by a cleric for pastoral use. The Liège manuscript *L* suggests use by a priest who, like Lambert of Liège, had the pastoral care of pious women, possibly beguines, in his charge. Its version of the *Abbaye* is framed as a letter of spiritual advice. In Pierre Basin's manuscript the textual allusion to the conversation is absent, but the manuscript context allows its participants to take a recognizable form — the queen and her chaplain — and demonstrates the continuing success of the *Abbaye* as a site for that conversation.

The *Abbaye* was not an isolated phenomenon. It was part of a wave of text production in northern France and the southern Low Countries dealing with the same set of questions about shaping interior dispositions and external behaviour in the pursuit of Christian perfection. It drew from the same pool of rhetorical structures, examples, and topoi, and was in turn drawn on by the authors of other texts. The patterns of transmission of the *Abbaye* constantly intersect with those of other texts from this period, even into the fifteenth century, where they appear in collections, like those of Margaret of York, that mined the production of the thirteenth century. Many of those texts were, like the *Abbaye*, modified in various ways during their transmission, the same text able to serve lay and religious, female and male, merchant and aristocrat, with minor adjustments to suit different ways of life and religious sensibilities. The *Abbaye*'s history is unusually rich in this respect. Its multiple readaptations in identifiable contexts show it moving from its initial audience among the urban merchant classes to the high aristocracy, in France and later in Burgundy, and from lay audiences to monastic and back again.

However, although it was sometimes adapted for male or mixed audiences, the *Abbaye* continued to be a text of choice for women, particularly in the fifteenth century. Perhaps the absence of concrete prescriptions of prayer and ascetic practices helped it to find a place among works presented to or chosen by aristocratic laywomen whose lives could not realistically embrace such practices. Instead of constraining its reader to a programme of observances, it allowed her to position herself imaginatively within an interior space constructed purposefully for the cultivation of virtue, and to align herself with those 'gens spirituels' who inhabited it. The possibility of narrative afforded by the allegorical personifications may also have made it more attractive than drier, sermon-like treatises. At the same time, the interior space constructed by the allegory remained perfectly suitable for nuns whose external space was more closely aligned with it. The construction metaphor at the heart of the *Abbaye* remained a powerful symbol of interior self-fashioning for both religious and lay.

The successive adaptations of the *Abbaye* also illustrate the multiple agendas at work in the development of vernacular theology. The base version represented by α_1 presents a model of religious life in which the penitential is important because it underpins a progression through contemplative prayer to spiritual union with the divine. It marshals teaching originally designed for monastic novices to open the way for laywomen who aspire to similar spiritual goals. All the adaptations, from β onwards, to a certain degree shift the balance between penitential and contemplation in the direction of penitential, whether by playing down contemplation, increasing the penitential matter (as in the case of α_2), or both. If we consider this only within the textual history of the *Abbaye*, it is tempting to regard it as a trend reflecting increasing anxiety about women and mysticism and a desire to impose greater control over female spirituality. This may indeed have been part of the agenda of individual adapters. However, when viewed in the context of the manuscript anthologies it forms a part of, the picture is more complex. They often contain other texts with a markedly contemplative tone, meaning that the penitential aspect is not privileged in the overall collection. Rather, the internal balance of the earliest version of the *Abbaye* is maintained between the elements of the collection, with the ascetic and regulatory possibilities inherent in the cloister allegory aligning the *Abbaye* adaptation more closely with the penitential element.

It is clear also that, in many of the choices that governed both the adaptations of the *Abbaye* and the constitution of the manuscript anthologies in which they appear, pastoral care and spiritual direction were not the only motives. For groups of elite women, the *Abbaye* became part of their repertoire of self-representation, in displays of spiritual and social capital. In the case of the *Sainte abbaye*, the text was incorporated into a luxurious object adding to the prestige of a royal abbey, where its architectural framework provided a stimulus for the innovative illuminations. Under the title of the *Cloistre de l'ame*, it was co-opted into a project which allowed a series of aristocratic women to present themselves as models of piety and virtue, and then as the *Abbaye du saint Esperit* it became part of Margaret of York's efforts to strengthen her position as she defended the duchy of Burgundy's interests in Flanders. In all of these cases, the heightened penitential tone played into models of female piety, particularly for women whose obligations to maintain the prestige of their position through public displays of consumption left them open to accusations of profligacy and vanity. It is in the use of the *Abbaye* by and for women whose wealth and power make their agency more visible that we can see most clearly how deeply the production of vernacular theology was embedded in the social and political concerns of its users.

Part II

Introduction to the Editions and Translation

The transmission history of the *Abbaye* is much more complex than the simple picture in four stages that emerged from Kathleen Chesney's study of the nine manuscripts known to her, with the six distinct states of the text presented here.[1] Already at the end of the thirteenth century there were at least two traditions (here called α and β). One was already geographically spread (Lorraine, Picardy, and Wallonia), and in the fourteenth century travelled to England, while in the fifteenth it was present in Picardy and Flanders. The other remained confined to the area around Paris and the Loire valley. The known manuscripts are listed below by group, each group corresponding to a redaction of the text.

Redaction	Siglum	Manuscript
α₁	M	Metz, Bibliothèque municipale, MS 535, fol. 63, Metz, late thirteenth or early fourteenth century
	L	Louvain, Bibliothèque de l'Université, MS G.53, fols 186va–187vb, Liège, 1311
	C	Munich, Bayerische Staatsbibliothek, MS cod. gall. 914, fols 91va–94rb, diocese of Cambrai, first decade of fourteenth century
	A	Paris, Bibliothèque de l'Arsenal, MS 3167, fols 50ra–52rb, Lorraine (probably Metz), mid-fourteenth century
	R	London, British Library, MS Royal 16 E XII, fols 132va–139vb, Paris or nearby, mid-fourteenth century

[1] Chesney, 'Notes on Some Treatises of Devotion', pp. 14–16. The groups α₁, α₂, β₁, and β₂ correspond to Chesney's versions *c*, *d*, *a*, and *b* respectively; the γ manuscripts, as well as *C* and *Q*, were unknown to her.

α_2	V	Vesoul, Bibliothèque municipale, MS 91, fols 1^r–28^r, Ghent, fifteenth century (before 1476)
	O	Oxford, Bodleian Library, MS Douce 365, fols 1^r–16^v, Ghent, March 1476
β_1	Y	London, British Library, MS Yates Thompson 11 (formerly MS Additional 39843), fols 2ra–7ra, Paris, 1293–95[2]
	N	London, British Library, MS Additional 20697, fol. 29^{ra-vb} (incomplete), Neuphle, before 1398
β_2	D	London, British Library, MS Additional 29986, fols 149vb–152vb, Paris, $c.$ 1407–10
	B	Brussels, Bibliothèque Royale de Belgique, MS 9555–58, fols 151ra–154rb, Paris, $c.$ 1410[3]
	P	Paris, Bibliothèque nationale de France, MS nouvelles acquisitions françaises 5232, fols 169^r–172^v, fifteenth century
	Q	St Petersburg, National Library of Russia, MS fr. Q. v. III. 1, fols 191ra–194vb, first half of fifteenth century
γ	X	Paris, Bibliothèque nationale de France, MS fonds français 2095, fols 29^r–34^v, Picardy, early fifteenth century
	Z	Paris, Bibliothèque nationale de France, MS fonds français 19397, fols 97^r–101^r, fifteenth century
δ	S	Brussels, Bibliothèque Royale de Belgique, MS 9106, fols 233va–234vb, Ghent, 1475 (fragments worked into a new text)

The α group is widely spread temporally and geographically. The earliest α_1 manuscripts are from Metz (M) and Picardy (C), and date from around the years around 1300, while the latest manuscript of α_2 (O) is from Ghent and dates from 1476. There is a second α_1 manuscript from Metz (A) and one from Liège (L), which, for the *Abbaye* and some accompanying French texts, was copied from M. One manuscript comes from the Paris area (R). There is some evidence of three versions of α_1, represented in the stemma below by x, y and z. R, though closely aligned with AC, shares some readings with Y, which suggests that Y's adaptation was made to a model that may have also been used by R. Notably, R and Y both make the chapel, rather than the dormitory, the part of the abbey that is elevated above the cares of the world, and both refer to the verse of the *Veni creator* hymn, 'hostem repellas longius', as the cue for the Holy Ghost to come to the rescue of the nuns.

---

[2] Rouse and Rouse, *Manuscripts and their Makers*, pp. 155–57. Chesney dated this manuscript to $c.$ 1300.

[3] The dates for D and B are those given by Meiss on the basis of the miniatures: *French Painting in the Time of Jean de Berry: The Limbourgs*, I, 408–09.

At some point during the second half of the fourteenth century a copy of α_1 made its way to England, where it was translated into English and enjoyed some success.[4] None of the three surviving α_1 manuscripts could have been the source of the translation, so at least one other manuscript must have existed. That manuscript may have also given rise to α_2, which is represented by two manuscripts created in the third quarter of the fifteenth century in Ghent (*V* and *O*). *V* is the earlier of the two and is closer to α_1 than *O*, whose scribe often altered wordings. It cannot be related directly to any of the α_1 manuscripts, but it agrees in some places with the English translation in ways that suggest it was copied from a manuscript very close to the one the translation was made from. The common readings of *V* and the English version are shown in bold in the table on the next page. *V* also often agrees with *A* and *C* against *R*, which suggests that both its source and that of the translation (which may have been the same manuscript) were related to *AC*. All of these observations indicate that there were more manuscripts of the α_1 group that have not survived.

The β group is relatively contained, both geographically and in terms of manuscript variants. All were probably produced in Paris, and most were owned by people in royal circles. No representative of this tradition is independent of *Y*. Apart from *Y*, they cluster around the early fifteenth century. Two of them (*Y* and *N*, which may have been copied directly from *Y*) preserve a version of the text which begins 'La sainte abbaie et la religion doit estre fondee esperituelment en la conscience' (The holy abbey and its order should be founded spiritually in the conscience). The β_2 manuscripts are all copies of the same anthology of texts of spiritual and moral advice for noblewomen, produced in the first decade of the fifteenth century. Their version of the *Abbaye* text is derived from β_1.

Two other groups are clearly derived from α_1, but have modified it to such a degree that I have treated them as separate versions, γ and δ. Of the two γ manuscripts, *X* probably represents the original version, made for Franciscan nuns in Picardy in the early fifteenth century, with *Z* containing a copy that has been further modified. δ is represented by a single manuscript, *S*, although there may be copies yet to be identified in other miscellanies. *S* gives a text made up of clearly identifiable extracts from α_1, recombined in a different order and interspersed with other material. *S* comes from the same workshop as *V* and *O*, but it is based on a manuscript of α_1 that included the reference, also found in *R*, to the lark swooning as it sings, which is not present in the version used by *VO*.

---

[4] There are twenty-four known manuscripts and five incunabula: Consacro, 'The Author of *The Abbey of the Holy Ghost*', p. 20.

French readings unique to *V*	English translation⁵
En largement donner aux poures (3ʳ)	**largeliche ʒeuynge to þe pore and to þe meseyse** (5/7–8)
Et ne mesprisiés par vostre grace souveraine les piz que vous avez creez (6ʳ)	**and folfulle þe brestes with þi grace þat þou has ifoormed** (10/8–9)⁶
Le pere, le filz, et le saint Esperit les **confortera** et aidera, (8ʳ)	þe Fader, þe Sone, þe Holi Gost hem schal **cumforten** with moni gostli joyes (14/6–7)
dame Jalousie gouverne par **saveur** de perfection (V 24ᵛ)	And þat is gelesye, and þat is **sauour** of perfeccion. (E36/2–3)
Or vous prye je tous et toutes que ceste sainte religion voeulliés tenir et soyés dilligens et dilligentes a vostre pouoir que chascune des bonnes dames quy en cestuy present traittié ont estee nommees fachent leur office en voz coeurs chascun jour espirituellement. Et bien vous gardez que point ne trespassez la riegle de la religion ne l'obedience des souverains. Et s'il advenoit par aucune mescheance que aulcune des dessus dittes [16ᵛ] quatre filles a l'ennemi d'enfer s'embatissent en voz cœurs, faittes par le conseil de madame Discretion et incontinent recourez a oroison, en appellant par tres ardant desir le tresdebonnaire saint Esperit. Lequel incontinent comme treshumble et tout charitable visiteur viendra et boutra hors de vous toute l'ordure par telle maniere que le couvent de vostre conscience demourra paisible et a bon droit, car elle sera temple du beneoit saint Esperit. Ainsi soit il. A.M.E.N.	Now I preye ow alle par charite of God, þat alle þo þat of þis religion reden or heeren, þat þei beo buxom qith al heore miht and to suffren þeose gode ladies bifore nempned don heore offys vche day, gostliche withinne ʒoure hertes. And loke vchone bisyliche þat ʒe don no trespas aʒeyn þe reule ne þe obedience of þe religion and, nomeliche, of þe souereyns. And ʒif it, þorw eny vnhap, falle þat eny of þeose foure douʒtren sechen in eny kun wyse to haue entre withinne ʒor hertes to dwelle, doþ aftur þe counseil of þe gode Ladi Discrecion and ʒiueþ ow to deuocion, with hertliche preyere, in hope of Godes help and of his socoures. And ʒe schul beo dilyuered þorw þe merci and þe grace of Almihti God. And he hit vs graunte þoruʒ þe besechynge of his deore moder. Amen.

---

⁵ Quoted from Consacro, 'A Critical Edition of "The Abbey of the Holy Ghost"'. Line references are given as page/lines.

⁶ Here both *V* and the English text are translating a part the *Veni creator* hymn which the English translation quotes in Latin: 'imple superna gratia que tu creasti pectora' (fill with grace the breasts that you have created). None of the French versions quote this part of the hymn in Latin, and *V* and its copy *O* are the only manuscripts to have it in French.

Stemma

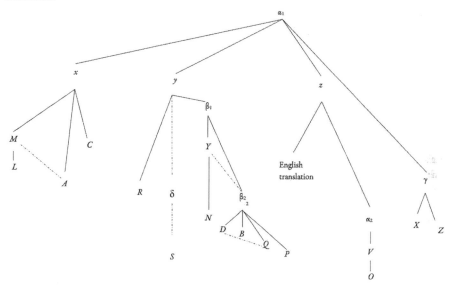

The Editions and Translation

The complex transmission history of the *Abbaye* also raises editorial challenges. Some states of the text are represented by disparate copies with a high degree of variance, while others are more stable.[7] They demonstrate a wide range of scribal practices, from obvious miscopying, through attempts to make sense of an unclear exemplar, to embellishment and stylistic variation. Although all states of the text visibly share an underlying structure, and repeat some content, there can be no question of a single edition; to attempt one would be to create an artificial entity which no medieval reader ever encountered. I have chosen to edit each state separately, but my editorial approach has varied a little from one edition to another because of differences in the nature of the manuscript groups involved. The editorial approach is set out at the beginning of each edition. In all editions normal editorial practice for editing Old and Middle French prose texts has been followed: the use of *i* and *j*, *u* and *v* has been standardized; the acute accent is used to indicated when an *e* is stressed, or to distinguish between homonyms; and the cedilla is used to mark a sibilant *c*. Abbreviations are expanded, and some modern punctuation has been added to facilitate reading. Latin quotations, which in some manuscripts are written in

---

[7] Cerquiglini, *Éloge de la variante.*

red or underlined, are given in italics. Where a word is divided by the move to a new folio or column, the folio number is placed at the beginning of the word. Where the source for a scriptural or patristic quotation can be identified, it is provided in a footnote.

I have provided one modern English translation of the text. Because of the many overlaps between the French versions, it seemed unnecessary and indeed repetitive to translate each one. I have chosen the earliest version, since it is probably of the widest interest to readers. The translation is made from the edition of *La religion dou cuer de l'Abbaie dou saint Esprit* (α_1) and, like the edition, uses bold type to indicate where the text of *C* has been supplemented from other manuscripts.

La religion dou cuer
de l'abbaie dou saint Esprit (α_1)

and translation

The Religion of the Heart of the
Abbey of the Holy Ghost

Two of the earliest known manuscripts of the α tradition (*M* and *L*) were destroyed during the Second World War and are known only from the short initial and final passages that were transcribed by Paul Meyer and Arthur Långfors.[1] The oldest surviving manuscript of this group is now *C*, from the beginning of the fourteenth century — older than *L* and possibly contemporary with *M*. The other manuscripts are *A* and *R*, both from the mid-fourteenth century. Unfortunately, each of the three surviving manuscripts has features that make it a less than perfect representative. The *A* text may be a copy of *M* — its language indicates that it was written in Metz and it matches the passages transcribed from *M* word for word. Unfortunately, it is a very careless copy, full of misreadings and omissions, but it occasionally provides readings, attested also by later witnesses, that are not present in *R*. *R* gives a much more careful rendering of the text, but it has clearly been deliberately modified in some places by the scribe, for example substituting 'temporele' for 'corporele' and suppressing of most of the addresses to a female reader. *C*, from the diocese of Cambrai, agrees with *A* in many places and often provides good readings for passages confused or omitted by *A*. However, *C* has some omissions of its own, and one serious piece of miscopying, where it mixes up the builders of the refectory, chapel, and dormitory and the order of the buildings. Like *R*, it is part of an anthology destined for male religious and suppresses the addresses to a female reader, although it retains some feminine grammatical forms. In spite of its shortcomings, however, I have chosen *C* as the base manuscript for this edition to provide access to the earliest available version of the text. Variants are supplied from *A* and *R* (and *M* and *L* where possible), with occasional corroboration from *V* (which is closer to α_1 than *O* is), and from *Y*, which, in spite of its modifications, shares many readings with *R*, and some with *A* and *C*.

For this edition, however, I am departing slightly from the principle of showing only what the reader of the base manuscript would have seen. Because a picture of what was available in the early tradition is essential for interpreting the changes made in later versions, including the Middle English translation, I have inserted in bold type the main passages that *C* omits, drawing on *A* and *R*. The title is taken from the full description of the work in the prologue in *M* and *A*, and reflected in *VO* and the Middle English translation, although it is shortened in *C*. The edition is accompanied by a modern English translation.

---

[1] Meyer, 'Notice du ms. 535 de la Bibl. Mun. de Metz', p. 43; Långfors, 'Notice des manuscrits 535 de la bibliothèque municipale de Metz et 10047 des nouvelles acquisitions du fonds français de la bibliothèque nationale', p. 143.

[no rubric]

(91va) **Fille, je regarde que**[2] mout de gent couvoitent et vauroient entrer en
religion, mes il ne pueent, ou c'est par povreté, ou pour ce qui sont retenu par
le loien de mariage ou par autre reson, et pour ce je fes une abeie de relegion
c'on apele dou saint Esperit. Et si le fes de cuer[3] que tout cil qui ne puent estre[4]
en relegion corporelment soient en relegion esperituelment.[5] He biaus sire
Diex ou sera cest religions fondee, ceste abeie plantee? Je di qu'ele sera fondee et plantee en une place c'on apele conscience. Souvent est avenu et bien
avons veu que ore a biau liu, ou de Meneurs ou de Preescours, qui soloit estre
mout hors. Ainsi avient il esperituelment en conscience ou li saint Esperit veut
demourer.[6] Ore couvient donc la place de conscience netoier et purgier, par coi
le sains Esperis i envoie .ii. demoisieles preus, vaillans et sages. La premiere a a
non Damoisile Verités, qui purgera tout ce liu par confession. L'autre si a a non
Amors de Purté, qui gardera cel cuer de toute ordure et de toutes mauvaises
pensees si que jamés honis ne sera. Et quant la place de conscience est bien
netoié et purgié si convenra fere les fondemens larges et parfons, et ce feront .ii.
damoisieles. L'une a a non Humilités et l'autre Povretés. Humilités les fera bas
et parfons. Et Povretés les fera grant et larges et jetera la terre de sa et de la, en
largement donner[7] quant qu'ele porra avoir et tenir. Hé, benoite soit relegions
qui est fondee en humilité et en povreté. Et c'est encontre aucuns mauvais relegieus (91vb) orguelleus et couvoiteus.

Ceste religions si doit estre fondee sor bone riviere, c'est de larges lermes et
de plors. Vile ou abeie qui est[8] sor bone riviere si est plus aaise et plus deliteuse.
Et pour ce la Magdalainne fu fondee sor bone riviere, dont grans biens li vint. Et
de ce dist David: *Tanquam lignum quod plantatum est secus decursus aquarum,*[9]

---

[2] Passages in bold are supplied from *A* unless otherwise indicated. *CR om*, *M* Fille je res-
garde (*L* regarde) que, *AVO* Fille regarde que.

[3] *MA* Ce te fas un livre de la religion dou cuer de l'abaie dou saint Esperit, *R* Pour ce si fes
.i. livre.

[4] *C om* estre.

[5] *R* que cil ou celes qui ne pueent entrer en religion temporele soient en religion espirituele,
A Que tuit cil qui ne pueent estre en religion corporel soient en la religion espirituel.

[6] *AR* ouvrer.

[7] *C om* donner, *RY* en largement donner, *A omits this sentence.*

[8] *C om* est.

[9] Psalm 1. 3.

Daughter, I see that many people would like to be in a religious order, but they cannot, either through poverty or because they are held back by the bonds of marriage, or for some other reason, and that is why I am making an abbey of the religion that is called that of the Holy Ghost. And I make it in the heart so that those who cannot corporally be in a religious order may spiritually be in one. Ah fair Lord God, where will this order be founded, this abbey established? I say that it will be founded in a place called the conscience. It has often come about that there are fair places, whether of the Friars Minor or Friar Preachers, which were once very ugly. The same happens spiritually in the conscience where the Holy Ghost would dwell. Now it is therefore necessary to purge and clean the place of the conscience, for which the Holy Ghost sends two excellent, valiant, and wise ladies. The first is called Lady Truth, who will purge the place with confession. The other is called Love of Purity, who will keep this heart from all filth and from wicked thoughts so it will never be shamed by them. And when the place of the conscience is well cleaned and purged it is necessary to make the foundations wide and deep, and this will be done by two ladies. One is called Humility and the other, Poverty. Humility will make them low and deep, and Poverty will make them great and broad, and will cast earth this way and that by giving generously whatever she might possess. Ah, blessed be an order of religion that is founded in humility and poverty; this is against certain bad religious who are proud and covetous.

This order of religion must be founded beside a good river, that is, of abundant tears and weeping. The city or the abbey that is by a good river is more delightful and at ease. And for that reason the Magdalene was founded on a good river, from which great good came to her. And of this David says: *Tanquam lignum quod plantatum est secus decursus aquarum,*

c'est-à-dire, ainssi que li arbres qu'est plantés selons le cors des iaues. Et encore: *Fluminis impetus letificat ciuitatem dei.*[10] C'est li bruis de la riviere resbaudist et esleesce la cite, et si le fet nete et pure, et seure et habundant de marchandise.

Damoisiele Obedience d'une part et Damoisiele Misericorde d'autre part si feront les murs grans et haus. Hé Diex, quantes bones ouvres nous fesons par le conmandement de Diu et le conseil de sainte eglyse, et quantes helesomosnes nous fesons, tantes pieres metons nous en nos defisces[11]. Nous lison[12] que Salemons fist[13] se meson de grans pierres precieuses. Ce sont grans aumosnes et saintes ouvres, qui doivent estre de bone cauch vive jointes ensamble. C'est de bone foi, et por ce dist David: *Omnia opera eius in fide.*[14] C'est-à-dire, toutes ces ouvres soient en foi et tout aussi[15] que murs ne puet durer sans boin chiment, tout aussi ouvres ne valent rient sans la foi de Diu, dont quanque li mescreant font est tout perdu. Damoisiele Passience et Damoisiele Force feront les piliers pour bien soustenir et pour (92ra) apoier que nus vent de tribulation ou de temptention ou de parole cuisant ne les puist abatre. L'escripture dist que une grant dame fist une meson, si i mist .vii. pillers.[16][17]

Or couvient fere le cloistre a .iiii. corniers. Pour ce a il a non cloistres qu'i[l] est clos et doit estre clos et bien gardés. **Fille, se tu vulz**[18] estre bien relegieuse si **te**[19] doit tenir close bien garder **ton**[20] cloistre. Clorre les ex de legerement regarder. Clorre les oreilles d'autrui mal oïr, la bouce tenir de parler et de rire, le cuer clorre de toute mauvaise pensee. Qui bien gardera et tenra ces .iiii. choses, ele sera bone nonmee et bien religieuse.[21]

[10] Psalm 46. 5 (45. 5).

[11] *AR* edifices.

[12] *C om.*

[13] *C* dist.

[14] Psalm 33. 4 (32. 4).

[15] *C* aussi aussi.

[16] *C* pierres, *AR* pillers.

[17] Proverbs 9. 1.

[18] *C* Qui veut, *AR* Fille se tu vulz (*R* vueux).

[19] *C* se.

[20] *C* son.

[21] *AR* elle sera bien religiuse.

that is, just like the tree which is planted by the course of the river. And again: *Et fluminis impetus letificat ciuitatem dei*. That is, the sound of the river cheers and enlivens the city, and makes it clean and pure, and secure and abundant in trade.

Lady Obedience on the one hand and Lady Mercy on the other make the walls thick and high. Ah God, however many good works we perform according to the commandment of God and the counsel of Holy Church, and however many alms we give, that is how many stones we add to our edifice. We read that King Solomon made his house from great precious stones. These are great alms and holy works, which must be joined together with good quicklime. That is, good faith, and for this reason David said: *Omnia opera eius in fide*. That is to say, may all these works be in faith. And just as a wall cannot last without good cement, in the same way works are worth nothing without faith in God. Thus however much unbelievers do, it is all lost. Lady Patience and Lady Fortitude will make pillars as a strong support, so that no wind of tribulation or temptation or wounding words can blow them down. Scripture says that a great lady made a house, and put seven pillars in it.

Now the cloister must be made, with four corners. The reason it is called cloister is that it must be closed and well-guarded. **Daughter, if you want** to be a religious woman, keep **yourself** close and guard **your** cloister. Close your eyes to frivolous looking, your ears to listening to ill of others, hold back your mouth from speech and laughter, close your heart to all wicked thoughts. She who guards and keeps these four things will be called good and truly religious.

Damoisiele Confessions fera le capistre, **car ele dist verité**,[22] **Damoisele predication fera le refecteur car ele past les ames.**[23] Contemplacions le dortoir, et devés savoir que le dortoir doit estre haus par souslevemens de grans desirriers et hors de noise et de triboul et d'ensonniement[24] de cest siecle. Damoisele Orisons[25] fera la capele. Compassion l'enfremerie, Devocions le celier, Meditations le grenier, et devés savoir que ces .ii. offices doivent tousdis estre plainnes et abondans par desseure les autres.

Quant les offices sont issi fetes si i couvient metre le couvent des vertus et des grasces et des dons dou saint Esperit, qui de ceste relegion est garde et visiteres. Ceste grande abeye li Peres par sa grand poissance le fonda. Et ce dist David: *fondavit eam altissimus.*[26] Li tres haus sires le fonda, li Fiex par sa sapience l'ordena. Et ce dist sains Pols: *Que a deo* (92rb) *sont* [sic] *ordinata sont* [sic].[27] Les choses qui sont de Diu sont ordenees. Li sains Esperis le garde et le visete, et de ce cantons nous: *Veni spiritus mentes tuorum visita.* Creerres Esperis vien visiter les pensees des tiens. Or disons dont de par Diu.

Madame Carités qui est la plus vaillans de toutes les autres si sera abeesse. Et tout aussi c'on ne doit riens fere sans le congié de s'abesse, ne nule part aller, ne prendre, ne donner, tout aussi espirtuelment ne doit on riens fere, ne nule part aller, sans le congié de Madame Carité. Et ainssi le commande sains Pols: *Omnia uestra in caritate fiant.*[28] C'est a dire, toutes vos choses soient fetes en carité. **Hé filhe, com**[29] ci a .i. fort commandement, mes il est boins et si sauve les ames. Toutes nos pensees, paroles, regars, alees, venues soient fetes par carité et en carité. Je voi moult de gens en relegion qui moult sont relgions petis.[30] Et mout de choses font et dient et en mout de lieus vont, qui moult de choses prendent et donent encontre le commandement de Madame Carité. Si est tout perdu devant Dieu. Prendés garde et si pensés bien parfont que quanque vous ferés soit fet pour Diu et en carité.

---

[22] *C om*, *RY* car ele dist verité.

[23] *C om*, *RY* Damoisele predication fera le refecteur car ele past les ames.

[24] *A* causassion, *R* l'achoison.

[25] *C* predications, *ARYVO* orison, *RY* Oroison fera la chapele qui doit estre haute par douce contemplacion.

[26] Psalm 87. 5 (86. 5).

[27] Romans 13. 1.

[28] 1 Corinthians 16. 14.

[29] *C om*, *A* Hé filhe com, *V* Hé fille, *R* Hee comment.

[30] *A* moult poy en religions, *R* qui sont mout po religieus.

Lady Confession will make the chapter house, **for she speaks the truth. Lady Preaching will make the refectory, for she feeds the soul**. Contemplation will make the dormitory, and you should know that the dormitory must be high, raised up by great desire and out of the disturbance and trouble and clamour of the world. Lady Prayer will make the chapel, Compassion the infirmary, Devotion the cellar, Meditation the granary, and you should know that these two storerooms must be always more abundantly stocked than any others.

When the buildings have been thus constructed, it is time to install the community of virtues, graces, and gifts of the Holy Ghost, who is the guardian and visitor of this order of religion. God the Father by his great power founded this great abbey. And David said: *fondavit eam altissimus*. The highest Lord founded it, the Son by his wisdom ordained it, and of this Saint Paul said: *Que a deo sunt ordinata sunt*. Those things which belong to God are ordained. The Holy Ghost guards it, and visits it, and of this we sing: *Veni spiritus mentes tuorum visita*. Come, Spirit, into the minds of your own. Let us say this in God's name.

My lady Charity, who is the most worthy of all, shall be abbess. And just as one should do nothing without the leave of one's abbess, nor go anywhere, nor take, nor give, likewise in the spiritual realm, one should not do anything nor go anywhere without the leave of my lady Charity. And thus Saint Paul commands it: *Omnia uestra in caritate fiant*. That is to say, let all that you do be done in charity. **Ah, daughter, how** hard a commandment this is! But it is good and saves souls. All our thoughts, words, looks, goings, and comings are to be carried out by and in charity. I see many in religion who do not hold it in high regard, and who act and speak, and go to many places, and take and give many things against the commandment of my lady Charity, and all of it is lost before God. Take heed and think well and deeply so that whatever you do, may be done for God and in charity.

Madame Sapience si sera prieuse. Car elle en est bien digne, et c'est escrit ou livre Salemon: *Prior omnia creata est sapiencia*.[31] C'est a dire, premiere de toutes choses est sapience créé. Par le conseil et par l'obedience[32] de ceste dame et prieuse devons nous (92ᵛᵃ) fere nos choses; si en serons miex prisié. Et por ce dist David: *Omnia in sapiencia fecisti*.[33] C'est a dire, Sire, tu as fet sagement ce que tu as fet.

Madame Humilités, qui tous dis se met au dessous, si ert souprieuse. Car ele s'abaisse mout et a li devons nous honor et obedience. Or veés **fielle**[34] donc se a .i. sainte abaye. Hé, certe tres moult bone relegion, ou il a si saintes damoisieles, si dignes et si souffisans abeesse com est Carités, prieuse comme Sapience, sousprieuse comme Humilités. **Hé filles**,[35] benoites soient les nonnains et benoites soient les ames qui bien gardent les commandemens de Madame Carité, les commandemens de Sapience et d'Umilité, qui les feront et manront toute leur vie caritablement, sagement, et humlement. Li Peres et li Fiex et le saint Esperit les sauvera, **li mondes les honorera**.[36]

Nous lisons u livre Daniel que .i. tres bien grans hons fu qui avoit a non Nabugodonosoyr.[37] Si establi sor trestout son regne .iii. homes qui tout fesoit et ordenerent et estoient bailliu de tout. Si que li rois n'avoit en son palais ne noise ne moleste, ains estoit em pais, en joie et en repos. Ou regne esperituel[38] ou ces .iii. baillie sont[39] n'ara ja plet ne nose, mes tous dis joie et repos. Hé, benoit soit li païs, li ordenes et li regnes ou ces .iii. roines sont[40] et tout est fet par amors, par sens et par humilité.

Damisiele Discrecions, qui moult est sage, si ert (92ᵛᵇ) tresoriere, et tout gardera et de tout prendera garde que tout voist a point.

Damoisiele Orisons si sera chantre et si levera les chans de jor et de nuit por Diu loer. Damoisiele Jubilations si ert sa compaigne. Vous savés bien qu'est orisons. Jubilations, ce dist sains Grigoires, si est une tres grans joie qui est conceue

---

[31] Ecclesiasticus 1. 4.

[32] *AY* Par le conseil, *R* Et par obedience ele conseille.

[33] Psalm 104. 24 (103. 24).

[34] *C* Or vees, *R* Or gardez, *Y* Or esgarde, *A* Or esgardeis fielle, *VO* Ha doulce fille.

[35] *CRY om*, *A* Hé filles, *VO* Fille.

[36] *C om*, *AR* li mondes les honorera.

[37] Daniel 2. 49.

[38] *A adds* ceu est la sainte arme, *R adds* de la sainte ame.

[39] *AR add* et la religion ou ces .iii. prelaz sont.

[40] *A* .iii. regnent, *R* trois dames regnent.

My lady Wisdom shall be prioress for she is worthy of it, and it is written in the book of Solomon: *Prior omnia creata est sapiencia*. That is to say, of all things wisdom was created first. We should obey this lady prioress's counsel in whatever we do; we will be thought better for it. And for this reason David says: *Omnia in sapiencia fecisti*. That is to say: Lord, whatever you have done, you have done wisely.

My lady Humility, who always places herself in a lowly position, shall be sub-prioress, for she abases herself greatly and we owe her honour and obedience. Now see, **daughter**, whether this is a holy abbey. Ah, certainly a most holy order of religion, where there are such holy ladies, such a worthy and capable abbess as Charity, prioress as Wisdom, sub-prioress as Humility. **Ah, daughter**, blessed be the nuns and blessed be the souls who keep the commandments of my lady Charity, the commandments of Wisdom and Humility, who carry them out and lead their whole life charitably, wisely, and humbly. The Father and the Son and the Holy Ghost will save them, **the world will honour them**.

We read in the book of Daniel that there was a very great man called Nebuchadnezzar. He set up three men who ordained and took care of everything over his whole kingdom, and were stewards of all there was. In this way the king had no commotion or disturbance in his palace; rather, all was peaceful, joyful, and calm. In the spiritual realm, wherever these three stewards are, there will be no commotion or complaint, but always peace and joy. Ah, blessed be the land, the order, and the realm where these three are sovereign, and where everything is done in love and wisdom and humility.

Lady Discretion, who is very wise, shall be treasurer, and look after everything and take care that all runs smoothly.

Lady Prayer shall be the choir-mistress and lead the singing, day and night, to praise God. Lady Jubilation shall be her companion. You know what prayer is. Jubilation, Saint Gregory said, is a great joy conceived

en ame par grasce aprés orison par amor et par ferveur d'esperite, qui ne puet estre dou tout moustree ne dou tout celee.[41] Si comme il avient aucune fois en aucune gent esperituel aprés oroison, que si sont si lié et si joiant et si fervent que lor cuers va cantant et murmurant une chanson parmi la sale ou parmi le chambre, et aucune fois la langue ne se puet tenir qu'ele ne chant ne les dois qui ne se muevent, **et li orteil qu'il ne dansent et s'envoisent. Si puet bien estre avenu que aucunes ont esté si ravies la ou eles se seoient que li fuisiaus leur cheoit d'une part et la quenoille d'autre, u livre, u sautier, et cheoient pasmés ausi comme l'alöese pasme en chantant.**[42]

Demoisiele Devocions si sera ceneliere. Si gardera les blans vins et les vermaus, rosés et fierés en la ramembrance de la bonté de Diu et de sa benoite passion et de la compaignie de Paradis. **Le ferré sont la remembrance du grant tourment d'enfer.**[43]

Damoisele Penitance fera la quisine et moult traveillera, car ele puet assés painnes pour fere satifaction et pour suer contricion.[44] Ele fet les bones viandes et peu en megue par astinence. Damoisiele Atemprance si ert refoituriere et si servira a mesure si que il n'i ara ne trop but ne trop mengié. (93ra) Damoisiele Soubrietés lira a tauble les belles et les saintes vies des peres et lor chantera a l'oreille quel vie il menerent pour aussi fere et pour prendre boin example.[45]

Damoisiele Pietés si sera pitanciere et si fera de bien selon ce qu'ele porra et qu'ele avera. Misericorde sa suer si sera aumosniere; c'est cele qui tout donne et riens ne retant.

Demisiele Paors si sera portiere et si gardera bien le cloistre de conscience. Si chassera hors les mauvais et apelera les bons, en tel manière que par le cremor des boins[46] li mauvais n'oseront entrer en cloistre dou cuer parmi la porte de la bouce, ou des iex, ou des oreilles.[47]

Demisiele Honestés sera maisteresse de nosvisces et enseignera a honestement vivre et aller et a saintement parler en tel manière que tout cil qui les ver

---

[41] Gregory the Great, *Moralia in Job* 28. 15.

[42] Supplied from *R. A* ne li orteis des piés qu'il ne se meuvent S'en puet estre avennu que teilz ou telle ierent sosprise et s'oblioit et ierent ravie. *S* Il est aucunes fois advenu que ame qui a esté ravye se paulme ainsi comme la liache qui se paulme en chantant.

[43] *C om*, *R* Le ferré sont la remembrance du grant tourment d'enfer, *Y* Li ferrez des tormenz d'enfer qui durent sanz fin.

[44] *R adds* en laquele ne puet plorer au moustier.

[45] *R* pour ce que eus y prennent essample a la uie des sainz.

[46] *AR om* par le cremor des boins.

[47] *RY add* Timor domini expellit peccatum.

in the soul by grace after prayer by love and by fervour of the spirit, which cannot be entirely shown nor hidden. And thus it happens sometimes to spiritual people after prayer, that they are so happy, joyful, and fervent that they go about through the hall or chamber, singing and murmuring a song in their heart, and sometimes their tongue cannot refrain from singing, nor their fingers from moving, **nor their tocs from dancing and making merry. It can happen that some have been so rapt that they dropped their spindle to one side and their distaff to the other, or their book, or their psalter, and they fell in a swoon, just as the lark swoons when it sings.**

Devotion shall be the cellarer. She will keep the white wines and the red, rosé, and ferrous,[48] in remembrance of the goodness of God and of his blessed Passion, and of the company of Paradise. **The ferrous wines are the remembrance of the great torments of Hell.**

Lady Penance shall do the cooking and work hard, for she can make enough effort to give satisfaction to God and to sweat for contrition. She cooks the good meats and eats little of them through abstinence. Lady Temperance shall be refectress and serve in such measure that there will not be too much eaten or drunk. Lady Sobriety shall read at table from the beautiful and holy Lives of the Fathers, and tell the sisters of the life they led, so they can do likewise and follow their good example.

Lady Pity shall be pittancer and do all the good she can with what she has. Lady Mercy her sister shall be almoner; it is she who gives all and holds nothing back.

Lady Fear shall be doorkeeper and guard the cloister of the conscience well. She will chase out the wicked, and call the good back, in such a way that through fear of the good, the wicked will not enter the cloister of the heart through the door of the mouth, or of the eyes, or of the ears.

Lady Honesty shall be novice mistress and teach them to live and behave honestly and have holy speech, in such a way that those who see them

---

[48] The meaning given by the *Altfranzösisches Wörterbuch* for *vin ferré* is wine with added iron, made by quenching hot iron in the wine.

ront i prignent bon example. Et por ce dist li Apostres: *Honeste ambulemus.*[49] Alons honestement.

Demisiele Cortoisie si sera hosteliere, qui les alans et les venans herbergera et rechevra gentement, en tel maniere que chascun s'en loera. Et pour ce que une nonne ne doit mie estre seule entre gent, si porroit avenir que Demisiele Cortoisie seroit trop hardie et trop baude. Si ara aveuc lui a compaigne Simplicité. Ce sont bones compaignes Cortoisie et Simplicités. Et bien sachiés que l'une sans l'autre vaut petit. Car trop grant cortoisie si est trop baude et trop hardie, et trop grant simplesce si est (93rb) soteriele, mes elles .ii. ensamble serviront bien et bel.

Demisiele Resons si sera pourverresse et pourverra et dehors et dedens si qui n'i ara nule defaute. Demisiele Loiautés si sera enfremiere et servira les malades et travellera mout et loiaument. Et pour ce que moult de malades i a plus assés que de haitiés, et plus de febles que de fors, Demisiele Largesce si sera sa compaigne et se li aministerra tout.

Une vaillans demisiele qui a a non Meditations si sera grenetiere. C'est cele qui assamle le boin grain de forment et des autres blés pour avoir soustenance a plenté. Meditations si est une vertus qui est de bien penser **a Deu**[50] et a ses fes et a ses dis,[51] c'est a criatures et a ses escriptures. Ceste grenetiere avoit li rois David. Si fu tous dis riches et mueblés,[52] de coi il dist ou Sautier: *Meditabor in omnibus operibus.*[53] Sire, dist il, je penserai tousdis a vos ouvres. Et en autre liu dist il: *In lege domini meditabiant die ac nocte.*[54] Il pensera et jor et nuit en la loi nostre seignor. C'est li commencement de toute perfection quant cuers se set metre en bien penser a Diu. Et tout aussi que li fruis vaut miex des fuelles, tout aussi vaut miex une boine pensee en sainte meditation que moult de paroles dire en oroison. Et si di encore plus,[55] que quant cuers est pris et eslevés en oroison il ne puet bien dire. Et tant a afere de penser a ce qu'i[l] (93va) sent et qu'i[l] voit et qu'il ot, qu'i[l] ne puet mot[56] dire et parole li faut; si se test por mieus crier et pour mex parler aprés. Et de ce dist David: *Quoniam tacui dum*

---

[49] Romans 13. 13.

[50] *R* a dieu.

[51] *C* asses f. et asses d.

[52] *AR* combles.

[53] Psalm 77. 13 (76. 13).

[54] Psalm 1. 2.

[55] *AR* Mes je di encore plus haut.

[56] *AR* riens.

can follow a good example. And for this reason the Apostle said: *Honeste ambulemus*. Let us go along honestly.

Lady Courtesy shall be hosteller and graciously receive and lodge those who come and go, so that each will rely on her. And since a nun should never be alone with other people, it could happen that Lady Courtesy might be too bold and forward, and so she will have Lady Simplicity with her as a companion. Courtesy and Simplicity make good companions. Know that one without the other is of little value. For too great courtesy is too bold and forward, and too great simplicity is foolishness, but these two together will perform the service well.

Lady Reason shall be steward and supply within and without so there will be no lack. Lady Loyalty shall be infirmarer and serve the sick, and work hard and loyally. And since there are more of the sick than of the well, and of the weak than of the strong, Lady Generosity shall be her companion, and administer everything for her.

A worthy lady called Meditation shall be the granarer. It is she who gathers the good wheat and other grains, so there is a plentiful supply of food. Meditation is a virtue which consists of thinking **about God** and his deeds and words: that is, about creation and Scripture. King David had this granarer and was always rich and had everything he needed. About this he spoke in the Psalter: *Meditabor in omnibus operibus*. Lord, he said, I will think always about your works. And in another place he said: *In lege domini meditabant die ac nocte*. Day and night he will think about the law of Our Lord. It is the beginning of all perfection, when the heart is able to begin thinking about God. And just as the fruit is worth more than the leaves, one thought in holy meditation is worth more than saying many words in prayer. And I say it is even more than this, that when the heart is engrossed and lifted up in prayer, it cannot speak. It is so occupied by what it feels and sees and hears, that it can say nothing and words fail it; thus it is silent the better to cry out, and in order to speak better afterwards. And of this David said: *Quoniam tacui dum*

clamarem.[57] Et la dist la glose, li grans cris que nous crions a Diu si est li grans desiriers que nous i avons. Et de ce dist S. Denis *in Mistica Theologia: Quantum superius ascendimus quantum contemplantibus nobis verba coartancur. Et postea: sine uoce erit totus vinctus immobilis.*[58][59] C'est a dire, quant cuers est bien soulevés et par grant desirier d'amor il ne puet dire ce qui sent, qu'il est si merveilleus et si esbahis que parole li faut. Et c'est sainte Meditations qui garde le grain de fourment qui est rouges par dehors et blans par dedens et fendus ou costé **dont on fait le boin pain. C'est Jhesucrist qui fut roges de son sanc en sa passion et blanc per dedens**[60] **par innocence, et fenduz u costé**[61] en la benoite mort de la lance. Et c'est li pains que prendons ou benoit sacrement.

Et si devés savoir que li greniers doit estre sour le celier, tot aussi meditation est avant devocion, et pour ce di je que Meditation est grenetiere, et Devocion ceneliere, et Pietés est pitanciere. Et de ces .iii. choses dist David ou Sautier: *A fructu frumenti uini et olei multiplicati sunt.*[62] Et en mout de liex en la Bible fet Diex ceste promesse: Servés me bien, ce dist, et je vous donrai habondance de forment, de vin et d'oiles. Et habundance de forment si est bien habundanmant penser au cors et a la benoite passion nostre seignor Jhesucrist. Et c'est meditations. (93vb) Habundance de vin si est parfetement de cuer et de grant desirier plourer, et c'est devotion. Habundance d'oile si est quant li cuers se delite et se soulasse en bien plourer,[63] et c'est consolacions. Car l'oile si donne savor et reluist en l'eglise[64] et art en la lampe, et aussi quant uns cuers[65] a bien pensé et bien plouré pour ses defautes si en a Dieu pité et se li fet pitance et confort ou delit qui le envoie. Or est donc premierement sainte meditation, c'est le forment, et aprés devocions, c'est le vin, et aprés consolacion, c'est l'oile qui donne savor en afection, et enlumine en connaissance et en revelacion, et art en ferveur, et est toudis esveillie pour bien fere.[66]

---

[57] Psalm 32. 3 (31. 3).

[58] *C* in nobili, *R* in noniabili, *Y* immobilis.

[59] Pseudo-Denis, *Mystica Theologia* 3. 2.

[60] Supplied from *A*; *R* et en fait on le bon pain. C'est Jhesucrist qui fu rouge de son sanc en pacience.

[61] Supplied from *R*; *A* au son batime per ignorance et fendus ou costeit.

[62] Psalm 4. 8.

[63] *A* por bien desirier, *R* pour bien loer.

[64] *AR* et si luist en l'eglise et si art en la lampe.

[65] *A* cuers espiritez, *R* cors bien espirituex.

[66] *AR om* et est toudis esveillie pour bien fere.

clamarem. And there the gloss says that the great cry we cry out to God is the great desire that we have. And of this Saint Denis said *in Mystica theologia*: *Quantum superius ascendimus quantum contemplantibus nobis verba coartancur. Et postea: sine uoce erit totus vinctus immobilis*. That is to say, when the heart is lifted up by desire of love, it cannot speak what it feels, because it marvels and is so astounded that speech fails it. And it is holy Meditation who keeps the good wheat which is red on the outside, and white within, and split along the side, **from which we make good bread. This is Jesus Christ, who was red from his blood in his Passion, and white within from innocence, and split in the side** by the lance in blessed death. And this is the bread we take in the sacrament.

And you must know that the granary must be above the cellar, and thus meditation comes before devotion, and for this reason I say that Meditation is granarer, and Devotion cellarer, and Pity pittancer, and of these three things David says in the Psalter: *A fructu frumenti uini et olei multiplicati sunt*. And in many places in the Bible God makes this promise: Serve me well and I will give you an abundance of wheat, wine, and oil. Abundance of wheat is thinking about the body and the Passion of Our Lord Jesus Christ. This is meditation. Abundance of wine is weeping heartily with perfect desire, and this is devotion. Abundance of oil is when the heart delights and finds solace in weeping, and this is consolation. For oil gives flavour, and shines **in the church** and burns in the lamp, and likewise when a heart has thought and wept well for its faults, God takes pity on it, and sends it a portion of comfort or delight. So holy meditation comes first; it is the wheat, and after it comes devotion, which is the wine; and after that, consolation is the oil that gives flavour in affection and illuminates in knowledge, in revelation, and burns with fervour, and is always alert in order to do good.

Une sage demisiele qui a a non Jalousie,⁶⁷ et qui tous dis veille pour bien fere, si atempera l'ologe⁶⁸ et esveillera tous dis les autre pour Dieu servir et loer. Ore i a ologiere de vile qui esveille les paisans. C'est li cos.⁶⁹ Si i a ologe de cité qui esveilles les marceans. C'est la gaite.⁷⁰ Si i a ologe de relegion qui esveille a matines.⁷¹ Si i a ologe de contemplation et de saint beguinage, et c'est jalousie et amors de perfeccion.⁷² Si est mainte fois avenu en l'ordre, que avant que ologe sonnast que maintes personnes avoient ploré mainte lerme et espandu devant Dieu.⁷³ Hé **fille**, benoite soit l'arme que amors esveille et qui n'est endormie ne parceuse. Et de ce avons nous ou livre des Chanssons:⁷⁴ *Ego dormio et cor* (94ʳᵃ) *meum uigilat.*⁷⁵ C'est a dire, quant je dor corporelment por men cors et mon cief reposer, mes cuers veille en jalousie et en soucist, en amor et en desir. Et tele ame a tousdis le cuer tendu et entendu a Diu, et ainssi puet dire la chansson du siecle: J'ai .i. cuer a cloquetes resveillié par amors. Les cloquetes dou cuer sont li plain et li souspir et li boin desirier c'on a en oroison.

Quant ceste abaye eust esté si bien fete et ordenee et Dex i eut esté⁷⁶ si bien servis et si bel, si vint uns grans usirriers, si fist tant par son avoir qu'il i mist .iiii. de ses filles mout ledes qu'il avoit. Et c'est li diables. L'une de ces filles si avoit a non Orguels Presomtions,⁷⁷ et ceste si estoit bochue et enflee ou cuer et ou pis car elle quidoit trop valoir et trop savoir, si comme il parut en Naaman. L'autre de ces filles si estoit Envie. Et ceste si estoit borgne ne ne daignoit ne ne pooit regarder a droit, mes tousdis en travers, si comme il parut en Saul et en David. L'autre si avoit a non Murmure Detraction. Et ceste si estoit bauberresse et ne savoit parler ne bien ne bel. Et tous dis voloit d'autruy murmurer, et esmouvoit tenchons et descorde parmi l'abeye. L'autre si estoit boiteusse ne ne pooit aller adroit. Si avoit a non Faus Jugements d'Autrui, que nulle bien ne pensoit, ne

---

⁶⁷ *C* joiouse, *RY* jelosie, *A* jacobise.

⁶⁸ *R* si est segresteine et tent l'orloge, *A* Celle tient la religion.

⁶⁹ *RY* coq, *A om.*

⁷⁰ *A* la gaite qui corne et dist je voi le jour, *R* la guete qui corne le jour et chante je voi le jour dorenlot.

⁷¹ *A* qui enveillent les moines a matines, *R* qui chiet a matinet.

⁷² *C* cele a vois de p., *R* amours de contemplation, *Y* amor de perfection, *A om.*

⁷³ *AR add* et avoient eut maintes devotions. Car li orloges d'amors les auoit esveilliez.

⁷⁴ *C* chassons, *AR* cantiques.

⁷⁵ Song of Songs 5. 2.

⁷⁶ *C* est.

⁷⁷ In all other manuscripts, Envie is the first daughter and Orgueil is the second.

A wise lady called Zeal, who always watches for opportunities to do good, sets the clock, and wakes the others every day to serve and praise God. Now, there is a timekeeper for the village that wakes the peasants: the cock. Then, there is a timekeeper for the town that wakes the merchants: the watch. Then, there is the clock of religious life which tells the time for matins. And there is the clock of contemplation and holy beguinage, which is zeal and love of perfection. It has happened many times in religious orders, that before the clock struck for matins, many persons had wept many tears, before God. Ah, **daughter!** blessed be the soul woken by love, for it is neither asleep nor lazy. And about this we find in the book of Songs: *Ego dormio et cor meum uigilat*. That is to say, when I sleep to rest my body and my head, my heart is still awake in zeal and in care, in love and in desire. Such a soul always has her heart stretched and turned towards God, and she can recite the worldly song: I have a heart woken to love with bells. The bells of the heart are the laments, sighs, and good desires one has in prayer.

When this abbey had been completed and arranged so well, and God had been so well served there, a great usurer of the country used his riches to place four of his ugly daughters there. And this was the Devil. One of these daughters was called Pride and Presumption, and she was a hunchback, and swollen about the heart and breast for she thinks she is better than others and knows more, as was seen in the case of Naaman. Another of these daughters was Envy. She is one-eyed and will not and cannot look straight ahead, but must always look sideways, as it appeared in the case of Saul and David. Another was called Murmuring and Detraction. She stammered, and could not speak well or fairly. She always wanted to spread rumours about others, and sowed contention and discord around the abbey. Another was lame and could not go straight. She was called False Judgement of Others, because she did not believe any good or

loiauté, ne (94rb) verité. Ces .iiii. filles a l'usurier, qui par malisce i furent mises, torblerent si le couvent de la consience que tout ala a mal.

Quant ce vit ma dame Carités l'abeesse et ma dame Sapience le prieuse et ma dame Humilités le sousprieuse et les autres boinnes demisieles, si sonnerent capistre et si s'i conseillererent qu'eles feroient. Ma dame Discrecion conseilla que toutes alassent en oroison et priassent au saint Esperit qui les venist viseter, car moult en estoit grans mestiers. Et par grant devocion et par grant desir de cuer commencierent a chanter : *Veni creator spiritus mentes tuorum uisita*. Et en aprés vint li sains Esperis et descendi mout tost[78] et par sa grasce geta ces .iiii. mauvaises filles au dyable hors — Orguels, Envie, Faus Jugements, Murmuracion — et aussi fu l'abaye reformee et ordenee miex que devant.

Ci defaut l'abeye du saint Esperit.

---

[78] *RY add* quant eles vindrent a cest vers Hostem repellas longius.

loyalty or truth-telling of them. These four daughters of this usurer, who were placed there with evil cunning, upset the entire convent of the conscience, to its great detriment.

When my lady Charity the abbess and my lady Wisdom the prioress and my lady Humility the sub-prioress and the other good ladies saw this, they rang the bell for chapter and took counsel as to what they would do. My lady Discretion advised them all to go and pray to the Holy Spirit to come and visit them, for there was great need. And with great devotion they sang: *Veni creator spiritus mentes tuorum uisita*. And then the Holy Spirit came quickly, and by his grace drove out these four wicked daughters of the Devil — Pride, Envy, False Judgement, Murmuring — and the abbey was reformed and better ordained than before.

Here ends the Abbey of the Holy Ghost.

LA SAINTE ABBAYE (β₁)

This version of the Abbaye is only represented by Y and its copy, N, which is now incomplete. The edition gives the text of Y.

[no rubric]

(2ʳᵃ) La sainte abbaie et la religion doit estre fondee esperituelment en la conscience. Souvent est avenu que li lieu qui suelent estre mout lait et gaste, la sunt les religions fondees, s'en sunt li lieu plus bel et plus delitable. Einsi avient il de la conscience, mais il la convient purgier, et a ce faire li sainz esperiz i envoie .ii. de ses damoiseles, preuz et vaillanz et saiges. La premiere est Veritez qui purgera le lieu par confession. L'autre est Amour qui purté gardera en cuer de toute ordure, que il ne soit honiz par mauvaise pensee.

Quant la place est bien purgiee, si convient faire les fondemenz larges et parfonz, et ce feront .ii. damoiseles, Humilitez qui les fera parfonz et Povretez qui les fera granz (2ʳᵇ) et larges, et getera la terre d'une part et d'autre, en largement doner quanque ele ara. Hé! beneoite religion fondee en povreté et en humilité, c'est contre aucuns mauvés religieus, qui sunt orgueilleus et convoiteus.

Ceste religion doit sooir seur iaue courant de larmes et de pleurs. Vile et abbaie qui sieent seur riviere sunt mout aaisiees et mout delicieuses. Tele fu l'abbaie la Magdelene. *Psalmi: Tamquam lignum quod plantatum.*[1] *Et illud. Fluminis impetus letificat.*[2] La bone riviere fait la vile nete et liee, et seure et habondant de marcheandises.

Damoisele Obedience d'une part, et Misericorde d'autre, feront les murs granz et hauz. Tant de bones oevres com nos faisons, et tant d'aumosnes com

[1] Psalm 1. 3.

[2] Psalm 46. 5 (45. 5).

nos donons, autant de pierres metons nos en noz edefices. Nos lisons que Salemons fist sa maison de granz pierres. Et (2ᵛᵃ) qui sunt ces granz pierres fors que bones oevres, granz et precieuses, qui doivent estre jointes ensemble a bon mortier de vive chauz, c'est d'amour en vive foi. *Psalmi: Omnia opera eius in fide.*[3] Et aussi comme li murs ne puet durer longuement sanz bon mortier, aussi oevres ne valent rien qui ne sunt fortes, et faites en amour, et en la foi de Dieu, dont tuit cil qui sunt mescreant sunt perdu.

Damoisele Pacience et damoisele Force feront les pilers por soustenir et pour apoier, que nus venz de tribulacion ne de temptacion, ou de parole cuisant, ou de grant domaige, ne les puisse abatre. Il est escrit ou Livre de Sapience d'une maison qui fu faite a .vii. pilers,[4] et ce sunt les trois vertuz theologiques qui ordenent quant a Dieu, et les quatre cardinaus quant a son prochien.

Or convient faire le (2ᵛᵇ) cloistre a quatre corons; pour ce a il non cloistre que il doit estre clos et bien gardez. Fille, veuz tu estre bien religieuse? Tien te close, garde ton cloistre, clo ton cuer de mauvaisement penser, tes eulz de folement regarder, tes oreilles de males paroles escouter, ta bouche de rire legierement et de folement paller. Cele qui se tient close en ces quatre choses est bien religieuse.

Confession fera le chapitre, car ele dit verité. Predicacion fera le refectoir, car ele repaist les ames. Oroison fera la chapele qui doit estre haute par douce contemplacion, et dessevree de touz soussiz du monde. Compassion fera l'enfermerie. Devocion fera le celier, Meditacion le guernier. Ces offecines doivent estre touz jourz pleines et habundanz.

Or i convient metre des vertuz, des graces, et des dons du saint Esperit, qui de ceste religion est garde et (3ʳᵃ) visiterres. Dieus li peres ceste abbaie fonda par sa poissance. *Psalmi: Fundauit eam altissimus.*[5] Li filz Deu l'ordena par sa sapience. *Apostolus: Que a deo sunt ordinata sunt.*[6] Et *Psalmi: Omnina in sapientia fecisti.*[7] Li Sainz Esperiz la garde et la visete par sa bonté, et s'amour et sa vaillance, dont nous chantons: *Veni creator spiritus et cetera.*

Ma dame Charitez, qui est la plus granz vertuz et la plus vaillanz — *Apostolus: Maior autem harum est caritas*[8] — sera abbaesse. Et tout aussi comme l'en ne doit rien faire, paller, ne aler, prendre ne doner sanz le congié de l'abbaesse,

---

[3] Psalm 33. 4 (32. 4).

[4] Proverbs 9. 1.

[5] Psalm 87. 5 (86. 5).

[6] Romans 13. 1.

[7] Psalm 104. 24 (103. 24).

[8] I Corinthians 13. 13.

aussi esperituelment ne doit l'en sanz le congié de charité. *Unde Apostolus: Omnia opera uestra in caritate fiant.*⁹

Sainte Sapience sera prieuse, car ele en est bien digne, si comme dist Salemons: *Prior omnium creata est sapientia.*¹⁰ Par le conseil de ceste prieuse doit l'en faire quanque l'en fait, si en sera l'en mielz prisiez. *Psalmi:* (3ʳᵇ) *Omnia in sapientia fecisti.*¹¹ C'est a dire: Sire, tu as fait par scn quanque tu as fait.

Dame Humilité qui de touz jourz se met au dessouz et s'abaisse en sera souprieuse. Or esgarde comme ci a sainte abbaie, et bone religion, ou si saintes dames sunt, et si dignes persones. Beneoites seront les ames qui bien garderont le commandement de Charité, le conseil de Sapience, l'enseignement de Humilité. C'est qui menront leur vie charitablement, saigement et humblement.

Dame Discrecion, qui mout est saige, sera tresoriere, et gardera le profit de l'ostel. Oroison sera chantre et levera le chant de nuiz et iourz pour Dieu loer, et Jubilacion sera sa compaigne, et li aidera si comme dist sainz Gregoires: Jubilacion est une granz joie qui est conceue en l'ame après oroison par ferveur d'esperit, qui ne puet estre du tout monstree (3ᵛᵃ) ne du tout celee,¹² si comme il avient aus genz esperituels.

Devocion sera celeriere, qui gardera les bons vins et blans et vermaus, rosez et ferrez. Li vin blanc sunt la remembrance de Dieu et de la joie de paradis. Li vermaus et li rosez de la passion et de la mort Jhesu Crist et des martyrs. Li ferrez des tormenz d'enfer qui durent sanz fin.

Penitance sera cuisiniere et mout se travaillera, car ele puet assez de paine soufrir pour faire a Dieu gre et satifacion et souvent suera pour ses pechiez. Ele fera les bones viandes et pou en mengera. Atemprance sera refroituriere et Abstinence li aidera, et serviront le couvent si amesureement qu'il n'i aura ne trop beu ne trop mengié. Sobrietez lira a la table les vies des peres queles vies il menerent, pour ce que eles i preignent example.

Pitiez sera pitanciere et leur fera de bien ce que (3ᵛᵇ) ele porra. Misericorde sa suer sera aumosniere, qui tant donra que riens ne retenra.

Peeur sera portiere; si gardera bien le cloistre de la conscience, et chacera hors les mauvais, et apelera bel les bons, et gardera que nus mauvais n'entre ou cloistre par la porte de la bouche ne par les fenestres des euz, ne des oreilles. Salemons dist: *Timor domini expellit peccatum.*¹³

⁹ 1 Corinthians 16. 14.

¹⁰ Ecclesiasticus 1. 4.

¹¹ Psalm 104. 24 (103. 24).

¹² Gregory the Great, *Moralia in Job* 28. 15.

¹³ Ecclesiasticus 1. 21.

Honestez sera maistresse des novices, et les enseignera a penser a Deu devotement et doucement, a regarder et paller saigement, a aler gentement si que ceus qui les verront i preignent bon example.

Courtoisie sera osteliere et recevra les alanz et les venanz lieement, si que chascuns s'en loera. Et pour ce que femme de religion ne doit pas estre seule entre genz, privez et estranges, et que bien porroit avenir que damoisele Cortoisie seroit trop baude et trop hardie, si aura aveques li (4ra) damoisele Simplece, car trop granz simplece est folie, et granz courtoisie aucune foiz outraiges, et pour ce les .ii. ensamble feront bien la besoigne.

Raison sera pourveerresse et pourverra dedenz et dehors qu'il n'i ait nule defaute. Leautez sera enfermiere et traveillera mout entre ces malades, de jourz et de nuiz. Et por ce qu'il i a plus de malades que de saines, et de foibles que de forz, Largece sera sa compaigne, et li amenisterra tout sanz nule defaute.

Meditacion sera guernetiere qui assamblera le bon grain de froment et d'autres blez. Meditacion est une vertuz qui est en bien penser a Deu et a ses faiz et a ses diz, c'est aus creatures et aus escritures. Ceste guerneteriere avoit li rois David qui dist *Psalmi*: *Meditabor in omnibus mandatis tuis*,[14] *et item*: *In lege domini meditabitur*.[15] C'est le commencement de toute perfection, quant li cuers se met a bien penser a Deu. Et tout aussi comme (4rb) li fruiz vaut mielz des fueilles, vaut plus une pensee en sainte meditacion que mout de paroles dire en oroison. Li cuers en meditacion se repose pour mielz crier, et c'est pour mielz paller. Et ce dist li prophetes David *Psalmi*: *Quoniam tacui inueterauerunt ossa mea*.[16] La dist la glose que li granz criz que nos crions a Deu, est li granz desirriers que nous avons. Et que ce soit voirs, sainz Denises le tesmoigne: *Ibi quantum superius ascendimus, tantum in nobis contemplantibus uerba coartantur. Et postea: Sine uoce erit animus uinctus immobilis*.[17] C'est a dire: quant li cuer est bien soulevez par desirrier d'amour en meditacion, il ne puet dire ce qu'il sent. Ceste damoisele garde le bon grain de froment qui est rouges par dehors, et si est blans dedenz, et fenduz en costé, dont li bons pains est faiz. C'est Jhesu Criz nostre sauveor qui fu rouges (4va) dehors du sanc qu'il espandi pour nous, et blans par dedenz par purté de innocence, et fenduz au costé du fer de la lance. C'est li pains que nous recevons ou sacrement de l'autel.

Li guerniers doit estre seur le celier. Aussi meditacion seur devocion. Et de ceste guernetiere, pitanciere, celeriere dist David: *Psalmi. A fructu frumenti uini*

---

[14] Psalm 77. 13 (76. 13).

[15] Psalm 1. 2.

[16] Psalm 32. 3 (31. 3).

[17] Pseudo-Denis, *Mystica Theologia* 3. 2.

et olei sui multiplicati sunt.[18] Et en mout d'autres lieus en l'escriture promet Dex ceste promesse. Servez moi bien, ce dist Dex, et je vous donrai plenté de froment, de vin et d'uile. Plenté de froment est en bien penser a Jhesu Crist, et a sa passion, et ce fait Meditacion. Plenté de vin est en bien plorer, et ce fait Devocion. Plenté d'uile est de bien loer Deu, de quoi l'ame reçoit grant consolacion et ce fait Piticz et Compassion. Oile done bone saveur, et si luist en l'eglise, et art en la lampe. Aussi com uns cuers bien (4ᵛᵇ) esperituels a bien pensé et bien ploré, si en a Dex pitié, et li fait pitance en confort, et en delit, et c'est quant il li envoie saveur en affection et enlumine sa conoissance en revelacion, et l'embrase de dilection.

Damoisele Jalousie, qui touz jourz est esveillie pour bien faire, sera secretaine et tendra l'auloge. Ceste esveille toutes les autres, et se soussie qu'il n'i ait nule defaute ou servise Deu; pour toutes veille, pour toutes se soussie, et les fait lever aus matines pour Deu servir. Et devons savoir qu'il i a auloge de vile pour esveillier les paisanz, c'est le coq, si a auloge de cité pour esveillier les marcheanz, c'est la gueite qui corne le jour, et auloge de religion qui chiet aus matines, et auloge de contemplacion et de saint beguinaige, c'est jalousie et amor de perfection. Si est mainte foiz avenu en religion, que avant que l'auloge de matines sonast, que maintes persones avoient (5ʳᵃ) plouré maintes larmes devant Deu, de doleur et de contriction quant a soi, de pitié et de compassion quant a leur prochien, d'amour et de devocion quant a Deu, car li auloges d'amour les avoit esveilliez. Hé! beneoite soit l'ame que amour esveille, car ele n'est pas pereceuse, ne endormie, et tele ame chante en Cantiques, quant je dor et mon cuer veille. *Ego dormio et cor meum uigilat.*[19] C'est a dire: quant je dor por mon cors reposer, mes cuers veille en jalousie, en soussi, et en desir de Deu amer. Tele ame a touz jorz l'auloge de son cuer tendu, et estendu a Deu. Et pour ce si puet bien dire, et chanter: J'ai un cuer a clochetes esveillié pour bien amer. Les clochetes de son cuer sunt li plaint, li souspir, li gemissement, li desirrier que ele a en oroison. Cest auloge doit chanter par trois manieres de chanz: par nature, par bequarré, par bemol. C'est a dire qu'ele doit chanter par nature, que ele doit (5ʳᵇ) penser et regarder la nature dont ele est, qui est vilz et abhominable, par bequarré a la mort d'enfer, qui est fort et pardurable, par bemol qui est uns chanz plus douz, a la joie de paradis qui est douce et delitable. Pour la premiere chose se doit on humiliier, pour la seconde tout pechié fuir et eschiver, pour la tierce bien faire, pour gaaignier et desservir si grant loyer.

Lors sera l'abbaie bien fondee, bien gardee, bien ordenee, car Humilitez la fondera, Peeur la portiere la gardera, et ma dame Charitez l'abbaesse lordenera.

---

[18] Psalm 4. 8.

[19] Song of Songs 5. 2.

Mais aucune foiz est avenu, et avient souvent, que quant ceste abbaie est si bien fondee, gardee, et ordenee, et Dex i est si bien servis comme vous oez, que la portiere par negligence, et par sa defaute, i laisse entrer et demourer quatre filles a un mauvais userier du païs, que il a mout laides. C'est li deables d'enfer, qui est le plus (5va) fort userier qui soit, car pour un pou d'oneur, un pou de joie, un pou de delit qu'il preste en cest monde qui si pou dure voudra que l'en li rende en l'autre qui touz jourz durra si grant usure que chascuns de ses deteurs li rendra honte et confusion, doleur et affliction, sanz fin et sanz consolacion. Icil meismes useriers par sa malice, et par la defaute de la portiere qui mauvaisement garde les portes, les huis et les fenestres, et toutes les entrees, met souvent en ceste abbaie ses quatre filles qui tant sunt laides. Dont l'une a non Envie, et ceste est borgne, qu'ele ne puet regarder droit, mais touz jorz de travers, si comme il parut de Saul contre David. L'autre a non Presumption, et ceste est enflee ou piz, car ele cuide plus savoir que les autres, et est boçue seur les espaules, car ele cuide mielz valoir. La tierce a non Murmure et Detraction, et ceste est begue, qu'ele ne set (5vb) paller, ne dire nul bien d'autrui, ainçois met contenz et dissension par l'abbaie. La quarte a non Faus Jugement et Soupeçon, et ceste est boiteuse, car ele ne puet aler droit, ne nul bien penser d'autrui, ne verité ne leauté, si que par ces quatre filles a ce mauvais userier laides et mauvaises, est toute l'abbaie et la religion du cuer troublee et destourbee.

Mes ma dame Charitez l'abbaesse, quant ele voit et aperçoit ceste chose, si doit tantost soner chapitre, et assambler tout le couvent, et damoisele Discrecion leur donra conseil, que eles aillent toutes en oroison, et prient le saint Esperit que il par sa grace les viegne visiter, car granz mestiers leur est, et adonc doivent chanter en grant devocion: *Veni creator spiritus et cetera*, qui doucement et volentiers vendra et descendra. Et quant ce vendra a cest ver: *Hostem repellas longius*, il les getera hors de l'ordre comme mauvaises garces, ces .iiii. filles a (7ra) ce mauvais userier, les filles au deable.[20] Et einsi sera l'abbaie ordenee et renformee comme devant.

---

[20] Fol. 6^{r} is blank, and 6^{v} is occupied by a full-page miniature.

Le cloistre de l'ame (β_2)

Of the three copies of β_2 I have been able to consult, the two oldest, *D* and *B*, are very similar. It looks as though both were copied from a fair copy of the revised version based on *Y*. *D* is in general the closer of the two to *Y*, and in general, but not always, it has fewer omissions and abbreviations and is fuller than *B*. On these grounds, I have chosen *D* as the base manuscript for this edition. Clear mistakes have been corrected with reference to *B* and occasionally to *P*.

(149vb) Cy comence le livre du cloistre de l'ame que Hue de Saint Victor fist

La sainte abaye et la religion a parler esperituelment doit estre fondee en la conscience d'omme et de femme. Et si come vous veez que es liex qui sont desert et gaste seult l'en fonder les abbaies, si en sont le lieu plus bel et plus delitable. Tout ainsi avient de la religion qui est faicte en la conscience, mais il convient primerement purger le lieu, dont les sains Esperitz a ce faire envoie .ii. damoiselles preux et sages. C'est assavoir Verité qui purge le lieu par confession, et Amour de Dieu[1] qui gardera le cuer que il ne soit ordoié par villainne pensee de delectation.

Quant la place est bien purgee si convient faire les fondemens parfons et largez et ce feront .ii. damoiselles de douce mainere. C'est Humilité de Cuer qui tousjours tent en bas et Povreté Volentive qui les fera larges quant elle gettera la terre ça et la en donant largement les biens terriens aux povres. Hé! benoite soit religion fondee en humilité et povreté. C'est encontre aucuns (150ra) religieux et convoiteux.

---

[1] *B* Amour.

Ceste religion doit estre² eaue courant de lermes de pitié et de devocion. Abbayes qui seent sur rivieres sont plus aisies et plus delitables que autres. Telle fu l'abbaye a la Magdalene. *Cuius oculi et cetera.³ Et fluminis impetus.⁴* C'est a dire que l'oeil de la Magdalene decouroit en l'amour de Dieu en lermes aussi come le ruissel d'une fontaine. Et telle riviere fait liee et fort la cité de Dieu, c'est le cuer. La bonne riviere fait la ville nette, liee et seure, habundant de marchandises.

Damoiselles Obedience et Misericorde feront les murs de ceste religion haus et grans. Tant de bonnes oeuvres come nous faisons et tant d'aumosnes come nous donnons aux povres, tant de pierres nous metons en noz oeuvres⁵, qui doivent estre jointes a mortier de chaux vive. C'est d'amour de Dieu en vive foy *Omnia opera eius in fide.⁶* Autressi come mur ne vault riens qui n'e fait de bon mortier, aussi ne valent riens oeuvres qui ne sont faites en amour et en foy de Dieu⁷, dont tant quanque mescreans font de bien ne vault une neffle.

Damoiselle Pacience et Force feront les pilliers pour soustenir que nulz vens de tribulacion, (150ʳᵇ) de mesaisse de cuer ne temptacion ne puist abbatre ceste abaye, ne vens de paroles cuisans ne puis faire chanceler ceste religion. Il est escript ou Livre de Sapience que Sapience fist une maison et l'apuia de .vii. pilliers. Ce nous signifient .iiii. vertus cardinaux – c'est assaver pourveance, attrempance, force et justice – et les .iii. vertus de theologie – c'est assaver foy, esperance, et charité. Dont l'escripture dit: *Venerunt flumina et cetera.⁸* C'est a dire que maison qui est puiee de telz pilliers n'a garde que de vent de tribulacion et de paroles cuissans li puissent nuire.

Or convient faire le cloistre a .iiii. corons. Pour ce a il non cloistre par ce que il doit estre bien clos et gardé. Fille, veulz tu estre bien religieuse, tien toy close, garde ton cloistre et l'uis. Clo ton cuer et le garde de mal penser, de mal juger, de haine, d'orgueil, d'envie, de acide, de vainne gloire, de toute male convoitise; tes yeulz garde de faulx regars faire; tes oreilles de mal escouter, qui puet grever a toy et a autrui; garde ta bouche de parler folement, de boire et de menger outrageusement⁹. Fille, tien toy close en ces iiii. choses, garde bien ces .iiii. pilliers, ne te muef, certes si seras religieuse.

---

² *P* estre environnee de.

³ Psalm 119. 136 (118. 136).

⁴ Psalm 46. 5 (45. 5).

⁵ *B* edefices, *P* euvres.

⁶ Psalm 33. 4 (32. 4).

⁷ *B* en amour de Dieu.

⁸ Matthew 7. 37.

⁹ *B* gloutement.

(150va) Confession si fera le chapistre car elle dit verité. Prédicacion si fera le refretouer car elle repaist les ames. Oroison fera la chapelle qui doit estre haute par contemplacion, desevree de toutez cures du monde. Compassion fera l'emfermerie, Devocion le celier, Meditacion le grenier. Ces .iii. offices doivent tousjours estre plainnes et ouvertes.

Or convient en ceste abbaie avoir un grant couvent de vertus, de graces et de dons du saint Esperit qui se prent garde et visite ceste abaye. Diex le pere fonde ceste abbaye par sa puissance: il est escript. *Fundauit eam altissimus.*[10] Le filz Dieu l'ordena par sa sapience, si come dit saint Pol: *Que a deo sunt ordinata sunt.*[11] *Omnia in sapiencia fecisti.*[12] Ce que Dieux fait est bien fait car il est tout fait en sapience. Le saint Esperit la visite par sa douceur, dont nous chantons: *Veni creator*, et prions le saint Esperit que il viengne visiter nos cuers.

Ma dame Charité sera abbesse, car c'est la plus noble, dont saint Pol dit: *Maior horum est caritas.*[13] Et dit l'Apostre que c'est la greignour vertu qui soit que charité. Et tout aussi come l'en ne doit riens faire ne dire contre l'abesse de une abbaye, ne riens faire sans congié, ne prendre ne donner, tout aussi – a parler esperituelment – l'en ne doit riens faire sanz charité. Si come dit (150vb) saint Pol: *Omnia in caritate fiant.*[14] Faites toutes voz choses en charité.

Ma dame Sapience sera prieuse car elle en est digne. Si come dit le sage: *Prior omnium est sapiencia.*[15] La sapience de Dieu doit estre devant toutes choses. Par le conseil de ceste dame doit l'en tout faire, si sera len plus prisié. Et il est escript: *Omnia in sapiencia fecisti.*[16] C'est a dire: fay par sens quanque tu feras.

Dame Humilité sera souprieuse par ce que elle s'abesse du tout, et donra exemple aux autres et gardera aussi come tousjours le couvent, dont saint Gregoire dit. *Qui ceteras virtutes sine humilitate congregat. quasi puluerem in ventum portat.*[17] C'est a dire que autant vault porter la poudre contre le vent come assembler toutes les vertus sans humilité.

Or regarde comme cy a sainte religion ou il a bonnes dames. Hé! benoit soit qui bien gardera le commendement de Charité, le conseil de Sapience, et

---

[10] Psalm 46. 5 (45. 5).

[11] Romans 13. 1.

[12] Psalm 104. 24 (103. 24).

[13] I Corinthians 13. 13.

[14] I Corinthians 16. 14.

[15] Ecclesiasticus 1. 4.

[16] Psalm 104. 24 (103. 24).

[17] Gregory the Great, *Homiliae in evangelia* 34. 23. 33.

l'exemple d'Umilité. Cest a dire, qui menra sa vie charitablement, sagement et humblement.

Dame Discrecion sera tresoriere et gardera le proufit de l'ostel. Saint Bernart dit: *Discrecions auriga virtutum*.[18] Discrecion, dit saint Bernart, est charretiere de vertus. Oroison sera chantre de jor et de nuit pour Dieu loer. (151ʳᵃ) Jubilacion li aidera. De laquelle dit saint Gregoire que Jubilacion si est une grant joie qui est conceue en l'ame aprés oroison par ferveur d'esperit, que l'en ne puet du tout monstrer ne du tout celer.[19] Ce scevent bien ces sages grans esperituelz.

Devocion sera celeriere, qui gardera les bons vins blans et vermeux, rosez et ferrez. Li blanc vin sont la douce remembrance de la passion nostre sire Jhesucristet des martirs. Li vin ferré sont la remembrance des tourmens d'enfer, qui sont cruel et sans fin.

Penitance sera cuisiniere et se eschaudera et suera souvent pour cuire la viande et petit en mengera. Atrempance sera refretouriere et servira le couvent si bien qu'il n'y aura ne trop beu ne trop mengé. Sobrieté lira a la table les vies des peres pour exemple prendre.

Pitée sera pitanciere et leur fera de bien ce qu'elle pourra especialment au couvent. Misericorde sa suer sera aumosniere, qui tout donra aprés sa necessité prise.

Paour de Dieu sera portiere, qui est propre a ceste office, et gardera si bien le cloistre de l'ame que il soit tousjours net, et chacera hors[20] la mardaille et les nuisars de pechié que ilz n'entrent en cloistre. Le sage dit: *Timor domini expellit peccatum*.[21] C'est a dire: la Paour (151ʳᵇ) de Dieu chace hors pechié et par la porte des oreilles et des yeulz, et de la bouche, et Confession sa chamberiere li aidera a tout ce faire.

Honnesté sera maistresse des novices et leur preschera, car elle enseignera comment on doit parler doucement, aler sagement, menger sobrement, donner bon exemple de soy a toutes gens.

Courtoisie sera chastelliere et Simplice li aydera, car trop grant courtoisie si est trop baude et espanue. Trop grant simplice si est folie, et pour ce ces .ii. ensemblez feront trop bien la besoingne.

Raison sera pourvoieresse que il n'y ait nul default dedans ne dehors.

Meditacion sera grenetiere qui assemble le bon grain des diverses vertus ou grenier de conscience. Meditacion si est une vertu qui est bien penser a Dieu et

[18] Bernard of Clairvaux, *Sermones super Cantica Canticorum* 49. 5.

[19] Gregory the Great, *Moralia in Job* 28. 15.

[20] *D* lors.

[21] Ecclesiasticus 1. 21.

a ses fais et aux escriptures. Ceste grenetiere avoit David, qui disoit: *Meditabor in mandatis.*²² Sire Diex, disoit David, je me pourpenseray en toutes tes voiez et oeuvres. C'est le comencement de toute perfeccion que metre son cuer a penser a Dieu, et tout aussi come le fruit de l'arbre vault mieulz que les fueillez, aussi vaut miex une bonne pensee que moult de paroles dites en oroison. Le bon cuer se repose en meditacion pour miex crier; la prent en (151ᵛᵃ) toutes choses et demende l'en tout ce que mestier est a Dieu. Saint Augustin dit que li grant cri que nous crions si sont le grant desir que nous desirons, dont quant li cuer est bien eslevé par sainte meditacion, par desirer d'amour, il ne puet dire la joie et le bien que il sent.

Cest damoisseille garde le froment blanc et vermeil et fenduz en costé. C'est le doulz Jhesucrist qui fu blanc par purté, vermeil par sa passion, fenduz en costé pour nous son cuer doner, dont saint Bernart dit: *Et vulnere lateris patet amor cordis.*²³ C'est a dire: par la plaie de son costé monstra bien le doulz Jhesucrist combien que il nous ama. C'est le pain que nous recevons en l'autel.

De ceste grenetiere dist David: *A fructu frumenti vini et olei multiplicati sunt.*²⁴ Cilz qui Dieu aiment, dit David, sont multipliez de fruit de forment, de vin et d'uille. Planté de forment est bien penser a Jhesucrist, a sa vie et a sa passion. Planté de vin est planté de lermes pleureez par devocion. Planté d'uille est planté de joie que Diex donne a ceulz qui le loent. Uyle donne saveur aux viandes et si luist en l'eglise et art en la lampe. Aussi quant cuer esperituel pense bien a Dieu et pleure, si en a Dieu pitie et li fait confort et saveur trouver en afection, (151ᵛᵇ) congnoissance et revelacion, et embrase son cuer de l'amour du feu de dilection.

Damoiselle Jalousie de bien faire sera secretainne, pour ce²⁵ que elle est bien esveilliee, et gardera que il n'y ait nul defaut en aucune maniere ou service de Dieu. Ceste esveille les autres et les fait lever a matines pour Dieu servir. Or faut orloge.

Amour de perfection sera orloge pour esveiller a matines. Il avient aucune foiz, aincois que matines sonent, que bonnes religieuses ont ja pleuré ou moustier maintes lermes devant Dieu avec douleur de contriction pour soy, lermes de compassion pour leurs pechiez, lermes de devocion quant a desirer de Dieu aver, car l'orloge d'amour les esveilloit. Hé! benoite soit l'ame qui amour esveille et n'est pas pereceuse, et telle ame chante es Cantiques: quant je dors et mon

---

²² Psalm 77. 13 (76. 13).

²³ Not identified.

²⁴ Psalm 4. 8.

²⁵ *D omits* ce. *Corrected from B.*

cuer veille. *Ego dormio.*²⁶ Quant mon corps dort pour soy reposer m'ame veille par jalousie de Dieu amer. Et puet dire ceste chanson: J'ay un cuer tout a clochetes; si sont li soupir, les lermes que l'en a en penser a Dieu.

Ceste nature doit chanter par nature, par bequarré, par bemol. C'est a dire que l'en doit penser a sa nature qui est abhominable, a la mort d'enfer qui est pardurable, a la joie de (152ʳᵃ) paradis qui est douce et delitable. Pour la premiere chose l'en se doit humilier, pour la seconde tout pechié fuir, pour la tierce tout bien faire pour paradis avoir.

Lors sera ceste abbaye bien fondee car Humilité la fondera, bien gardee quant Charité l'ordenera, bien ordenee quant Paour de Dieu la gardera.

Mais il avient aucune foiz que par la negligence de la portiere entrent en ceste abbaye et sont receuez .iiii. filles a un grant usurier. C'est le diable, qui pour un pou d'onneur un pou de joie que il preste qui si tost faut, voudra que l'en li rende en enfer chascun de ses debteurs honte, confusion et tribulacion sanz fin et sanz consolacion. Ce mauves usurier, par le defaut de la portiere qui mal garde les huis et les fenestres et les entreez de ceste abbaye, met souvent en ceste abbaye ces .iiii. filles, dont la premiere a nom Envie, et ceste si est borgne et louche si que elle ne puet droit regarder si come Saul David. La seconde²⁷ a nom Presompcion et ceste si est engrossie et si est boçue. Je di que ceste est grosse de son pere, de ses freres, et de ses oncles qui engendrent en lui une fille qui a nom Vantise .fi. de lignage en religion si est boçue ou (152ʳᵇ) dos, car elle est a l'ordure²⁸ de vainne gloire aussi come une boce en son cuer pour son sanz²⁹ ou pour les graces que Dieu li a prestez. La tierce a nom Detraction ou Mesdis. Ceste est boçue; c'est la cegoingne au diable, et boute son bec es ordures et vit des viandes envenimees et s'en paist. Elle ne dira ja de nullui bien. C'est celle qui seme discorde par ceste religion, et si met hainne entre ceulz qui s'entre aiment. Ceste si est la propre fille au diable. La quarte fille a nom Faire Jugement ou³⁰ Souspeçon. Ceste fait son mal preu de tout ce que elle voit. Ceste cloche de .ii. hanches et si vuelt que toutes les autres aillent droites. Ceste veult tout amander et tout reprendre; elle se maupaie de plorer et de rire et de jeuner et de manger. Elle parle de tout; elle quiert le poil dessoubz le cuir. Elle se malpaie de ce de quoy Diex et le monde se tien bien a paye. Elle ressemble un fol de Chastiaudun qui portoit sa massue et aloit la ou il veoit assez gens assemblez ou

---

²⁶ Song of Songs 5. 2.

²⁷ *D* tierce.

²⁸ *P* ha l'ordure.

²⁹ *B* pour son sens ou pour sa chastee.

³⁰ *B om* Faire Jugement ou.

marchié ou ailleurs et branloit sa massue par dessus les gens et crioit: tout arés!
res! arés! c'est a dire: que l'une teste ne passe l'autre, ou je vous ferray! Ces .iiii.
filles (152ᵛᵃ) au diable troublent la paiz de ceste abbaye³¹.

Et quant ma dame l'abesse s'en aperçoit – c'est Charité – si doit tantost son-
ner chapitre et assembler le convent, et les doit faire tantost aler en oroison et
prier le maistre de ceste abbaye – c'est le saint Esperit – que il viengne visiter
ceste abbaye car le soing³² en est grant. Et pour ce que il se haste de venir l'en
doit chanter: *Veni creator spiritus* devotement et li doit on prier: *Hostem repellas longius et cetera*. Ha sire! boute hors ces anemis et ces filles au diable de nostre religion si loing que jamés n'y entrent; si arons paix. C'est bien voir, car la
ou qu'elles sont ne puet paix avoir, et si commandez a la portiere que elle garde
miex desormés les huis du cloistre – ce sont les yeux, les oreilles, le cuer, et la
bouche – si bien que jamés ces .iiii. filles ne puissent en ceste abaye entrer pour
promesse ne pour don que leur pere – c'est le diable – promettre a doner. Et que
il commande a Confession, qui est chamberiere a la portiere, que elle tiengne
nette ceste abbaye et chace hors la mardaille quant elle y sera entree. Ainsi sera
la religion de graces et de vertus qui doit estre en la conscience bien et saintement gardee. *Benidicamus domino* qui (152ᵛᵇ) a ceste chose achevee.

Religion est dicte de relier, car la conscience si est le tonnel de vin de graces
du saint Esperit, qui doit estre si forment³³ relié que il n'espande pour nulle
achoison.

---

³¹ *B* de ceste abaye – mal y entrassent elles.

³² *P* le besoing.

³³ *B* forment estraint et.

La religion du benoit saint Esprit (γ)

Manuscript *X* contains the only full copy of this version and is therefore the basis of the edition. In the case of clear mistakes, the text is corrected and the manuscript reading shown in a note. The other manuscript, *Z*, is a close copy of the short part of the text it reproduces, and its few departures (other than stylistic padding) are indicated in the notes.

(29[r]) Chy s'ensieut la religion du benoit saint Esprit.

Audi filia mea et vide et inclina aurem tuam.[1] Tres doulce fille nostre seigneur, combien que les paroles precedantes en latin soient escriptes ou[2] livre de David qui est nommés le Sautier et dites du vray amant menseigneur Jhesucrist en parlant a s'amie et a son espouse l'ame devotte, nient mains je me sui arrestés espirituelment pour desclairier aucune chose qui vous est neccessaire a salut et pourtant je dys ainssy: *Audi filia etc.* Chiere fille vostre oreille voeulliés encliner a oïr cheste presente escripture et grandement porrés pourfiter se bien le regardés de boin esprit. Par moy considerant vostre tres boin desir et parfait, qui est que volentiers seriés en religion a che que plus parfaitement puissiés Dieu amer et servir tant de nuit comme de jour et a che aussy que vous fussiés hors de la solitude[3] mondaine et des empeschemens qui sont en chu monde, pour la quelle cause je vous segnefie par chu present escript qu'il est .ii. manieres de religion: l'une qui est corporelle et l'autre qui est espirituelle. En la religion corporelle tout ne poevent mie estre, ch'est assavoir tout cheuls et chelles qui volentiers

---

[1] Psalm 45. 11 (44. 11).

[2] *X* un.

[3] *Z* sollicitude.

y seroient et pour .ii. causes. Prumierement pour tant qui sont lyés du lien de mariage aucune foys. Secundemennt aucune foys pour trop grant povreté ou trop grant estroiteté[4] de vie. Toute foys en la secunde religion qui est espirituelle devons nous tous estre. Si vous fault savoir doulce fille comment de cheste religion serés et qui plus est comment en vous ferés un (29ᵛ) glorieux couvent.

Si entendés diligaument la plache ou cheste religion sera fondee: je vous dys que che sera vostre conscience pour la quelle cose et devant toute choses il la fault nettier de toutes ordures et pechiés et ainssy li benois saint Espris y anvoiera[5] .ii. de ses demoiselles, ch'est assavoir Verité qui par vraye confession nettiera tout, et aussy Creanche et Doubtanche de Dieu. *Quia timor domini expellit peccatum.*[6] Car la doubtanche de Dieu si encache tous pechiés de la conscience de creature.

Les fondemens de chu benoit couvent si seront humilité et povreté. O devote fille que benoite est la creature dont la conscience si est fondee sur chelles .ii. nobles vertus comme humilité contre tout orgueil et presumpcion car comme dist saint Pierre, *Deus superbis resistit humilibus autem dat gratiam.*[7] Dieu si est contraire as orgueilleus mais as humbles il donne sa grace, comme aussy de povreté. Éllas doulce fille, pourtant disoit saint Franchois preschant a ses freres eulx enortant d'estre fondés sus chu fondement de povreté, *Fratres mei noverint paupetatem esse specialem viam salutis.*[8] Mes freres sachiés que povreté si est l'especialle voye de salut.

Et doivent estre mis ches. ii. fondemens ychi sus ou dencoste une riviere habundante et plentureuse ch'est assavoir larmes pleurs et cris, soupirs et gemissemens, car sans chechy vostre conscience ne sera point habundante ne plentureuse des biens de grace et de vertus. O doulce fille que bien fondee fut la conscience de monseigneur saint Pierre (30ʳ) dencoste cheste riviere. *Quia fleuit amare.*[9] Quar si tost qu'il eust congnissanche qu'il l'avoit renié son seigneur il se departi et se bouta en une fosse ou il ploura amerement. Item aussi Marie Magdalene. *Quia effudit lacrimas cordis in obsequio salvatoris.*[10] Quar elle respandi les larmes de sen coeur u service de nostre seigneur quant de ses propres

---

[4] *X* auctorité *with* estroiteté *written in above, Z* austerité.

[5] *X* auoiera.

[6] Ecclesiasticus 1. 27.

[7] 1 Peter 5. 5.

[8] Bonaventure, *Legenda Maior* 7. 1.

[9] Matthew 26. 75; Luke 22. 62.

[10] Not identified.

larmes li lava les piés et pourtant disoit saint Augustin: *Cogitanti mi de Marie penitentia magis in libet flere quam aliquid dicer.*[11] Dist saint Augustin quant je pensse a le penitanche de Marie Magdalene il me prent plus grant volenté de plourer que de nulle chose dire. Vostre conscience doncques doulce fille si soit fondee sur la riviere de larmes et de cris et de gemissemens.

Aprés les murs de chu couvent et de cheste religion si seront obedience – obeir au commandement de Dieu et auls consauls de sainte Esglise – et aussy misericorde, en donnant piteusement et par charité de vos biens auls povres, car otant de boines euvres vous faite en obeissant a commandemens de Dieu et autant d'aumosgnes que vous faites par charité, autant de pierre mettés vous a vostre edefice espirituel, et doivent estre ches pierres ychi assamblees et jointes ensamble a boin chiment, par quoy j'entens vraye et ferme foy car comme dist David, *Omnia opera eius in fide.*[12] Tout de quanques vous faites si soit faite en vraye foy car autrement pour riens ne vous pourfiteroit (30ᵛ) dequanques vous feriés quant a salut.

Mes pour soutenir ches murs ychi fault il .ii. pillers a chest fin que nuls vens ne les puist abatre ne bouter jus, ch'est assavoir ne les vens de temptacions ne de tribulacion ne de parolles cuisantes ne de prosperité ne d'aversité ne de dommages, et ches .ii. pillers ychi seront pacience emportant passianment les adversité de chu monde. Pourtant dist sainte Esglise: *In paciencia vestra possidebitis animas vestras.*[13] En vostre pacience possederés vos ames, ch'est assavoir le salut de vostre ame. Et l'autre si sera forche en resistant contre toutes mauvaises temptacions dyaboliques, car comme dist saint Augustin, l'anemy n'a de puissanche sur nous fors che que nous ly en donnons: *Debilis est inimicus qui non potest vincere nisi volentem.*[14]

Et aprés che ferons le cloistre a .iiii. cornes et che cloistre sera vostre corps qui sera nommié cloistre portant car il doibt estre clos et bien gardés et les .iiii. cornes seront .iiii. de vo sens natureulx. Le prumier sera le sens de la veue comme vos yeulx qui seront clos a legierement regarder a che que point ne s'arreste a regarder la vanité du monde et pourtant disoit David: *Averte oculos meos ne videant vanitatem via tua vivifica me.*[15] A sire, mes yeulx voeulliés avertir a che que point ne voient du monde la vanité mays en ta voye me voeullés vivifier par ta grace. Le second sera le sens de l'oÿe que diligaument clorrés a mal oïr d'autrui

---

[11] Gregory the Great, *Homiliae in euangelia* 33. 1.

[12] Psalm 33. 4 (32. 4).

[13] Luke 21. 19.

[14] Probably Gregory the Great, *Moralia in Job* 5. 22. 18.

[15] Psalm 119. 7 (118. 7).

nient plus que vous vorriés oïr de vous meismes (31ʳ) et sera chu sens ouvert
a oïr la parole de Dieu et ses benois commandemens a che que parfaitement
y puissiés obeir et acomplir entierement et par ainssy Dieu sy porra dire de
vous: *In auditu auris obedivit michi.*[16] Le tierch sera le sens de gouster, par quoy
j'entens vostre bouche, qui doibt estre gardee de trop parler fors de che de quoy
il vous sera de neccessité, car de toutes paroles wiseuses il converra rendre raison
au jour du jugement, tant soit petite. Si vous prie, tres doulce fille, que vous
parlés peu et atrempeement a che que puissiés dire a le fin de vos jours: *Posui
ori meo custodiam.*[17] A ma bouche j'ai mis garde et frain de trop parler. Le quart
sera que vos alees et venues si seront atrempees et vous gardés bien que point
vous n'alés ne ne venés en compaignie de gens que bien ne congnissiés. N'alés
point avoeucques femmes dansseresses ne gengleresses, car comme dist le sage,
Con saltatrice ne assiduus sis nec audias illam ne forte pereas.[18] Garde toi bien,
dist le sage, que point ne te tiengnes avoeucques danseresses, ne aussy n'escoute
point ses paroles, a cheste fin, dist il, que par adventure tu ne perisses, car en
verité doulce amie, moult de jones gens ont esté perdus a cause de dansses et de
canchons dissolues qui sont faites et dittes, et vous dy bien que cheuls qui point
n'y vont ne ne veillent as dansses n'a carolles sont plus asseur de leur sauvement
que ne sont cheuls qui les frequentent. Pour tant doncques alés avoeucques les
boins et fuiés les mauvais et vos (31ᵛ) tenés secretement en vostre oratoire en
tamps convenable par devocion en orisons, en contemplacion et en jubilacion,
a che que seurement puissiés dire: *Pes enim meus stetit in via recta.*[19] Je me suis
tenue et arrestee en la droite voye de mon salut, et qui bien fait chechi je dis que
telle creature si doibt estre et est nommee pafaite religieuse espirituelle.[20]

Si ferés aprés en che couvent espirituel chappitre, refroitoir, dortoir, chapelle,
enfermerie, chelier, et grenier.

Le chappitre sera confession car tout aussi comme en chappitre tous boins
religieus recongnoissent leur coulpe et leur defaultes et rechoivent[21] discipline,
aussy en confession vraye apartient de recongnoistre tous ses pechiés et toutes ses
defaultes et de rechepvoir discipline, ch'est assavoir penitanche et correction et

---

[16] Psalm 18. 45 (17. 45).

[17] Psalm 39. 2 (38. 2).

[18] Ecclesiasticus 9. 4.

[19] Psalm 26. 12 (25. 12).

[20] *Z ends here with this added text* Et serez du nombre des oueilles qui seront mises es pastures tres plantureuses de paraïs. Que nous vueille octroyer le pere le filz et le benoist saint Esprit. Amen.

[21] *X* rechoinent.

volenté de soi amender et tout aussy comme le bon religieux humblement recong-
noissant sa defaulte en che faisant se justefie et purefie comme dist saint Augustin,
*Confessio homines iustificat confessio peccati veniam iuvat. Nam cessat vindicta div-
ina si confessio precuerat humana.*[22] Dist saint Augustin, confession est de si grant
value car elle justefie la creature et empietre a pecheurs pardon et remission et
cesse l'avenganche et rigeur divine puis quelle est faite dignement et saintement.

Le refroitoir sera predicacion car tout aussi comme en (32ʳ) refroitoir ly religieux prennent leur refection corporelle aussy en predicacion devotte creature
rechoipt refection espirituelle, ch'est assavoir la parole de Dieu qui est le nour-
rissement de l'ame, et pourtant dit la sainte Euvangille: *Non in solo pane vivit
homo sed in omni verbo quod procedit de ore Dei.*[23] Que non mie tant seulement
creature est sustentee et nourrie corporellement et espirituelment sans la parole
de Dieu de pain materiel, mais par la parole de Dieu seulement et corporellement et espirituellement sans pain materiel[24]. Predicacion doncques sera vostre
refroitoir, ch'est que diligaument orrés la parole de Dieu et la rechepverés en
creanche en honneur et en reverence.

Le dortoir sera contemplacion car tout aussi comme le dortoir si doibt estre
en hault eslevés et non mie parterre, aussi comtemplacion doibt estre en hault
eslevee u chiel et non mie par terre en regardant les choses terriennes et ch'est, tres
doulche fille, que vous devés contempler devotement les biens souverains de lassus
qui sont apparelliés as bons, ch'est assavoir a chuls qui aiment parfaitement Dieu
et pourtant dist saint Gregoire: *Si consideremus fratres karissimi que et quanta
fratres que nobis promittuntur in celis vilescunt animo omnia quae habentur terris.*[25]
O devote fille, se bien considerés quels biens et comme grans y sont qui nos sont
promis u chiel nous (32ᵛ) ariemes du tout en despit et en vieuté tout che qui est
en che monde car briefment tout che qui est en che monde se n'est fors que con-
cupiscence carnelle ou vaine plaisanche des yeuls en avarice et tout orgueil de vie.
Vostre contemplacion doncques douche fille si soit eslevee en hault lassus car yeuls
morteuls ne porroient regarder ne oreilles escouter ne coeur pensser n'entendre
ne comprendre les biens que Diex vous a apareilliés et promis, se loialment l'amés.

Le chappelle sera devocion en laquelle doibt estre tout entierement vostre volenté, car come dist saint Gerome, *Devocio est fervor bone voluntatis.*[26]

---

[22] Prosper of Aquitaine, *Liber sententiarum* 211. 3.

[23] Matthew 4. 4; Luke 4. 4.

[24] *X par* crossed out.

[25] Gregory the Great, *Homiliae in euangelia* 37. 1.

[26] Hugh of St. Victor, *De arca Noe* 3. 6.

Devocion si est une ferveur et .i. desir qui vient de tres parfaite et boine volenté sans nulle contrainte.

L'enfermerie sera compassion qui procedera de tres parfaite carité, car piteusement et caritablement devés visiter povres enfermés et malades, car je vous dys que se vous aviés en vous toutes les aultres vertus et charité pitié et compassion en defausist, riens ne vous pourfiteroit. *Quia qui non habet caritatem nichil habet.*[27] Quar qui n'a charité il n'a riens.

Le chelier sera orison qui envers Dieu empietre grace et pardon, pourquoy dist saint Jehan Crisothome: *Vis scire dignitatem orationis mox ut de ore processerit suscipiunt eam angeli in manibus suis et offerunt ante Deum.*[28] Veuls tu savoir, dis chu docteur, la dignité d'orison? Sache, dist il, que si (33ʳ) tost q'elle est yssue de la bouche et departie li angles de Paradis la rechoivent entre leurs mains et l'offrent devant la fache de nostre signeur.

Et le grenier ou les grains seront mis sera meditacion et ch'est vous devés mediter en la loy de nostre seigneur de quoy il est dit ou Psautier: *In lege domini meditabitur die ac nocte.*[29] A sire, sache que ta loy je mediteray et de jour et de nuit.

Et par ainssy, doulce fille loialle, poés vous veoir parfaitement tout entierement l'edefice du couvent espirituel que saintement devés faire en vostre conscience a che que soiés religieuse espirituelle en la religion du benoit saint Esprit, laquelle Dieu le Pere l'a fondee. *Fundavit eam altissimus.*[30] Dieu le Filz l'a ordonnee comme dist l'Apotle, *Ordinata per angelos in manu mediatoris.*[31][32] Ordonnee est par les angles en la main du mediateur qui est Jhesucrist, et est du saint Esprit visitee. Si devés maintenant dire devotement avoeucques nostre mere sainte Esglise: *Veni creator spiritus, mentes tuorum visita, imple superna gracia quae tu creasti pectora.* O benoit et glorieux saint Esprit, par ta doucheur et courtoisie vien maintenant visiter les pensees des tiens et leurs consciences, a che que de ta supernelle grace soient raemplis.

Mays aprés l'edefice fault il regarder qui sont et seront les dames qui en chest sainte religion demourront et quelles offices elle aront. Prumierement Charité (33ᵛ) sera abeesse, car tout aussi comme une boine religieuse ne doibt riens dire ne riens faire ne riens prendre ne riens donner sans la licence de dame abeesse, aussi di ge que creature devote ne doibt n'aler ne venir ne riens prendre ne riens

---

[27] Paul, 1 Corinthians 13. 2.

[28] Pseudo-Chrysostom, *Opus imperfectum in Mattheum* 13.

[29] Psalm 1. 2.

[30] Psalm 87. 5 (86. 5).

[31] *X* meditatoris.

[32] Galatians 3. 19.

donner sans charité, et pourtant dist l'Apotle: *Opera vestra in caritate fiant*.[33] Toutes vos oeuvres et vos operacions et tout che que vous faites si soit faites en charité et par charité.

La prieuse sera Sapience, car comme dist Salmin, *Prior omnium creata est sapientia*.[34] Devant toutes choses Sapience a esté creee, et par le conseil de cheste dame ichi devons nous tout faire a cheste fin que de vous soit dit, *Omnia in sapientia fecisti*.[35] Tout dequanques que tu as fait tu as fait sagement et prudaument et par grant discrecion.

Humilité sera souprieuse et a cheste dame ychi vous fault obeir humblement a che que par elle soyés eslevee en hault. *Quia qui se humiliat exaltabitur*.[36] Et non mie tant seulement humble creature est eslevee mais est en glore comme dist l'Apostle, *Qui humiliatus fuerit erit in gloria discrecionis*.[37]

Discression sera tresoriere et gardera tout.

Jubilacions sera chantre qui chantera haultement et de jour et de nuit en la chappelle de devocion.

Orison sera vinetiere qui gardera les boins vins blans et vermauls en remenbranche de la bonté et doucheur (34ʳ) de la passion de nostre seigneur Jhesucrist ou il respandi sang et yaue. O tres amee fille, contemplés chechi devotement et moult grandement pourfiterés.

Penitanche sera cuisiniere qui prendra moult de paines. Elle apparllera les viandes, mais peu en mengera par abstinences.

Atrempanche sera refroituriere et servira en refoitoir par mesure en telle maniere qu'il n'i ara ne trop but ne trop mengié.

Sobreté lirra a table la vie des Peres et comment par example doivent vivre.

Pité sera pitanchiere qui fera tant de biens comme elle porra.

Et misericorde sa seur aumosniere qui tout donrra et riens ne reterra pour soy.

Et Doubtanche sera portiere qui bien gardera le cloistre de la conscience que nuls n'y entre pour mal faire ne par la porte de la bouche, ne par les fenestres des yeuls ne des oreilles.

Ounesteté sera maistresse des jones, ch'est assavoir des .v. sens de vostre corps.

Courtoisie sera oteliere qui rechepvera les alans et les venans et servira en telle maniere qui chascun s'en loera. Mais pourtant que toute boine religieuse

---

[33] 1 Corinthians 16. 14.

[34] Ecclesiasticus 1. 4.

[35] Psalm 104. 24 (103. 24).

[36] Luke 14. 11, 18. 14.

[37] Job 22. 29.

ne doivent pas estre seules elle ara Simplesche qui sera sa compaigne. La cause si
est car Courtoisie si porroit estre trop baude et hardie et trop se porroit avanch-
ier et Simplesche trop soterelle, et pourtant seront elles[38] .ii. ensamble.

Raison sera prouveresse. Elle prouvera tout che q'il (34ᵛ) faurra raisonna-
blement en tant qu'il n'y ara nulle defaulte. Loiauté sera enfremiere. Elle gardera
les malades. Larguesche sera sa compaigne et par ainssi li malades n'aront nulle
defaulte.

Meditacion sera grenetiere qui gardera le boin grain de fourment. Qui est
rouge par dehors et blanc par dedens et fendu au costé, et par chu grain ychi est
entendu le pretieux corps de nostre seigneur Jhesucrist qui par dehors fu rouge
en l'efusion de son preciex sang et par dedens blanc par pureté et ignoscence et
a costé fendu d'une lanche engoisseusement.

Jalousie sera secretaine. Elle sonnera matines et esveillera les dames a minuit
pour loer Dieu saintement et tres devotement. Et ch'est, doulce fille, que sus
toutes choses vous devés avoir jalousie de vostre salut, et chest dame ychi si a
une aurloge qui l'esveille. Cheste aurloge si est amours a amere Dieu souveraine-
ment, car l'amour de Dieu si esveille le coeur devot et ne le laisse point endor-
mir en quelconques vanités mondaines, si comme le tesmongue la devote ame
es cantiques: *Ego dormio et cor meum vigilat.*[39] Combien, dist l'ame devote, que
mon corps si se repose et dorme, toutfoys par grant jalousie mon coeur si veille
a che que grace cha jus me soit donnee et glore lassus habandonnee. Amen.

Explicit

Chy fine le rieulle du benoit saint Esprit.

---

[38] *X* elle seront-elles.
[39] Song of Songs 5. 2.

L'ABBAYE DU SAINT ESPERIT (α_2)

I have chosen *O* as the base manuscript for this edition because of its status as the copy that was owned by Margaret of York and the culmination of the work of adaptation that began with *V*, which can perhaps be regarded as a first draft. To show this process of development, all the important variants from *V* are indicated in the notes. However, the scribe's constant 'polishing' in *O* sometimes led to worse readings rather than improvements, as when he replaced 'pelican' with 'pellerin' (see note 19), inserting it in a sentence which talks of Christ as the pelican feeding her young with her blood, apparently not noticing that it did not make sense. He sometimes made careless mistakes, which have been corrected where necessary with reference to *V*.

(1ʳ) Cy commence ung beau traittié jadiz compilé par maistre Jehan Jarson, docteur en theologie, et est intitulé l'Abbaye du saint Esperit. Premierement: Comment chascune personne poeult icelle abbaye et religion fonder en sa conscience. Le chapitre premier.

Fille, regarde que moult de gens voldroient bien estre en religion maiz ilz ne peuent ou par povreté ou par ce qu'ilz sont par loyen de mariage retenus ou par aultre raison. Et pour tant fay une religion en ton[1] coeur del abbaye du saint Esperit, pour quoy tous ceulz et celles qui estre ne peuent en religion corporelle puissent estre en religion espirituelle. Haa, beau sire Dieu, ou sera ceste religion fondee et ceste abaye (1ᵛ) plantee? Certes je dy en une place qui est appellee[2] conscience. Nous avons souvent veu et bien est advenu que aujourd'huy a bel et notable lieu de Prescheurs ou de Freres Mineurs en tel place quy souloit estre

---

[1] *V* en cœur.

[2] *V* quy a nom.

moult orde et inhabitee. Ainsi advient il espirituelment la ou le saint Esperit voeult ouvrer. Or convient il tout premierement la place, c'est a dire la conscience, purgier et nettoier de toutes ordures, de toutes espines et de tous chardons, par quoy la place soit tresbien appareilliee pour si noble et hault ediffice fonder comme est l'abaye du saint Esperit.

Comment le saint Esperit, pour clorre de bons murs son abbaye, y envoiera damoiselles Verité, Amour de Pureté, Humilité et Povreté. Le chapitre .iie.

Quant donques ce sera fait, le saint Esperit y envoiera deux damoiselles preuses, vaillantes et sages. La premiere si est damoiselle Verité. Et l'autre a nom Amour de Pureté. Et tant qu'elles seront en l'abbaye elles garderont le coeur de toute ordure et de mauvaises pensees, tellement que jamais honni ne sera tant qu'elles soient gouverneresses del habitation. Quant la place de la conscience est bien purgiee, si convient il faire les fondemens larges et parfons. Et ce feront deux damoiselles, c'est a savoir Humilité et Povreté. Humilité les fait bas et parfons et Povreté les fait grans et larges, et jette la terre deça et dela en largement donner (2^r) quanques elle poeult tenir et avoir. Haa fille, beneoite soit la religion qui est fondee en povreté et en humilité. C'est encontre aulcuns maulvais religieuz orgueilleuz et convoitteuz.

Comment les murs de celle abaye sont eslevez par deux damoiselles, c'est a entendre Obedience et Misericorde. Et comment par deux aultres damoiselles, Pacience et Force, sont les pilliers pour l'euvre asseurer illec estaurez. Le chapitre .iiie.

Ceste religion donques doibt estre fondee sur bonne riviere de larmes et de pleurs. Car ville ou cité ou abbaye qui siet sur bonne riviere est plus aysiee et plus delicieuse. La Magdalee fut fondee sur bonne riviere dont grant bien luy en vint. Et c'est ce que dit le Prophete: *Tanquam lignum quod plantatum est secus decursus aquarum.*[3] Et en ung aultre lieu dit il: *Fluminus impetus letificat ciuitatem dei.*[4] La bonne riviere fait la cité nette, lyé, sceure et habondant de marchandise.

Damoiselle Obedience d'une part et damoiselle Misericorde d'aultre part font les murs de la religion grans et haulz, en largement donner aux povres par la misericorde et compassion que l'on a de ses proismes, en l'obedience de nostre seigneur qui dist: Je vous donne ung nouvel commandement. C'est que vous

---

[3] Psalm 1. 3.
[4] Psalm 46. 5 (45. 5).

amez l'un l'aultre ainsi que je vous ayme. Car quantes bonnes oeuvres que nous faisons pour l'amour de Dieu (2ᵛ) par son commandement[5] et par le conseil de nostre mere sainte Eglise, et quantes aulmosnes que nous donnons, autant de bonnes pieres mettons nous en nostre edifice et en nostre mur.

Nous lisons que Salomon fist sa maison de grans pierres moult precieuses, de quoy l'abitation du saint Esperit doibt estre faitte. Ce sont grandes aulmosnes et devotes, et toutes bonnes operations, qui doibvent estre de bonne vifve et forte chaulx jointes ensemble. Mais quy est icelle vifve et forte chaulx sinon amour de Dieu et de son proisme, qui adjoint l'une amour a l'autre et l'une bonne operation a l'autre? Mais a ce que le mur soit bon et bien durant il est de necessité que il soit fait de bon cyment. Et quel est ce cyment fors vraye foy? Dont dit David: *Omnia opera eius in fide.*[6] Toutes operations, dit il, sont en foy. Et tout ainsi que le mur ne poeult longuement durer sans cyment, pareillement oeuvre nulle que l'on face riens ne vault sans foy de Dieu. Et pour tant toutes operations que mescroians fachent sont de nulle valeur quant a leur salut.

Damoiselle Pacience et damoiselle Force sont les pilliers pour soustenir et pour appuyer l'oeuvre par telle maniere que nul vent de tribulations ou de temptations ou de paroles cuisans ou de grans dommages ne le puissent abatre.

Cy parle de la maison que une noble dame fist asseurer par sept pilliers. Le chapitre .iiiiᵉ.

(3ʳ) L'escripture recorde que une dame fist jadis faire ung bel et grant manoir, et y fist estaurer sept haulz pilliers.[7] Mais quy sont iceulz sept pilliers synon les sept vertus? C'est a entendre : Foy, Esperance, Charité, Justice, Attemprance, Force et Prudence. Ce sont les sept pilliers par lesquelz l'abaye doibt estre soustenue en laquelle le saint Esperit habite.

Comment le cloistre d'icelle abbaye doibt estre scitué et conditionné. Et de la proprieté et edifications des offices de icelle. Le chapitre .vᵉ.

Or couvient il faire le cloistre del abbaye, qui doibt avoir quatre cornets. Et est nommé cloistre pour tant que il doit estre cloz et bien gardé. Fille, se tu voeulz estre bien religieuse, tiens toy close et enfermee et ainsi tu gardes bien ton cloistre. Baisses et clos tes yeulx et te abstiens de legierement regarder, tes oreilles du mal de aultruy oyr, ta bouche de trop parler et rire. Cloz ton cœur encontre

---

[5] *V* par le commandement de dieu.

[6] Psalm 33. 4 (32. 4).

[7] Proverbs 9. 1.

toute mauvaise pensee. Et qui bien se garde en ces quatre choses certes il est bien religieux.

Damoiselle Confession fera le chapitre. Damoiselle Prudence fera le refroitoir, Oroison la chappelle, Contemplation le dortoir, car le dortoir doibt estre hault par soubslievement de desir et hors de noise et de triboul et de la cure de cest siecle.

Compassion fait l'enfermerie, Devotion fait le celier, Meditation le grenier, car icelles (3ᵛ) trois damoiselles, c'est assavoir Compassion, Devotion, Meditation, doibvent estre habondantes.

Comment en celle abbaye du saint Esperit fault estaurer ung couvent, et comment Dieu le père, Dieu le filz, Dieu le saint Esperit la fonderent. Le chapitre .viᵉ.

Quant les officieres sont ainsi faittes si couvient y establir et ordonner le couvent de grace et vertus et du tres debonnaire saint Esperit qui de ceste religion est gardeur et deffenseur. Doncques ceste tres noble abbaye Dieu la fonda. Et de ce dist le prophete David: *Fundauit eam altissimus*.[8] Dieu le filz par sa sapience la ordonna, si comme dit saint Pol: *Que a deo sunt ordinata*.[9] C'est, dit il, tout certain que l'abaye et religion ainsi rieglee est de Dieu le filz ordonnee. Mais encoires y a il plus. C'est que le saint Esperit en est gardien et deffenseur ou visiteur. Car tout ce chantons nous disons[10]: *Veni creator spiritus*. Sire saint Esperit creeur, venez sire et si visitez les pensees de ceulz et de celles qui pour l'amour de vous tiendront en leurs cœurs la regle de vostre religion. Et par vostre grace souveraine [ne] mesprisiés[11] les piz que vous avez creez.

Comment dame Charité fut esleue abbaesse d'icelle abbaye du saint Esperit, et comment toutes oeuvres doibvent estre faittes par charité. Le chapitre .viiᵉ.

(4ʳ) Quant le doulz couvent a ainsi chanté, et le saint Esperit appellé, si voeult avoir une bonne abbaesse. Et esleut dame Charité, pour tant que elle vaillant et sage estoit, toute courtoise et playne de toutes bonnes meurs. Et se misrent du tout en obedience, car tout ainsi qu'en religion l'on ne doibt riens faire ne en nul lieu aler, ne prendre, ne donner congié, sans le congié de l'abbesse, aussi qui ceste sainte religion et ceste sainte abbaie voeult garder et en son cœur establir, il ne doibt riens faire et si ne doit en nul lieu aler, ne prendre ne donner, sans le

---

[8] Psalm 87. 5 (86. 5).

[9] Romans 13. 1.

[10] *V* quant nous disons.

[11] *O* mesprisies *V* ne (*inserted*) mesprisies.

congié de ceste sainte abbaesse, ma dame Charité. Et ainsi le commande saint
Pol, qui dit: *Omnia opera vestra in caritate fiant.*[12] Vous qui voulez, dist il, ceste
religion tenir et en voz cœurs establir, laquelle religion se elle est bien main-
tenue et souvent du saint Esperit visitee, confortee, et consolee, et emmuree,
gardez, dist il, que toutes voz operations soient faittes en charité. Hellas, sire,[13]
cy a grant commandement, mais certes il est bon. Et quy le fait ainsi qu'il est
commandé, i (il) saulve les ames. Grant est quant il dist: Toutes voz pensees,
voz paroles, vos regars, voz alers, et voz venues, et briefment a dire toutes voz
operations, quelles quelles soient, faittes les en charité. Hellas, que je voy de
gens en religion petit religieuz, et et font moult de choses, prendent et donnent,
encontre le conseil de ma dame Charité.

(4ᵛ) Comment ma dame Sapience fut esleue pour estre prieuse del abbaye du
saint Esperit, et dame Humilité soubz prieuse. Et d'aulcunes moult belles auc-
toritez. Le chapitre .viiiᵉ.

Ma dame Sapience doncques fut esleue pour estre prieuse de la noble abbaye
du saint Esperit. Et ce fut bien droit et raison, car elle en est bien digne, selon
ce qui est escript ou livre de Salomon, ou il dit: *Prior omnium creata est sapiencia.*[14] Sachés, dit il, que premierement devant toutes est créé sapience. Et par
l'obedience et le conseil de ceste prieuse nous debvons faire toutes noz œuvres.
Si en vauldront mieulz, et mieulz en seront prisiees par le visiteur. Et ce est ce
que dit David: *Omnia in sapiencia fecisti.*[15] Ainsi comme se il voulsist dire : O
tu ame qui de Charité as fait abbaesse de ton cœur et commanderesse et qui as
esleu Sapience ad ce que elle soit prieuse, en l'obedience et conseil desquelles
deux dames tu entierement voelz remanoir et demourer. Trop mieulz doivent
tes operations estre prisiees et trop plus chierement estre tenues pour la reverence de icelles dames, en qui obedience et par qui conseil elles sont faittes.

  Madame Humilité, qui tousjours se ravale, et en tous temps se met voulon-
tiers au dessoulz, sera soulz prieuse, et bien est droit que venez a elle en obedience car elle est bien amee du visiteur. Ha, doulce fille, que cy a sainte abbaye
et bonne religion, ou il a et demeure si vaillans gens, si saintes et si (5ʳ) dignes
personnes, et ou il a si souffissant abbaesse comme Charité, prieuse comme
Sapience, et soubz prieuse comme Humilité. Fille beneoittes soient les nonnains

---

[12] i Corinthians 16. 14.

[13] *V* fille.

[14] Ecclesiasticus 1. 4.

[15] Psalm 104. 24 (103. 24).

quy bien gardent les commandemens de Charité, les consaulz de Sapience, et les enseignemens de Humilité, et qui toute leur vie meneront, ordonneront, et riegleront charitablement, sagement, et humblement. Le Pere le Filz et le saint Esperit les confortera et aidera, mais le monde les despitera. Haa, quel merveilles! Et pour tant dit Jhesucrist en l'euvangile a ses disciples: Ne vous esmerveilliés pas se le monde vous hayt car il me a premier eu en hayne. Se vous feussiés du monde, certes le monde amast ce que sien fust. Et pour tant que vous n'estes pas du monde il vous hayt. Souviengne vous, dist il, de la parole que je vous di: C'est que le sergant n'est pas plus grant de son seigneur. Car il avoit devant dit que le disciple n'est mie plus grant de son maistre. Ne ainsi n'est le sergant plus grant de son seigneur. Si doibt souffire au disciple que il soit comme sont maistre, et au garchon que il soit comme son seigneur. Si ilz appellent le maistre Belzebus, quel merveilles si ainsi sont appellez. Comme s'il voulsist dire a tous ceulz et a toutes celles qui ses disciples voeulent estre et eulz ensieuvir: Vous savez bien que je suis le seigneur et maistre, et que je scay et puis tout. Et si scavez que avant que je venisse sur terre prendre char humaine, tout le monde estoit en misere grant (5ᵛ), et pour tant disoient les prophetes en tres ardant desir: Sire venez, Sire enclinez voz cieulz et descendez. Et ung aultre prophete disoit: Il vendra le seigneur que est desiré de toutes gens et en toutes contrees. Et moult d'aultres paroles disoient les sains peres. Et tant me requisrent que moy venant au monde je leur apportay paix.

Comment Jhesucrist nostre seigneur remoustre icy par moult de voyes la grant charité qu'il a en nous par sa venue au monde, et par sa passion et mort tres amere. Le chapitre ixᵉ.

Or te recorde, ma chiere fille, du commencement de ma vye, au moien et la fin, et tu trouveras qu'elle fut toute en povreté, en tribulation, en meschief, en angoisse, en dureté et en toute aspreté. Regardes orendroit en quel lieu je fus nez, de quoy ne comment je fus enveloupé, et la ou je fus couchié. Regardes pareillement comment le monde me commença tempre a hayr, et de si grant hayne que de mort. Car pour la doubte et hayne que Herode conchupt sur moy commanda il de occir les innocens et me cuida avoir entre eulz occis. Regardez comment ma mere me transporta en Egypte, et de lieu en aultre. Encoires regardes comment je conversay doulcement aveuc toy au monde, et non mie ung jour ou deux tant seulement, mais durant l'espace de trente et trois ans. Regardez comment je enseignay au monde la voye dirrecte de la vye pardurable par operations et enseignemens de bouche. Car tout ce que je y (6ʳ) preschay je le accompliz par oeuvre. Regardez comment le monde ne fut oncques saoule de moy mal faire, et comment il en a mal converty tous les biens que je luy

feys, et au contraire comment j'ay en bien converty tous les maulz que jamais il me fist. Et encoires tu poeulz lire et trouver comment le monde me trahist et vendi, comment il me prist et blaphema, buffia et decracha. Comment il me lya a la coulompne[16] et baty, puis me courrona d'espines. Et en la fin aprés tout ce comment il me condempna a mourir. Comment il me cruciffia, attachant mes piés et mes mains de groz clouz dc fcr a la croiz de bois[17]. Regardes encoires ma doulce fille que se toutes les voyes et chemins qui sont par tout le monde feussent chagiés de cordes, et tous les champs et tous les plains et monts et vaulz feussent chargiés de clouz, et de tout ce j'eusse esté loyé et cloué, si n'eiussent ilz eu nul povoir de moy tenir une minute contre le vouloir de mon pere, maiz le tresgrant amour que j'avoie a vous, ma chiere fille, et le tresgrant fain et soif que j'avoie de vostre salut, ce fut le souverain lyen qui a la coulompne me lya, et qui a la croiz me cloua et soustint par mes deux mains en l'ayr.

Comment aprés plusieurs belles remoustrances les nonnains del abbaye et religion du saint Esperit, c'est a entendre le monde, doibt recognoistre la grant charité que Jhesucrist nostre seigneur a eu a nous. Le chapitre .xᵉ.

(6ᵛ) Haa, mon tresdebonnaire et leal ami, et mon treschier redempteur Jhesucrist nostre seigneur et saulveur du monde, vous dittes toute pure verité, car je scay certainement, tresdoulz sires, que nul lyen quelconques ne vous eust jamais peu arrester ne retenir fors seulement le lyen de vraye amour et charité qui vous loya pour moy desloyer. Certes, treschier sire, vous avez esté mon champion sans point de conquest, et vous savez, chier sire, que j'estoye malade et trop agravé et que nulz ne me pouoit rendre bonne santé fors vous. Et pour tant que a vous je ne pouoie aller, par vostre debonnaireté vous venistes liberallement a moy, et me avez de vostre[18] et precieulz sang sané et guery. Lequel pour ma redemption et soulvement fut espandu par telle manere que les pierres et les roches qui vostre mort sentirent s'en fendirent et espartirent, combien que nul mestier n'avoient de rachat, ne point n'estoit ce sang pour elles espandu. Mais lasse moy, tres douloureuse et mescheante, qui tresgrant mestier en avoie et pour qui il fut espandu a mon tresgrant proufit, demeure toute entiere sans fendre et sans amolir en riens. Et a paynes le sens je. Et se aulcunement je le sens, si est ce tant seulement en passant oultre, et tant que le parler en dure.

Haa, mon tres debonnaire redempteur, mon Dieu et mon seigneur, il vous pleut par vostre grace tres benigne recepvoir mort tres cruelle et horrible pour

---

[16] *V omits* a la coulompne.

[17] *V omits* de bois.

[18] *V* vostre propre.

moy rachatter de mort eternelle et moy donner vye pardurable. (7ʳ) Et en ce vous estes moustré vray pellerin[19] qui se occist et oeuvre son costé pour rendre la vye a ses poullons. Vous scaviés, chier sire, que mon pere le tout puissant estoit a moy courrouchié par ma grant coulpe et desserte, et me avoit menachié de batre comme celle quy grandement l'avoie desservy. Mais vous, treshumble et tres charitable ami Jhesucrist, qui scaviés ma fragilité et foiblesse, certes eiustes trop plus pitié de moy, miserable creature, que n'avez eu de vostre tres excellente haulteur. Car a celle fin que la verge de mon dit pere ne parvenist jusques a moy, il vous pleut de aler et mettre entre deux. Et la vous avez recheu les grans horions sur l'escu de vostre propre corps tresprecieux, par telle maniere que icelluy escu fut perchié et cruellement mutillé ou service de ma deffense. Et tant avez enduré de vituperes et de tourmens pour l'amour de moy, que vous eustes mon pere a moy du tout appaisié, qui pour nul aultre fors par vous jamais ne l'eust esté.

Comment par l'auctorité de Dieu le pere Jhesu son filz et souverain juge des humains. Et comment toute grace et bonté nous vient seulement de luy par sa debonnaireté. Le chapitre onzieme

Mon treshonnouré redempteur et tresdoulz amy, encoires avez vous trop plus fait pour moy. Car le incomparable service que pour l'amour de moy il vouz pleut a faire, en vous presentant et faisant moienneur d'entre mon pere et moy, fut (7ᵛ) tant agreable et plaisant a luy qu'il me pardonna tout entierement quanques je luy pouoie avoir meffait. Et que plus est, encoires s'il advenoit que je de rechief luy offensasse, il luy plaisoit que vous, tres debonnaires sires, en seussiés juge en vous donnant plain pouoir et auctorité de jugier et condempner tout autant que je aroie meffait. Haa, tres humble et tresmisericordieuz sires Jhesuscrist, que vous pourroie je rendre et guerdonner pour tant de si grans biens que des ja vous m'avez fais. Car de moy meismes je n'ay riens fors pechiés et deffaultes. Et ainsi vous m'avez playnement donné a cognoistre comment tout est vostre. Et ce est droit, car toutes choses quelzconques a la verité viennent et procedent de vous, soient biens de fortune, ou biens temporelz, soient richesses ou avoir, ou soient biens de nature, si comme biaulté corporelle, eloquence ou soy scavoir contenir et retrouver entre toutes gens. Ou soient biens de grace, si comme sont les sainctes vertus quiconques les a, car tout ce vient de vous, et telz sont les dons que vous departez a vostre tresnoble ordonnance, dont tous ceulz et toutes celles qui telz biens ont, quelz que ilz soient, les doibvent tenir de vous sans aultre, et non point croire ne penser que ilz en possessent par leur sens ou

---

[19] *V* pellican.

par leur vertu ou vaillance, car l'on voyt bien moult de grans lignaiges et sages gens devenir et d'avoir[20] estre povres et malostrus.

(8ʳ) Comment l'on poeult courrouchier nostre seigneur par estre ingrat envers le povre quy a necessité. Et comment l'on en doibt user. Le chapitre .xiiᵉ.

Haa doulz sires Jhesucrist filz de dieu tout puissant, en toutes choses je cognois de avoir moult grandement fourfait a l'encontre de voz tres dignes commandemens. Car des biens de fortune, desquelz vous me avez fait garde pour en departir a voz creatures qui necessité en avoient, et je les ay encontre eulz moult destroittement et muchiés[21], combien que j'estoie tout adverty de leur estat, et comment ilz estioent mes freres et mes sereurs. Et trop plus me a pesé a eulz donner cinq solz pour l'amour et ramenbrance de vous que vingt solz ou plus despendus en oultrages et beubans. Et que pis est, ce tant petit que pour l'amour de vous je ay donné, je, lasse moy meschante, le ay par moult de foiz plaint et regretté tant qu'il sembloit que fort il m'en pezast et tellement que par mon ingratitude j'en perdoie le merite du don. Et aveuc ce je faisoye de vertu vice.

Las moy treschetive creature et pleine de presumption, combien chargié me sens de grant delsoiaulté quant je tresbien savoie mes povres freres et sereurs en moult grant douleur et meschief par povreté. Et nostre seigneur par chacun jour m'envoioit de ses biens largement pour a iceulz en distribuer et donner doulcement de bon coeur quant ilz pour l'amour de Dieu le me demandoient, (8ᵛ) ce que tout detenoie pour le attribuer a mon singulier prouffit, par telle maniere que ce tres petit que leur en donnoie malvaisement leur plaindoye en mon courage ingrat et desnaturel. Mais lasse moy tresmeschante pecheresse, en quoy puis je bien avoir toute ma vye durant employé tant des biens de fortune et de nature que nostre seigneur par sa grace m'a envoiez en si grant habondance? Certes en riens aultre chose, sinon en mon parentage[22] ou je me suis souvent enorguillye et gloriffiee et que j'ay porté et eslevé plus qu'il ne m'appartenoit.[23] Et de mon sens naturel et acquis j'ay trop tenu, et si ne l'ay mie despendu par enquerir et cherchier les voyes et[24] fachons comment je peusse a vous complaire mon tres debonnaire sire Jhesucrist. Ainchois ay regardé et advisé par toute dilligence et

---

[20] *V omits* d'avoir.

[21] *V* moult destroitement tenus.

[22] *V* hault parentaige.

[23] *V omits* et gloriffiee et que j'ay porté et eslevé plus qu'il ne m'appartenoit.

[24] *V omits* voyes et.

par moult de manieres²⁵ comment je pourroie au monde mieulz complaire, et a mon corps furnir²⁶ de toutes ses plaisances mondaines.

Comment nulz ne se doibt contrefaire plus bel ne advenant que nature ne a permis, ne attribuer a sa gloire les biens qui de Dieu luy viennent. Le chapitre .xiiᵉ.

Haa moy tres douloureuse charrongne ingrate, donnee et lynntee aux vers puans qui aprés ma mort tantost naistront et sauldront par tous les conduits²⁷ de mon corps, qui doncques poeult bien estre ditte charrogne. De la beaulté dont vous, mon benoit createur, me aviez departie²⁸, n'a pas eu souffissance. (9ʳ) Car par grant estude je ay pourpensé et quiz tous desguisemens et achesmemens et tous divers et esquiz²⁹ atournemens pour moy atourner et parer, et pour moy en iceulz le mieulz pollir mon corps et contenir, a celle fin que du monde j'en fusse a toute heure plus regardee. Certes, par telz exploiz j'ay droittement esté la dempnee muse en quoy les folz et musars ont musé, dont par aventure et a la verité plenté en sont cheüz en grant pechié dont j'ay esté cause et meute de leur dempnation, par telle maniere que ceulz ou celles pour lesquelz saulver il vous a pleu tresdebonnaire Jhesucrist vostre precieulz sang espandre, par le desvoiement³⁰ de mon tres fol et tant desordonné atour. Et pour les mauvais exemples que j'ay demoustrez³¹ par devant iceulz ou icelles, je les puis avoir mis ou chemin³² de eternelle dempnation. Et ainsi que vous, tres debonnaire Jhesucrist, avez rendu bonne dilligence pour eulz et toutes humaines creatures saulver, j'ay rendu toute puissance pour eulz et moy pardurablement dempner. Ainsi ma obstinee perversité a en tous temps contrarié vostre bonté inestimable. Et des dons du saint Esperit ainsi de toutes les graces et vertus et de tous les grans biens que sans nombre j'ay de vous recheuz, tant sur les sains fons de baptesme comme depuis, certes je les ay tous polus et de fait par mon iniquité³³ perdues. Et se j'ay fait (9ᵛ) ou dit aulcune chose quy ait eu ou rendu quelque couleur de bien, si en ay je bien voulu estre prisiee, et ainsi je vous en ay tollu la

---

²⁵ *V* advisé ententivement.

²⁶ *V* décorer.

²⁷ *V omits* et sauldront par tous les conduits.

²⁸ *V* impartie.

²⁹ *V omits* divers et esquiz.

³⁰ *V* l'espandement.

³¹ *V* et du mauvais example que j'ay espandu.

³² *V* je les ay mis en voye.

³³ *V* par pechiés.

gloire, et approprié a moy tout l'honneur. Se j'ay oy que l'on vous aist despité, a ce ay je peu ou neant acompté, mais se quelque ung m'a despité ou blasmé, vigoureusement et appertement m'en suis deffendu. Se aulcuns vous ont loué et recommandé[34] et en ma presence rendu graces, petit m'en a esté, mais se aulcuns me ont aulcunement loué[35] pour quelque chose de bien que je pourroie avoir fait, combien que je n'auroie mie fait la chose pourquoy l'on me prise, si en ay je a moy accepté la louenge sans la renvoier a vous, tresdebonnaire Jhesucrist, de quy tous biens viennent[36]. Et pour abregier, certes tresdoulz redempteur Jhesu, onques je ne me deportay de vous guerroyer et estre contraire en recompense de tous les biens que toute ma vye par grace vous m'avez fais. Et tout ce me vient par la grant desolation de mon ingratitude.

Cy devise les lechons et suffrages et les laudes que doibvent dilligamment lire les nonnains de ceste sainte abbaye et religion. Le chapitre .xiii^e.

Haa[37] lasse moy tres malleureuse pecheresse, quel desir ne talent doy je avoir de tout ce reveler, quant je scay que tant de maulz sont par moy souvent advenus. Lasse, quant seray je saolee[38] de mal faire? (10^r) Sire, quant vendra le jour et l'eure de ma conversion et amendement?[39] Quant pourra en mon coeur entrer si grant hayne encontre tous pechiés pour l'amour de vous, comment pour l'amour de moy vous eustes en hayne tous pechies, quant vous meismes vous livrastes vostre precieuz corps[40] a mort pour pechié mettre a mort? Quant porray je regarder l'abisme de mes deffaultes en tel despit et par telle hayne que jamaiz voulenté aucune ne me puist surmonter pour faire chose quy a vous mon doulz amy Jhesucrist puist tourner a desplaisir? Quant pourray je avoir de par vous plaine cognoissance des biens, lesquelz sans nombre et sans mesure je ay de vous recheuz, ne comment pourray je avoir toute vraye consideration[41] de la tres entiere amour que continuellement avez eue envers moy, par lesquelles choses je puisse contourner et mon corps et mon coeur et toutes mes intentions de faire chose quy a vous soit agreable? Sire je regarde et cognoiz tresbien

---

[34] *V omits* et recommandé.

[35] *V* louee.

[36] *V omits* tresdebonnaire Jhesucrist, de quy tous biens viennent.

[37] *O illuminated initial* L *instead of* H.

[38] *V* tanee.

[39] *V* de mon amendement.

[40] *V omits* vostre precieuz corps.

[41] *V* consideration et recordation.

que tout vostre regne au monde a esté demené en mesprisement, en aspreté et en grant povreté, et moy au contraire ay tousjours voulenté de conduire toute ma vye en richesses, en honneurs et en delices. Hellas, mon tres debonnaire et cordial ami Jhesucrist, comment poeult telle folie en mon coeur entrer ne demourer, qui voeul et demande promptement avoir en ce monde tout ce que jamais vous n'y avez eu, en demandant les (10^v) grans honneurs et beubans, la ou vous mon Dieu, mon roy, et mon tres souverain seigneur avez esté despité, en appetant les delices, et vous y avez eu et recheu tourmens inestimables et innombrables, et en desirant les richesses de cest monde, et vous y avez demouré tousjours en grant povreté.[42] Certes se il advenoit que le roy de France se transportast en aulcune contree de son regne et les habitans de icelle le constituassent prisonnier, puis le alaissent degabant et buffiant, puis sans pité nulle le loiassent et batissent, et finablement le menassent pendre au gibet sans aulcune desserte, ceulz quy ce feroient pas ne se debvroient par raison[43] nommer ses hommes liges et feables. Quy bien scauroient leur roy ou leur seigneur avoir fait endurer et soustenir si tres grant vitupere et douleurs et sans aulcunement le avoir desservy, le avoir tant cruellement et inhumainement[44] traittié comme de a tort le mettre a mort si tres cruelle et villaine, en luy tiranniquement usurpant les honneurs et les sirymonies royaulz, certes moult debvroit ung tel poeuple estre tenu pour fol et pour desvoié. Hellas mon treshonnouré seigneur, tout pareillement est il de nous a toy nostre tresbon roy Jhesucrist, comme il a esté dit dessus, et toutes telles doibvent estre les leçons, les laudes et les suffrages des religieuses de ceste sainte abbaye et religion. Premierement (11^r) elles doibvent lire ou psaultier de leur conscience tous leurs pechiés et leurs deffaultes pour mieulz elles humilier. Aprés elles doibvent chanter pour les biens que le souverain abbé a fait pour eulz tous, lesquelz sont sans nombre, et comment encoires il leur prommet, que se bien et entierement voeulent tenir tous les poins de la religion, elles aront auecques luy pardurable consolation.

Comment ou livre de Daniel est contenu del establissement de Nabugodonosor par tout son empire[45] pour sa vye deduire en repos. Le chapitre .xiiiie.

Comme dit est dessus doibt l'on commenchier de labourer en la vallee de ses deffaultes. Et parmi l'esperance que l'on a des biens quy sont a ton[46] ami, doibt

---

[42] *V* avez tousjours esté en pure povreté.

[43] *V omits* par raison.

[44] *V omits* et inhumainement.

[45] *V* royaulme.

[46] *V* son.

l'on monter en la montaigne de repos. Ad ce se accorde moult bien ce que nous lisons ou livre de Daniel la ou il dist que ung grant roy quy avoit a nom Nabugodonosor, roy de Babilonne, estably sur tout son roiaulme totalment trois hommes quy tout y gouvernoient et ordonnoient pour le bien de la chose publique. Et tellement que Nabugodonosor n'avoit en son palais molestation aulcune de proces ne de discort, ou question nulle. Ainchois conduisi son estat et sa vye par paix, et par consolation et repos.

Tout pareillement advient[47] il ou roiaulme espirituel de la sainte ame, ouquel sont trois ordonneurs, (11ᵛ) et les religions ou sont constituez ces trois prelats ne auront ne plaits ne noises, mais joye et paiz. Et beneoit soit le royaulme et la religion qui est faite et ordonnee par charité, par sens et par humilité.

Comment quatre damoiselles, c'est assavoir Discretion, Oroison, Devotion et Penitance ont office en l'abbaye du saint Esperit. Le chapitre .xiiiiᵉ.

En l'abbaye du saint Esperit, aveuc tous aultres offices dessus declairez y sont constituez pour tresoriere damoiselle Discretion, laquelle tout garde et de tout s'entremet pour tant que tout voit a point. Damoiselle Oroison si est chantre, et eslieve le chant de jour et de nuyt pour Dieu louer. Et Jubilation est sa compaigne. Saint Gregoire dist que jubilation est une tres grant joye qui est concheue en larmes par amour et par faveur d'esperit, qui ne poeult estre du tout moustree ne du tout cellee, si comme il advient aulcunes fois a gens espirituelz après leurs oroisons, quy sont tant joieulz et par consolation si ardans que leur coeur va chantant et murmurant une chanson parmi leur salle ou parmi leurs chambres, ou aulcunes fois advient que leur langue ne se scet tenir qu'elle ne chante. En oultre damoiselle Devotion est celerriere, laquelle a en sa garde les vins blans et vermaulz comme roses et flours soubz la (12ʳ) ramembrance de Dieu nostre redempteur[48] et de sa très beneoitte passion, et de sa trés grant bonté et glorieuse compaignie en Paradis. Et damoiselle Penitance fera la cuisine, car assez prent de payne pour satisfation. Elle prepare et fait les bonnes viandes et souvent sue par contrition et petit mengue par abstinence. En oultre madamoiselle Attemprance est reffroiteresse, laquelle excersant son office sert tant amesureement que ja n'y ara ne trop mengié ne trop beu. Damoiselle Sobresse list a la table les vyes des sains Peres, et leur chante a l'oreille comment ilz ont par cy devant vescu, en les enhortant par tout le couvent de ainsi faire pour y prendre bon exemple. Damoiselle Pitié est pitanchiere, et moult dilligamment visitte les malades en leur administrant toutes leurs necessitez, a chascune personne selon

---

[47] *V* Ainsi est.

[48] *V* seigneur.

sa faculté. Misericorde sa suer est aumosniere quy tant donne que gaires ne luy demeure. Madame Paour est portiere, quy moult bien garde le cloistre de la conscience en deboutant hors le mal et appellant le bien, par quoy nulles maulvaistiés ne puissent entrer dedens le cloistre du coeur et de la conscience parmi la porte de la bouche ou des oreilles ou des yeulz, quy toutes sont fenestres quy bien font a prendre garde de nuyt et de jour. Damoiselle Honnesteté est garde des novisses, et les enseigne de parler a point et de (12^v) aler saintement et honnestement pour tant que tous ceulz quy les regardent y puissent prendre bon exemple. Et c'est ce que l'Appostre nous admonneste, disant: *Honeste ambulemus*.[49] Maintenons nous, dit il, honnestement. Et damoiselle Courtoisie doibt bien estre hosteliere pour les alans et venans devement recepvoir, et tellement que tous et toutes s'en puissent loer. Mais pour tant que religieuse nulle ne doibt point estre seule entre les survenans exercant l'office de hostelaine, a celle fin que trop joieuse et trop liberalle ne soit, pour sa compaingne ara damoiselle Courtoisie une nommee damoiselle Symplesse.[50] Car moult bonnes sont ensemble et petit valent l'une sans l'aultre, consideré que trop grant simplesse poeult estre tenue pour sottie, et trop grant courtoisie poeult estre trop joieuse et trop hardie. Mais elles deux ensemble serviront bien et bel. Madame Raison si est pourveresse, car elle pourvoit par dedens et par dehors et si a point que nulle deffaulte ny est trouvee. Damoiselle Loialté est enfermiere, car moult loialment se traveille pour servir les malades. Et pour tant que il y a plenté de enfermes et de foibles plus que de fors ne haitiés, si est damoiselle Largesse sa compaigne quy par tout administre, car petit se cure des grans despens que elle fait pour furnir au bien et utilité des malades et paciens.

Madame Meditation quy moult est (13^r) prudente et sage est grenettiere, et assemble le bon fourment et les aultres bons grains a plenté a celle fin qu'en leur sustentation il ne ait deffaulte aucune. Certes meditation est une vertu qu'on appelle bien penser a nostre seigneur Dieu et a tous ses fais, et a ses dits pareillement. Ceste greneteire amoit moult bien le roy David, et pour celle cause fut il tout son temps riche a plenté, dont il dit ou Psaultier: *In omnibus operibus tuis meditabitur*.[51] Sire, dist il, je pensoie a toutes vos operations. Et encoires dit il: *Meditatus sum omnibus operibus tuis in factis manuum tuarum meditabar*.[52] Sire, dit il, j'ay pensé a toutes voz operations et si pensoie aux fais de voz mains.

---

[49] Romans 13. 13.

[50] *O* elle pour sa compaingnie ara damoiselle Courtoisie et une autre nommee damoiselle Symplesse, *corrected from V*.

[51] Psalm 77. 13 (76. 13).

[52] Psalm 143. 5 (142. 5).

Et si dit encoires que celluy est bien eureuz quy en la loy de Dieu pensera de jour et de nuyt. Et ce est le commencement de toute perfection, quant de bon coeur l'on commence de penser a nostre seigneur bien ententifvement. Car tout ainsi que le fruit vauls mieulz par[53] la feuille, ainsi trop est meilleure une bonne pensee et sainte meditation que moult de paroles dittes en oroison. Mais je touche encoires plus hault et vous di que quant ung bon coeur et devot est prins et en oroison eslevé il ne poeult riens dire; ainchois a tant a faire de penser a ce qu'il oyt, qu'il sent et qu'il voyt que la parole luy fault. Si se taist pour aprez mieulz cryer et mieulz parler. Et ce dist David le psalmiste: (13ᵛ) *Quoniam tacui dum clamarem tota die.*[54] Je me taisoye, dist il, a celle fin que adés je criasse. Illec dist la glose que le grant cry que nous crions a nostre seigneur ce sont les grans desirs que nous avons a Dieu. Et de ce dist saint Denys que quant ung coeur est saoule par grant desir d'amour, certes il ne poeult bonnement dire ce qu'il sent. Ainchois est tant esmerveillié et esbahy que bonnement la parole luy fault. Et ce est proprement ditte sainte Meditation quy garde les grains de fourment, lequel est rougeastre au par dehors et par dedens blanc et si est fendu au costé. Et de tel fourment fait on le bon et savoureuz pain lequel est signifié Jhesucrist nostre seigneur, car il nous dit: Je suis le pain de vye. Car sa tres digne humanité fut rouge de son sang tres precieuz en sa passion, et certes son ame fut toute blanche par pureté de innocence. Et si fut de la lange Longin fendu au costé. Cestuy pain nous prendons au tressaint sacrement del autel. Et de meditation parla saint Augustin quant il dist: Sire lors que je pense a la tres grant doulceur emmyellee du tres doulz miel, se tous ceulz quy vous veoient en vous guerroiant me veoient et je n'enveisse nulz, si seroient ilz tous convertis pour les inestimables biens que vous me faittes, tant en sont les delices vertueulz et grans sans comparroison.[55] Et veez icy moult bonne grenettrye. (14ʳ) Or devez vous savoir que le grenier est et doybt estre devant le celier. Et pareillement doibt estre meditation devant devotion. Et pour tant j'ay dit que Meditation est grenettiere et Devotion celleriere, et damoiselle Pitié est pitanciere. Et de ces trois damoiselles dist le psalmiste David: *Affructu frumenti vini et olei sui multiplicati sunt.*[56] Ces trois lieux, dist il, sont multipliés de fruit de fromment, de vin et d'huille.

---

[53] *V* que.

[54] Psalm 32. 3 (31. 3).

[55] Not identified.

[56] Psalm 4. 8.

Comment nostre seigneur en la bible a ceulx qui bien le servent prommet habondance de fruits, c'est a entendre sa gloire permanente. Le chapitre[57]

En moult de lieux en la bible nostre seigneur prommet ceste promesse en disant: Servez moy bien, dist il, et certes je vous donneray grant habondance de fromment. Ceste habondance de fromment est donnee par bien penser a la croix et a la passion de Jhesucrist nostre redempteur. Et ce est meditation. Habondance de vin est par grandement plourer et mediter et ce est devotion. Habondance d'huile est par soy bien delitter en nostre seigneur. Et ce est consolation. Car l'huile donne moult bon saveur et reluist en l'eglise, ardant en la lampe. Pareillement ung cœur, quant il a bien pensé et bien aouré, Dieu en a pitié et luy donne confort, pitance et delict. Premierement il luy envoye le doulz fromment de meditation. Aprés luy donne le (14ᵛ) vin de devotion, puis luy transmet le huile de pitié et de consolation. Et cest huile donne saveur et affection, et enlumine en cognoissance et en revelation, et art par ferveur de naturelle inflamation.

Une moult sage damoiselle qui est nommee Jalousie, et quy tousjours est esveilliee pour bien faire, tient et gouverne l'orloge pour resveillier toutes les aultres et les faire lever matin pour nostre seigneur servir. Par les bonnes villes sont orloges quy resveillent les passans et ce sont les galz quy de leur propre nature au plus matin et devant le jour se resveillent, donnans par leur chant cognoissance aux passans que la matinee est prouchaine. Et d'aultre part sont par les citez d'aultres orloges quy resveillent les citoiens et marchans, et ce est la guette qui corne le point du jour. Mais toute aultre orloge a en ceste religion et lieu saint de beguinage. Car ce est contemplation, que damoiselle Jalousie gouverne par saveur de parfection. Et pour tant est maintes fois advenu en religion que avant le son del orloge aux matines, devotes personnes avoient plouré larmes en grant habondance par amour et devotion devant la representation de nostre seigneur, car l'orloge d'amours les avoit resveilliés.

Comment le coeur de toute personne doibt veillier en grant jallousie, dilligence et en desir et parfait (15ʳ) amour a nostre seigneur. Le chapitre

Haa fille, que beneoitte soit l'ame que amour entiere dilligamment esveille, ne quy point n'est endormie ne parresseuse. Et ainsi l'avons nous ou livre de Cantiques: *Ego dormio et cor meum vigillat.*[58] C'est a dire, quant je dors corporellement et me acoute pour mon corps ung petit reposer, mon coeur continuel-

---

[57] Chapter numbering stops here in both *V* and *O*.
[58] Song of Songs 5. 2.

lement veille en jalousie en ardant amour et desir de Dieu. Telle ame a tousjours son entendement et son coeur a son debonnaire createur, par quoy elle poeult chanter une chanson mondaine disant: J'ay ung coeur resveillié a sonnettes par amours. Les sonnettes du coeur sont les regrets, les souspirs et les doubtes, les gemissemens et les desirs que la sainte ame a continuellement en ses orisons.

Comment l'ennemi d'enfer mist en l'abbaye du saint Esperit quatre de ses filles, c'est assavoir Orgueil, Envye, Presumption, et Murmure ou Detraction et Faulz Jugement d'Aultruy.[59] Le chapitre.

Quant ceste tant noble abbaye fut parfaitte et ordonnee comme dit est, et que nostre seigneur Dieu y fut haultement et bien servy et honnouré, et par grant estude et bonne diligence ung grant usurier du paiis fist tant par son avoir et malice qu'il y mist quatre filles qu'il avoit, lesquelles estoient moult laides. Mais quy fut cestuy mallicieux usurier? (15^v) Certes ce fut l'ennemi d'enfer. Et la premiere de ses filles fut nommee Envye, quy tant est borgne et lousce qu'elle ne poeult regarder.[60] Ainchois tousjours de travers, si comme il appert en Saul et en David. La seconde fille estoit appellee Orgueil et Presumption, laquelle est si bochue et emflee ou piz que merveilles, car elle cuide plus savoir ou valloir que les aultres, comme il appert en Naaman. La tierche se nommoit Murmure ou Detraction, car certes elle est si besgue qu'elle ne scet parler ne bien ne bel; ainchois est a toute heure dame de tenchons et de noyses, et semoit discorde parmi la religion. La quarte avoit a nom Faulz Jugement d'Aultruy. Et est ceste fille icy tant boiteuse qu'elle ne poeult aller droit, et si ne pense a nul bien, ne loyaulté ne verité.

Comment par oroison lesdittes quatre filles del annemi d'enfer furent boutees dehors l'abbaye du saint Esperit. Le chapitre.

Les quatre filles a l'usurier dessus dit, quy par malice furent mises en la noteble abbaye du saint Esperit, troublerent par telle maniere tout le couvent que tout y ala mal. Pour quoy voiant ce le couvent, Madame Charité l'abbaesse, Madame Sapience la prieuse, Madame Humilité soubz prieuse, et toutes les aultres bonnes dames s'esmeurent et sonnerent chapitre, puis se conseillierent pour savoir qu'elles feroient. Et adont madame Discretion (16^r) leur conseilla que diligamment elles alassent a oroison en priant le tres doulz saint Esperit qu'il de sa grace les venist secourir, car moult en avoient grant besoing, et que par grant

---

[59] *O* Orgueil, Envye, Presumption et Murmure ou Detraction et Faulz Jugement d'aultruy sont comprins.

[60] *V* regarder a droit.

devotion chantassent *Veni creator spiritus et cetera*, ce que tantost elles firent de bon coeur. Et adont leur sourvint le beneoit saint Esperit, qui par sa grace et haulteur jetta hors de son abbaye icelles quatre filles au dyable, c'est a entendre Orgueil, Envie, Faulz Jugement d'Aultruy et Murmure ou Detraction, comme faulses malvaises garses et ordes, indignes de jamaiz avoir repair entre honnestes gens car a tousjours en vauldroit trop grandement piz la compaignie.

La fin et conclusion de ce present traittié intitulé L'abbaye du saint Esperit.

Adont fu la noble abbaye du saint Esperit reformee et de rechief trop mieulz ordonnee que par avant n'avoit esté. Or vous prie je tous et toutes que ceste sainte religion voeulliés tenir et soyés dilligens et dilligentes a vostre pouoir que chascune des bonnes dames quy en cestuy present traittié ont estee nommees fachent espirituellement leur office chascun jour en voz coeurs. Et bien vous gardez que point ne trespassez la riegle de la religion ne l'obedience des souverains. Et s'il advenoit par aucune mescheance que aulcune des dessus dittes (16ᵛ) quatre filles a l'ennemi d'enfer s'embatissent en voz cœurs, faittes par le conseil de madame Discretion et incontinent recourez a oroison, en appellant par tres ardant desir le tresdebonnaire saint Esperit. Lequel incontinent comme treshumble et tout charitable visiteur viendra et boutra hors de vous toute l'ordure par telle maniere que le couvent de vostre conscience demourra paisible et a bon droit, car elle sera temple du beneoit saint Esperit. Ainsi soit il. A.M.E.N.

Cy fine le livre intitulé L'abbaye du saint Esperit.

Enseignement (δ)

This is a transcription from *S*, fols 233ᵛᵃ–234ᵛᵇ.

(233ᵛᵃ) Aprés s'ensieult plusieurs beaulz exemples et enseignemens.

Se tu voeulz estre bon religieuz, tien toy cloz, garde le cloistre de tes yeulz de follement regarder, cloz ton coeur de malvaises pensees, ayme quy bien se garde. Car qui se teint en ces trois choses parfaitement, il ara beau commencement d'estre religieuz. Il advient a la fois aprés les oroisons aux gens espirituelz que ilz sont lies et si joieulz et constans a Dieu amer que leur coeur a clochettes ressonnans. Pour Dieu ayme les clocettes de ton cœur. Ce sont les plours, les souspirs, les gemissemens, le desirier, et les larmes quy viennent (233ᵛᵇ) en oroison de bon cœur.

Le juste homme pensera a la loy de nostre seigneur Jhesucrist nuyt et jour. C'est le commencement de perfection quant coeur se met a bien penser a Dieu. Et aussi comme le fruit vault bien mieulz des fueilles, ainsi vault mieulz pensee et sainte meditation que moult de paroles dire en oroison. Mais je dy encoires que quant l'esperit est levé en oroison il ne poeult riens dire, et tant a cure de penser a ce qu'il sent et qu'il voyt que parole lui fault. Si se repose pour mieulz plourer, si se taist pour mieulz parler. Ung saint homme dit que le grant cry que nous faisons et crions a Dieu est[1] le grant desir que nous avons a Dieu de luy veoir. Il est aucunes fois advenu que ame qui a esté ravye se (234ᵛᵃ) paulme ainsi comme la liache qui se paulme en chantant. C'est joye a l'ame repuse, que nulz ne scet que c'est fors celluy qui de Dieu est desiré.

Jubilation est une grant joye quy est par grace conceupte en l'ame aprés l'oroison, quy ne poeult estre du tout moustree ne du tout cellee. A meditation

---

[1] *S* et.

est[2] habondance divine pour bien plourer, devotion est habondance double pour Dieu bien amer et louer. Ainsi comme bon coeur espirituel a bien penser et a bien plourer si en a Dieu pitié, si lui fait pitance en confort et en delit que luy envoie. Gardez vous de toutes oiseuses paroles, pensees, regarts, venus et a venir, que ilz soient faits par charité pour plaire a Jhesucrist, (234ʳᵇ) car il est jalouz de nous amer. Dieu souffry pour nous povreté honteuse, honte douloureuse, douleur angoisseuse, angoisse amoureuse, amour oultrageuse. Coeur qui se voeult garder de pechié doibt regarder la dignité a quoy il est fait, et le pris que il vault, et l'amour que Dieu en luy a mis, et la promesse que Dieu luy a faitte, et de quoy l'ame sera douee. C'est que elle amera Dieu parfaitement, elle verra Dieu appertemet, elle le sentira doulcement, et goustera sa tresdoulce misericorde. Quant l'on fait offrande a Dieu, l'on doibt dire: je offre a Dieu le pere et a la sainte Trinité a quy je supplie que voeulle recepvoir mon povre coeur que je offre en la souvenance de la tres grant amour que ai tousiours eu aux pecheurs, quant il de sa (234ᵛᵃ) grace nous fait vivre. Saint Jehan dist que Dieu est dedens toutes choses et si n'est point encloz. Dieu est dehors toutes choses et si n'est point eslevé. Dieu est dessoubz toutes choses et si n'est point abaissié. Coeur qui languist pour Dieu amer est en charité, et si diffinist et appalist et devient povre des biens temporelz. Si le guerpissent ses amiz charnels. Si pleure quant il voye joie faire, si devient pale, si pert sa couleur, si se confesse voulentiers pour plaire a Dieu, si pert le goust de boire et mengier, si affoiblist, si ne voeult jamais reposer fors a Dieu. Par tout ou vous alez tenez vous closement, les yeulz bas, a peu de parole, en humilité pour bon exemple donner a aultruy, et principalement pour (234ᵛᵇ) plaire a Dieu qui tant est jalouz des ames que il moustrer semblant a aultre d'amour fors a luy. Je vous prie, mon tresdoulz espeuz Jhesuz qui morustes pour moy en la croyz, que me donnez vous embraser par doulce pensee et par tendre et bon amour, que je puisse sentir en grant reverence et compassion la grant durté de vostre precieuse mort. Telz est preudhoms qui n'est religieuz, si doit estre tel qu'il porte en paix de coeur tous mesdites, tous meffais, maladies, pouretez, desplaisir, et tous les fais de tribulation doulcement et en paix. Et se il ne fait ainsi, certes il n'est mie parfait.

[2] *S* et.

BIBLIOGRAPHY

Manuscripts and Archival Documents

Brussels, Bibliothèque Royale de Belgique, MS 9106
Brussels, Bibliothèque Royale de Belgique, MS 9272–76
Brussels, Bibliothèque Royale de Belgique, MS 9411–26
Brussels, Bibliothèque Royale de Belgique, MS 9555–58
Canterbury, Cathedral Library, MS Lit. B. 6
Chartres, Bibliothèque municipale, MS 1036 (largely destroyed)
Città della Vaticano, Biblioteca Apostolica Vaticana, MS Latinus Reginensis 444
Lille, Bibliothèque municipale, MS 452 (795)
London, British Library, MS Additional 15606
London, British Library, MS Additional 20697
London, British Library, MS Additional 28162
London, British Library, MS Additional 29986
London, British Library, MS Additional 54180
London, British Library, MS Royal 16 E XII
London, British Library, MS Royal 20 B III
London, British Library, MS Yates Thomson 11
Louvain, Bibliothèque de l'Université, MS G.53 (destroyed)
Lund, Universitetsbibliotek, MS Medeltidhanskrift 53
Metz, Bibliothèque municipale, MS 535 (destroyed)
Montpellier, Bibliothèque de l'École de médecine, MS 43
Montpellier, Bibliothèque municipale, MS Fonds C. Cavalier 216
Munich, Bayerische Staatsbibliothek, MS cod. gall. 32
Munich, Bayerische Staatsbibliothek, MS cod. gall. 914
Oxford, Bodleian Library, MS Douce 365
Paris, Bibliothèque de l'Arsenal, MS 2058
Paris, Bibliothèque de l'Arsenal, MS 3167
Paris, Bibliothèque Mazarine, MS 788

Paris, Bibliothèque Mazarine, MS 870
Paris, Bibliothèque nationale de France, MS fonds français 423
Paris, Bibliothèque nationale de France, MS fonds français 926
Paris, Bibliothèque nationale de France, MS fonds français 1802
Paris, Bibliothèque nationale de France, MS fonds français 2093
Paris, Bibliothèque nationale de France, MS fonds français 2095
Paris, Bibliothèque nationale de France, MS fonds français 6447
Paris, Bibliothèque nationale de France, MS fonds français 19397
Paris, Bibliothèque nationale de France, MS fonds français 19531
Paris, Bibliothèque nationale de France, MS nouvelles acquisitions françaises 4276
Paris, Bibliothèque nationale de France, MS nouvelles acquisitions françaises 5232
Paris, Bibliothèque nationale de France, MS nouvelles acquisitions françaises 10246
Poitiers, Bibliothèque municipale, MS 83 (187)
St Petersburg, National Library of Russia, MS fr. Q. v. III. 1
Tours, Bibliothèque municipale, MS 399
Urbana, University Library, MS 98
Vesoul, Bibliothèque municipale, MS 91

Primary Sources

Aelred of Rievaulx, *De institutione inclusarum*, ed. by C. H. Talbot, CCCM, 1 (Turnhout: Brepols, 1971)

Augustine, *Enarrationes in Psalmos*, ed. by E. Dekkers and J. Fraipont, CCSL, 38 (Turnhout: Brepols, 1956)

——, *Expositions of the Psalms*, trans. by Maria Boulding, ed. by John E. Rotelle, vol. III.16, *The Works of Saint Augustine: A Translation for the 21st Century* (New York: New City Press/Augustine Heritage Institute, 2000)

Bayot, Alphonse, *Poème Moral: Traité de vie chrétienne écrit dans la région wallonne vers l'an 1200*, Académie Royale de Langue et de Littérature françaises de Belgique, Textes anciens, 1 (Brussels: Académie royale de langue et de littérature françaises de Belgique, 1929)

Bechmann, E., 'Drei Dits de l'ame aus der Handschrift Ms. Gall. Oct. 28 der Königlichen Bibliothek zu Berlin', *Zeitschrift für romanische Philologie*, 13 (1890), 35–84

Bernard of Clairvaux, *On the Song of Songs I*, vol. II of *The Works of Bernard of Clairvaux*, trans. by Kilian Walsh, Cistercian Fathers Series, 4 (Cistercian Publications, 2005)

——, 'Sermones super Cantica Canticorum', in *Bernardi opera*, ed. by J. Leclercq, C. H. Talbot, and H. M. Rochais (Rome: Editiones Cistercienses, 1957–58)

Biblia sacra iuxta Vulgatam versionem, ed. by B. Fischer, J. Gribomont, H. F. D. Sparks, W. Thiele, and R. Weber (Stuttgart: Deutsche Bibelgesellschaft, 1975)

Boeren, Petrus Cornelis, *La Vie et les oeuvres de Guiard de Laon, 1170 env.–1248* (The Hague: Nijhoff, 1956)

Brisson, Marie, *A Critical Edition and Study of Frere Robert, Chartreux: 'Le Chastel Perilleux'*, Analecta Cartusiana, 19–20 (Salzburg: Institut für Englische Sprache und Literatur, 1974)

Chevallier, Ph., *Dionysiaca: Recueil donnant l'ensemble des trad. latines des ouvrages attribués au Denys de l'Aréopage etc.* (Paris: Desclée de Brouwer, 1937–51)

Christ, Karl, 'Le Livre du Palmier, ein Beitrag zur Kenntnis der altfranzösischen Mystik', in *Mittelalterliche Handschriften, Festgabe Hermann Degering* (Leipzig: Hiersemann, 1926), pp. 57–81

——, 'La Regle des fins amans, eine Beginenregel aus dem Ende des XIII. Jahrhunderts', in *Philologische Studien aus dem romanisch-germanischen Kulturkreise: Karl Voretzsch zum 60. Geburtstage und zum Gedenken an seine erste akademische Berufung vor 35 Jahren*, ed. by B. Schädel and Werner Mulertt (Halle an der Saale: Max Niemeyer Verlag, 1927), pp. 173–213

Consacro, Peter, 'A Critical Edition of "The Abbey of the Holy Ghost" from All Known Extant English Manuscripts with Introduction, Notes and Glossary' (unpublished doctoral dissertation, Fordham University, 1971)

Delisle, Léopold, *Testament de Blanche de Navarre, reine de France*, Mémoires de la Société de l'histoire de Paris et de l'Île de France, 12 (Paris: Société de l'histoire de Paris, 1886)

Denis the Carthusian, *Doctoris ecstatici D. Dionysii Cartusiani Opera Omnia*, 43 vols (Monstreux, Belgium: Typis Cartusiae S. M. de Pratis, 1896–1935), vol. XXXVII (1909)

Durand de Champagne, *Speculum dominarum*, ed. by Anne Flottès-Dubrulle, with Constant J. Mews, Rina Lahav, and Tomas Zahora (Paris: École des Chartes, 2018)

Friesen, Erika, 'The Seven Gifts of the Holy Spirit: Ten Anonymous 13th Century French Sermons' (unpublished doctoral dissertation, University of Toronto, 1999)

Glorieux, P., *Jean Gerson, Œuvres complètes*, vol. VII: *L'Œuvre française* (Paris: Desclée, 1967)

Gregory the Great, *Homiliae in euangelia*, ed. by R. Etaix, CCSL, 141 (Turnhout: Brepols, 1999)

——, *Moralia in Job*, ed. by M. Adriaen, CCSL, 143B (Turnhout: Brepols, 1079)

——, *Morals on the Book of Job by St Gregory the Great, Translated with Notes and Indices*. trans. by James Bliss and Charles Marriott (Oxford: J. H. Parker, 1844)

Hilka, A., 'Altfranzösische Mystik und Beginentum', *Zeitschrift für romanische Philologie*, 47 (1927), 121–70

Hugh of Fouilloy, *De claustro animae*, PL, 176, cols 1017–1182

Hunt, Tony, 'An Allegory of the Monastic Life', *Neophilologus*, 87 (2003), 3–10

Jacques de Cessoles, 'Le jeu des eschaz moralisé': Traduction de Jean Ferron (1347), ed. by Alain Collet, Classiques français du Moyen Age, 134 (Paris: Honoré Champion, 1999)

John of Ford, *Super extremam partem Cantici canticorum sermones CXX*, ed. by Edmund Mikkers and Hilary Costello, CCCM, 17 (Turnhout: Brepols, 1970)

Langlois, Ernest, *Recueil d'arts de seconde rhéorique* (Paris: Imprimerie nationale, 1902)

Laurent d'Orléans, *La Somme le roi par Frère Laurent*, ed. by Edith Brayer and Anne-Françoise Leurquin (Paris: Société des anciens textes français, 2008)

Lazar, Moshé, ed., *Bernard de Ventadour, troubadour du XIIᵉ siècle, Chansons d'amour, édition critique avec traduction, introduction, notes et glossaire*, Bibliothèque française et romane. Série B: Éditions critiques de textes, 4 (Paris: Klincksieck, 1966)

Lemoine, H., ed., *Inventaire sommaire des Archives Départementales antérieures à 1790. Archives ecclésiastiques – série H.*, vol. II (Corbeil: Département de Seine-et-Oise, 1944)

Liber de modo bene vivendi ad sororem, PL, 184, cols 1199–1306

The manere of good lyvyng: A Middle English Translation of Pseudo-Bernard's 'Liber de modo bene Vivendi ad sororem', ed. by Anne E. Mouron (Turnhout: Brepols, 2014)

Mechthild of Magdeburg, *The Flowing Light of Godhead*, trans. by Frank Tobin (New York: Paulist Press, 1998)

Morawski, J., 'Deux poèmes en quatrains monorimes', *Neuphilologische Mitteilungen*, 28 (1927), 32–37

Otto, Richard, 'Altlothringische geistliche Lieder', *Romanische Forschungen*, 5 (1890), 583–618

Philippe de Novare, *Les Quatre Âges de l'homme: Traité moral publié pour la première fois d'après les manuscrits de Paris, de Londres et de Metz*, ed. by Marcel de Fréville, Société des anciens textes français (Paris: Firmin-Didot, 1888)

Reypens, L., *Vita Beatricis: De Autobiografie van de Z. Beatrijs van Tienen O. Cist. 1200–1268* (Antwerp: Ruusbroec-Genootschap, 1964)

Speculum virginum, ed. by Jutta Seyfarth, CCCM, 5 (Turnhout: Brepols, 1990)

Secondary Works

Allen, Hope Emily, *Writings Ascribed to Richard Rolle* (New York: Heath, 1928)

Baron, Françoise, 'Le Maître-autel de l'abbaye de Maubuisson', *Comptes-rendus des séances de l'Académie des inscriptions et belles-lettres*, 114 (1970), 538–44

Baron, Roger, 'Note sur le *De Claustro*', *Sacris Eruderi*, 15 (1964), 249–55

Barratt, Alexandra, *The Book of Tribulation*, Middle English Texts, 15 (Heidelberg: Carl Winter Universitätsverlag, 1983)

Bauer, Gerhard, *Claustrum animae: Untersuchungen zur Geschichte der Metapher vom Herzen als Kloster* (Munich: Wilhelm Fink Verlag, 1973)

——, 'Herzklosterallegorien', in *K. Ruh, Die deutsche Literatur des Mittelalters Verfasserlexicon*, ed. by W. Stammler and K. Langosch (Berlin: Walter de Gruyter, 1981), pp. 1153–67

Bawcutt, Priscilla, 'The Lark in Chaucer and Some Later Poets', *Yearbook of English Studies*, 2 (1972), 5–12

Beaucourt, Gaston Du Fresne de, *Histoire de Charles VII*, 6 vols (Paris: Librairie de la société bibliographique, 1882–91)

Beaune, Colette, and Élodie Lequain, 'Marie de Berry et les livres', in *Livres et lectures de femmes en Europe entre Moyen Âge et Renaissance*, ed. by A.-M. Legaré (Turnhout: Brepols, 2007), pp. 49–65

Bell, Kimberly K., and Julie Nelson Couch, *The Texts and Contexts of Oxford, Bodleian Library, ms. Laud misc. 108: The Shaping of English Vernacular Narrative* (Leiden: Brill, 2011)

Blockmans, Wim, 'The Devotion of a Lonely Duchess', in *Margaret of York, Simon Marmion, and the Visions of Tondal*, ed. by Thomas Kren (Malibu: J. Paul Getty Museum, 1992), pp. 29–46

Boffey, Julia, 'The Charter of the Abbey of the Holy Ghost and its Role in Manuscript Anthologies', *Yearbook of English Studies*, 33 (2003), 120–30

Bolton, Brenda, 'Some Thirteenth-Century Women in the Low Countries: A Special Case?', *Nederlands archief voor kerdgeschiedenis*, 61 (1981), 7–29

Bondéelle-Souchier, Anne, 'Les Moniales cisterciennes et leurs livres manuscrits dans la France d'Ancien Régime', *Citeaux: Commentarii cistercienses*, 45 (1994), 194–337

Boriosi, Marc, 'Saint François en vers: Les Premières Légendes rimées en français (XIIIᵉ siècle)', *Etudes franciscaines*, n.s., 3 (2010), 55–77, 241–71

Bousmanne, Bernard, Frédérique Johan, and Céline Van Hoorebeeck, *La Librairie des ducs de Bourgogne: Manuscrits conservés à la Bibliothèque royale de Belgique. Textes didactiques*, 3 vols (Turnhout: Brepols, 2003)

Buettner, Brigitte, 'Le Système des objets dans le testament de Blanche de Navarre', *Clio*, 19 (2004), 37–62

Busby, Keith, *Codex and Context: Reading Old French Verse Narrative in Manuscript*. 2 vols (Amsterdam: Rodopi, 2002)

Carruthers, Leo, 'In Pursuit of Holiness Outside the Cloister: Religion of the Heart in the Abbey of the Holy Ghost', in *Models of Holiness in Medieval Sermons: Proceedings of the International Symposium (Kalamazoo, 4–7 May 1995)*, ed. by Beverly Mayne Kienzle, Edith Wilks Dolnikowski, Rosemary Drage Hale, Darlene Pryds, and Anne T. Thayer (Louvain-la-Neuve: Fédération Internationale des Instituts d'études Médiévales, 1996), pp. 221–27

Carruthers, Mary, *The Craft of Thought: Meditation, Rhetoric, and the Making of Images*, ed. by Alastair Minnis, Cambridge Studies in Medieval Literature, 34 (Cambridge: Cambridge University Press, 1998)

Caviness, Madeline, 'Patron or Matron? A Capetian Bride and a Vade Mecum for her Marriage Bed', *Speculum*, 68 (1993), 333–62

Cerquiglini, Bernard, *Éloge de la variante: Histoire critique de la philologie*, Des travaux, 8 (Paris: Éd. du Seuil, 1989)

Charles-Gaffiot, Jacques, and Dominique Rigaux, eds, *Beauté et Pauvreté: L'Art chez les clarisses de France* (Paris: Centre culturel du Panthéon, 1994)

Chesney, Kathleen, 'Notes on Some Treatises of Devotion Intended for Margaret of York', *Medium Aevum*, 20 (1951), 11–39

Clark, Robert L. A., 'Constructing the Female Subject in Late Medieval Devotion', in *Medieval Conduct*, ed. by Kathleen Ashley and Robert L. A. Clark (Minneapolis: University of Minnesota Press, 2001), pp. 160–82

Cockshaw, Pierre, 'Some Remarks on the Character and Content of the Library of Margaret of York', in *Margaret of York, Simon Marmion and the Visions of Tondal*, ed. by Thomas Kren (Malibu: J. Paul Getty Museum, 1992), pp. 57–62

Collet, Olivier, and Yasmina Foehr-Janssens, eds, *Le Recueil au Moyen âge: Le Moyen âge central*, Texte, codex et contexte, 8 (Turnhout: Brepols, 2010)

Conlee, John W., 'The Abbey of the Holy Ghost and the Eight Ghostly Dwelling Places of Huntingdon Library HM 744', *Medium Aevum*, 44 (1975), 137–44

Consacro, Peter, 'The Author of *The Abbey of the Holy Ghost*: A Popularizer of the Mixed Life', *Fourteenth Century English Mystics Newsletter*, 2 (1976), 15–20

Crassons, Kate, *The Claims of Poverty: Literature, Culture, and Ideology in Late Medieval England* (Notre Dame: University of Notre Dame Press, 2010)

De la Selle, Xavier, *Le Service des âmes à la cour*, Mémoires et documents de l'École des Chartes, 43 (Paris: École des Chartes, 1995)

De Marsy, Arthur, *Les Abbesses de Maubuisson* (Paris: J.-B. Dumoulin, 1868)

Debae, Marguerite, *La Bibliothèque de Marguerite d'Autriche: Essai de reconstitution d'après l'inventaire 1523–24* (Louvain: Éditions Peeters, 1995)

Delmaire, Bernard, 'Les Béguines dans le Nord de la France au premier siècle de leur histoire (vers 1230 – vers 1350)', in *Les Religieuses en France au XIIIᵉ siècle: Table ronde / organisée par l'Institut d'études médiévales de l'Université de Nancy II et le CERCOM 25–26 juin 1983*, ed. by M. Parisse (Nancy: Presses universitaires de Nancy, 1985), pp. 121–62

Desobry, Jean, *Un aspect peu connu de la Révolution française de 1789 à Amiens*, Mémoires de la Société des antiquaires de Picardie, 54 (Amiens: Société des antiquaires de Picardie, 1986)

Dohrn-van Rossum, Gerhard, *Die Geschichte der Stunde: Uhren und moderne Zeitordnungen* (Cologne: Anaconda, 2007)

Echard, Siân, and Stephen Partridge, eds, *The Book Unbound: Editing and Reading Medieval Manuscripts and Texts* (Toronto: University of Toronto Press, 2004)

Evdokimova, Ludmilla, 'Deux types de traduction au milieu du XIVᵉ siècle: Jean de Vignay et Jean Ferron, traducteurs du *Libellus de ludo scachorum* de Jacques de Cessoles', in *In principio fuit interpres*, ed. by Alessandra Petrina (Turnhout: Brepols, 2013), pp. 49–61

Farmer, Sharon A., *Surviving Poverty in Medieval Paris: Gender, Ideology, and the Daily Lives of the Poor*, Conjunctions of Religion & Power in the Medieval Past (Ithaca: Cornell University Press, 2001)

Félibien, Michel, *Histoire de la ville de Paris*, 5 vols (Paris: Guillaume Desprez et Jean Desessartz, 1725)

Fery-Hue, Françoise, 'Gossuin de Metz', in *Dictionnaire des lettres françaises: Le Moyen Âge*, ed. by Geneviève Hasenohr and Michel Zink (Paris: Fayard, 1992), pp. 555–56

Field, Sean L., 'From *Speculum anime* to *Miroir de l'âme*: The Origins of Vernacular Advice Literature at the Capetian Court', *Mediaeval Studies*, 69 (2007), 59–110

——, 'Marie of Saint-Pol and her Books', *English Historical Review*, 125 (2010), 255–78

——, 'Reflecting the Royal Soul: The *Speculum anime* Composed for Blanche of Castile', *Mediaeval Studies*, 68 (2006), 1–42

Galloway, Penelope, '"Discreet and Devout Maidens": Women's Involvement in Beguine Communities in Northern France, 1200–1500', in *Medieval Women in their Communities*, ed. by Dianne Watt (Cardiff: University of Wales Press, 1997), pp. 92–115

Geybels, Hans, *Vulgariter Beghinae: Eight Centuries of Beguine History in the Low Countries* (Turnhout, Belgium: Brepols, 2004)

Gobry, Ivan, 'Hugues de Fouilloy', in *Dictionnaire de spiritualité ascétique et mystique* (Paris: Beauchesne, 1969), cols 880–86

Green, Karen, 'Christine de Pizan: Isolated Individual or Member of a Feminine Community of Learning'?, in *Communities of Learning: Networks and the Shaping of Intellectual Identity in Europe, 1100–1500*, ed. by Constant J. Mews and John Crossley (Turnhout: Brepols, 2011), pp. 229–50

——, 'What Were the Ladies in the City of Ladies Reading? The Libraries of Christine de Pizan's Contemporaries', *Medievalia et Humanistica*, 36 (2010), 77–100

Hall, Kathryn A., 'The Abbey of the Holy Ghost: The French Manuscripts and their Relationship to the English Tradition' (unpublished doctoral dissertation, Florida State University, 1999)

Hammond, Eleanor Prescott, 'Latin Texts of the Dance of Death', *Modern Philology*, 8 (1911), 399–410

Hasenohr, Geneviève, 'Aspects de la littérature de spiritualité en langue française', *Revue d'histoire de l'église de France*, 77 (1991), 29–45

——, 'D'une "poésie de béguine" à une "poétique des béguines": Aperçus sur la forme et la réception des textes (France, xiiie–xive s.)', *Comptes-rendus des séances de l'Académie des inscriptions et belles-lettres*, 150 (2006), 913–43

——, 'Un Enseignement de vie chrétienne du xiiie siècle et sa postérité: La Règle des coeurs ordonnés', *Romania*, 124 (2006), 324–60

——, 'Un Faux Pierre de Luxembourg, un vrai Arnoul de Bohéries et un Isidore travesti dans la bibliothèque de Marguerite d'York', in *Miscellanea in memoriam Pierre Cockshaw (1938–2008): Aspects de la vie culturelle dans les Pays-Bas méridionaux (xive–xviiie siècle) / aspecten van het culturele leven in de Zuidelijke Nederlanden (14de–18de eeuw)*, ed. by Frank Daelemans and Ann Kelders (Brussels: Archives et Bibliothèques de Belgique, 2009), pp. 175–93

——, 'Isidore de Séville, auteur ascétique "français"?', *Romania*, 128 (2010), 299–351

——, 'Les Prologues des textes de dévotion en langue française (xiiie–xve siècles): Formes et fonctions', in *Les Prologues médiévaux: Actes du colloque international, Rome, 26–28 mars 1998*, ed. by Jacqueline Hamesse (Turnhout: Brepols, 2000), pp. 593–638

——, 'Les Recueils littéraires français du xiiie siècle: Public et finalité', in *Codices miscellanearum: Brussels Van Hulthem Colloquium 1999 / Colloque Van Hulthem, Bruxelles 1999*, ed. by R. Jansen-Sieben and H. Van Dijk (Brussels: Archives et bibliothèques de Belgique / Archief- en Bibliotheekwezen in België, 1999), pp. 37–50

——, 'La Seconde vie du Miroir des simples âmes en France: Le Livre de la discipline d'amour divine (xve–xviie s.)', in *Marguerite Porete et le Miroir des simples âmes: Perspectives historiques, philosophiques et littéraires*, ed. by Sean L. Field, Robert E. Lerner, and Sylvain Piron (Paris: Vrin, 2013), pp. 263–317

——, *Textes de dévotion et lectures spirituelles en langue romane (France, xiie–xvie siècle)* (Turnhout: Brepols, 2015)

——, 'La Vie quotidienne de la femme vue par l'Eglise: L'Enseignement des "journées chrétiennes" de la fin du Moyen-Age', in *Frau und spätmittelalterlicher Alltag (Internationaler Kongress, Krems an der Donau, 2. bis 5. Oktober 1984)* (Vienna: Verlag der Österreichischen Akademie der Wissenschaften, 1986), pp. 19–101

Holladay, Joan A., 'The Education of Jeanne d'Evreux: Personal Piety and Dynastic Salvation in her Book of Hours at the Cloisters', *Art History*, 17 (1994), 585–611

——, 'Fourteenth-Century French Queens as Collectors and Readers of Books: Jeanne d'Evreux and her Contemporaries', *Journal of Medieval History*, 32 (2006), 69–100

Hollywood, Amy M., *The Soul as Virgin Wife: Mechthild of Magdeburg, Marguerite Porete, and Meister Eckhart*, Studies in Spirituality and Theology, 1 (Notre Dame: University of Notre Dame, 1995)

Huot, Sylvia, 'A Book Made for a Queen: The Shaping of a Late Medieval Anthology Manuscript (B. N. fr. 24429)', in *The Whole Book: Cultural Perspectives on the Medieval Miscellany*, ed. by Stephen G. Nichols and Siegfried Wenzel (Ann Arbor: University of Michigan Press, 1996), pp. 123–43

Keane, Marguerite A., *Material Culture and Queenship in 14th-Century France: The Testament of Blanche of Navarre (1331–1398)*, Art and Material Culture in Medieval and Renaissance Europe, 5 (Leiden: Brill, 2016)

Kinch, Ashby, *Imago mortis: Mediating Images of Death in Late Medieval Culture*, Visualising the Middle Ages, 9 (Leiden: Brill, 2013)

Kinder, Terryl, 'Blanche of Castile and the Cistercians: An Architectural Re-evaluation of Maubuisson Abbey', *Cîteaux: Commentarii cistercienses*, 27 (1976), 161–88

Kocher, Suzanne, *Allegories of Love in Marguerite Porete's Mirror of Simple Souls*, Medieval Women: Texts and Contexts, 17 (Turnhout: Brepols, 2008)

Kren, Thomas, Scot McKendrick, Royal Academy of Arts (Great Britain), and J. Paul Getty Museum, *Illuminating the Renaissance: The Triumph of Flemish Manuscript Painting in Europe* (Los Angeles: J. Paul Getty Museum, 2003)

Kumler, Aden Welles, *Translating Truth: Ambitious Images and Religious Knowledge in Late Medieval France and England* (New Haven: Yale University Press, 2011)

Laborde, Alexandre de, *Les Principaux Manuscrits à peintures conservés dans l'ancienne Bibliothèque publique de Saint-Petersbourg* (Paris, 1936–38)

Laemers, Jeroen W. J., 'Claustrum animae: The Community as Example for Interior Reform', in *Virtue and Ethics in the Twelfth Century*, ed. by István P. Bejczy and Richard G. Newhauser (Leiden: Brill, 2005), pp. 119–30

Landes, David S., *Revolution in Time: Clocks and the Making of the Modern World* (Cambridge, MA: The Bellknap Press of Harvard University Press, 1983)

Långfors, Arthur, 'Notice des manuscrits 535 de la bibliothèque municipale de Metz et 10047 des nouvelles acquisitions du fonds français de la bibliothèque nationale', *Notices et extraits des manuscrits de la Bibliotheque nationale*, 42 (1933), 139–288

Lauwers, M., and W. Simons, *Béguines et Béguins à Tournai au Bas Moyen Age*, Publications d'histoire de l'art et d'archéologie de l'Université Catholique de Louvain, 63 (Tournai: Archives du Chapitre Cathédral; Louvain-la-Neuve: Université Catholique de Louvain, 1988)

Leclercq, Jean, *The Love of Learning and the Desire for God: A Study of Monastic Culture*, 3rd edn (New York: Fordham University Press, 1982)

Lefèvre, Sylvie, 'Jean le Court, dit Brisebarre', in *Dictionnaire des lettres françaises: Le Moyen Âge*, ed. by Geneviève Hasenohr and Michel Zink (Paris: Fayard, 1992), pp. 801–02

Legaré, Anne-Marie, 'Les Bibliothèques de deux princesses: Marguerite d'York et Marguerite d'Autriche', in *Livres et lectures de femmes en Europe entre Moyen Âge et Renaissance*, ed. by A.-M. Legaré (Turnhout: Brepols, 2007), pp. 253–64

Leroux, Xavier, ed., *La Mise en recueil des textes médiévaux*, Babel: Littératures plurielles, 16 ([Toulon]: Université de Toulon, 2007)

Lester, Anne E., 'Suburban Space and Religious Reform', *Parergon*, 27.2 (2010), 59–87

McCurry, Charles, 'Religious Careers and Religious Devotion in Thirteenth-Century Metz', *Viator*, 9 (1978), 325–34

McDonnell, E. W., *The Beguines and Beghards in Medieval Culture, with Special Emphasis on the Belgian Scene* (New Brunswick, NJ: Rutgers University Press, 1954)

McGinn, Bernard, 'The Changing Shape of Late Medieval Mysticism', *Church History*, 65 (1996), 197–219

——, *The Flowering of Mysticism: Men and Women in the New Mysticism (1200–1350)*, vol. III of *The Presence of God: A History of Western Christian Mysticism* (New York: Crossroad, 1998)

——, *The Growth of Mysticism*, vol. II of *The Presence of God: A History of Western Christian Mysticism* (London: SCM Press, 1994)

——, ed., *Meister Eckhart and the Beguine Mystics: Hadewijch of Brabant, Mechthild of Magdeburg, and Marguerite Porete* (New York: Continuum, 1994)

Meiss, Millard, *French Painting in the Time of Jean de Berry: The Late Fourteenth Century and the Patronage of the Duke*, 2nd edn, Kress Foundation Studies in the History of European Art, 2, 2 vols (London: Phaidon, 1969)

——, *French Painting in the Time of Jean de Berry: The Limbourgs and their Contemporaries*, 2 vols (London: Thames and Hudson, 1974)

Mews, Constant J., 'Apostolic Ideals in the Mendicant Transformation of the Thirteenth Century: From Sine Proprio to Holy Poverty', in *Poverty and Devotion in Mendicant Cultures, 1200–1450*, ed. by Constant J. Mews and Anna Welch (London: Routledge, 2016), pp. 24–39

——, ed., *Listen, Daughter: The 'Speculum virginum' and the Formation of Religious Women in the Middle Ages* (New York: Palgrave, 2001)

——, 'The *Speculum dominarum* (*Miroir des dames*) and Transformations of the Literature of Instruction for Women in the Early Fourteenth Century', in *Virtue Ethics for Women, 1250–1500*, ed. by Karen Green and Constant J. Mews (Dordrecht: Springer, 2011), pp. 12–30

Mews, Constant J., Karen Green, Charmaine Manuel, and Janice Pinder, 'Introducing the *Miroir des dames*', *Revue d'histoire des textes*, 14 (2019), 313–51

Meyer, Paul, 'Notice du ms. 535 de la Bibl. Mun. de Metz', *Bulletin de la Société des anciens textes français*, 12 (1886), 41–76

——, 'Notice du MS Royal 16 E XII du Musée Britannique', *Bulletin de la Société des anciens textes français*, 38 (1912), 43–63 and 95–97

——, 'Notice d'un manuscrit lorrain appartenant a une collection privée', *Bulletin de la Société des anciens textes français*, 10 (1884), 73–79

——, 'Notice sur le manuscrit du Musée britannique Add. 20697', *Bulletin de la Société des anciens textes français*, 18 (1892), 94–95

Michalove, Sharon, 'Women as Book Collectors and Disseminators of Culture in Late Medieval England and Burgundy', in *Reputation and Representation in Fifteenth-Century Europe*, ed. by Sharon D. Michalove, Albert Compton Reeves, and Douglas Biggs (Leiden: Brill, 2004), pp. 57–79

Mikhaïlova-Makarius, Milena, ed., *Mouvances et jointures du manuscrit au texte médiéval [actes du colloque international, 21–23 novembre 2002]*, Medievalia, 55 (Orléans: Paradigme, 2005)

Newman, Barbara, *From Virile Woman to WomanChrist: Studies in Medieval Religion and Literature*, Middle Ages Series (Philadelphia: University of Pennsylvania Press, 1995)

——, *God and the Goddesses: Vision, Poetry, and Belief in the Middle Ages* (Philadelphia: University of Pennsylvania Press, 2003)

——, 'The Mirror and the Rose: Marguerite Porete's Encounter with the Dieu d'Amours', in *The Vernacular Spirit: Essays on Medieval Religious Literature*, ed. by Renate Blumenfeld-Kosinski, Duncan Robertson, and Nancy Bradley Warren (New York: Palgrave, 2002), pp. 105–23

Nichols, Stephen G., and Siegfried Wenzel, eds, *The Whole Book: Cultural Perspectives on the Medieval Miscellany* (Ann Arbor: University of Michigan Press, 1996)

Normore, Christina, *A Feast for the Eyes: Art, Performance, and the Late Medieval Banquet* (Chicago: University of Chicago Press, 2015)

Oliver, Judith, 'Devotional Images and Pious Practices in a Psalter from Liège', *Latrobe Library Journal*, 13 (1993), 24–29

——, 'Devotional Psalters and the Study of Beguine Spirituality', *Vox Benedictina*, 9 (1992), 198–225

——, 'Je pecherise renc grasces a vos: Some French Devotional Texts in Beguine Psalters', in *Studies for Keith Val Sinclair*, ed. by Peter Rolfe Monks and D. D. R. Owen (Leiden: Brill, 1994), pp. 248–66

Omont, Henri, Auguste Molinier, and Ernest Coyecque, *Chartres*, vol. XI of *Catalogue Général des manuscrits des bibliothèques publiques de France* (Paris: Plon, 1890)

Oury, G., 'Le "De Claustro Animae" de Jean, prieur de Saint-Jean-des-Vignes', *Revue d'Ascétique et de Mystique*, 40 (1964), 427–42

Pächt, Otto, 'The Illustrations of St Anselm's Prayers and Meditations', *Journal of the Warburg and Courtauld Institutes*, 19 (1956), 68–83

Pagan, Martine, 'Les Légendes françaises de Claire d'Assise (XIIIᵉ–XVIᵉ siècle). I. Inventaire et classement des manuscrits', *Etudes franciscaines*, n.s., 7 (2014) 5–30

Passenier, Anke, '"Women on the Loose": Stereotypes of Women in the Story of the Medieval Beguines', in *Female Stereotypes in Religious Traditions*, ed. by Wouter J. Hanegraaff (Leiden: Brill, 1995), pp. 61–89

Pearson, Andrea G., 'Gendered Subject, Gendered Spectator: Mary Magdalen in the Gaze of Margaret of York', *Gesta*, 44 (2005), 47–66

——, 'Productions of Meaning in Portraits of Margaret of York', in *Women and Portraits in Early Modern Europe: Gender, Agency, Identity*, ed. by Andrea G. Pearson (Aldershot: Ashgate, 2008), pp. 35–49

Pedersen, Else Marie Wiberg, 'Can God Speak in the Vernacular? On Beatrice of Nazareth's Flemish Exposition of the Love for God', in *The Vernacular Spirit: Essays on Medieval Religious Literature*, ed. by Renate Blumenfeld-Kosinski, Duncan Robertson, and Nancy Bradley Warren (New York: Palgrave, 2002), pp. 185–208

——, 'The In-carnation of Beatrice of Nazareth's Theology', in *New Trends in Feminine Spirituality: The Holy Women of Liège and their Impact*, ed. by Juliette Dor, Lesley Johnson, and Jocelyn Wogan-Browne, Medieval Women: Texts and Contexts, 2 (Turnhout: Brepols, 1999), pp. 61–79

Peltier, Henri, 'Hugues de Fouilloy: Chanoine régulier; Prieur de Saint-Laurent-au-Bois', *Revue du Moyen Âge latin*, 2 (1946), 25–44

Pinder, Janice, 'The Cloister and the Garden: Two Visions of Religious Life from the Twelfth Century', in *Listen, Daughter: The 'Speculum virginum' and the Formation of Religious Women in the Middle Ages*, ed. by Constant J. Mews (New York: Palgrave, 2001), pp. 159–79

——, 'Food for the Journey: The Thirteenth-Century French Version of Guiard of Laon's Sermon on the Twelve Fruits of the Eucharist', in *Intellectual Dynamism in the High Middle Ages*, ed. by Clare Monagle (Amsterdam: Amsterdam University Press, forthcoming)

——, 'A Lady's Guide to Salvation: The *Miroir des dames* Compilation', in *Virtue Ethics for Women, 1250–1500*, ed. by Karen Green and Constant J. Mews (Dordrecht: Springer, 2011), pp. 45–52

——, 'Love and Reason from Hugh of Fouilloy to the *Abbaye du Saint Esprit*: Changes at the Top in the Medieval Cloister Allegory', *Parergon*, 27.1 (2010), 67–83

——, 'Un recueil picard de lectures spirituelles pour des sœurs franciscaines: Paris, Bibliothèque nationale de France, français 2093 et 2095', *Etudes franciscaines*, n.s. 9 (2016), 273–87

Quentel-Touche, Cécile, 'Charles V's Visual Definition of the Queen's Virtues', in *Virtue Ethics for Women, 1250–1500*, ed. by Karen Green and Constant J. Mews (Dordrecht: Springer, 2011), pp. 53–80

Quéruel, D., ed., *Les Manuscrits de David Aubert 'escripvain' bourguignon*, Cultures et civilisations médiévales, 18 (Paris: 1999)

Reynaert, Joris, 'Hadewijch: Mystic Poetry and Courtly Love', in *Medieval Dutch Literature in its European Context*, ed. by Erik Kooper (Cambridge: Cambridge University Press, 1994), pp. 208–25

Rice, Nicole R., *Lay Piety and Religious Discipline in Middle English Literature*, Cambridge Studies in Medieval Literature, 73 (Cambridge: Cambridge University Press, 2009)

——, 'Spiritual Ambition and the Translation of the Cloister: The Abbey and Charter of the Holy Ghost', *Viator*, 33 (2002), 222–60

Richards, Joan Marie, 'Franciscan Women: The Colettine Reform of the Order of Saint Clare in the Fifteenth Century' (unpublished doctoral dissertation, University of California, Berkeley, 1989)

Rigaux, Dominique, 'Claire et le livre, parcours iconographique', in *Beauté et Pauvreté: L'Art chez les clarisses de France*, ed. by Jacques Charles-Gaffiot and Dominique Rigaux (Paris: Centre culturel du Panthéon, 1994), pp. 41–44

Rivers, Kimberly A., *Preaching the Memory of Virtue and Vice: Memory, Images, and Preaching in the Late Middle Ages*. Sermo: Studies on Patristic, Medieval, and Reformation Sermons and Preaching, 4 (Turnhout: Brepols, 2010)

Roest, Bert, *Order and Disorder: The Poor Clares between Foundation and Reform* (Leiden: Brill, 2013)

Rouse, Richard A., and Mary A. Rouse, *Manuscripts and their Makers: Commercial Book Producers in Medieval Paris, 1200–1500*, 2 vols (London: Harvey Miller, 2000)

Rubin, Miri, *Corpus Christi: The Eucharist in Late Medieval Culture* (Cambridge: Cambridge University Press, 1991)

Rychner, Jean, 'Les Traductions françaises de la Moralisatio super Ludum scaccorum de Jacques de Cessoles: Étude comparée des traductions en tant que telles', in *Recueil de travaux offerts à M. Clovis Brunel par ses amis, collègues et élèves* (Paris: Société de l'École des Chartes, 1955), pp. 480–93

Sandler, Lucy Freeman, 'John of Metz, the Tower of Wisdom', in *The Medieval Craft of Memory: An Anthology of Texts and Pictures*, ed. by Mary Carruthers and Jan M. Ziolkowski (Philadelphia: University of Pennsylvania Press, 2002), pp. 215–25

Scheepsma, Wybren, *The Limburg Sermons: Preaching in the Medieval Low Countries at the Turn of the Fourteenth Century*, trans. by David F. Johnson, Brill's Series in Church History, 34 (Leiden: Brill, 2008)

——, 'Het oudste Middelnederlandse palmboomtraktaat en de Limburgse semoenen', *Ons Geestelijk Erf*, 75 (2001), 153–81

Simons, Walter, *Cities of Ladies: Beguine Communities in the Medieval Low Countries, 1200–1565* (Philadelphia: University of Pennsylvania Press, 2001)

——, '"Staining the Speech of Things Divine": The Uses of Literacy in Medieval Beguine Communities', in *The Voice of Silence: Women's Literacy in a Men's Church*, ed. by Thérèse de Hemptinne and María Eugenia Góngora (Turnhout: Brepols, 2004), pp. 85–110

Smith, Jeffrey Chipps, 'Margaret of York and the Burgundian Portrait Tradition', in *Margaret of York, Simon Marmion, and the Visions of Tondal*, ed. by Thomas Kren (Malibu: J. Paul Getty Museum, 1992), pp. 47–56

Smith, Julie Anne, 'Clausura Districta: Conceiving Space and Community for Dominican Nuns in the Thirteenth Century', *Parergon*, 27.2 (2010), 13–36

Smith, Nathaniel B., 'The Lark Image in Bondie Dietaiuti and Dante', *Forum Italicum: A Journal of Italian Studies*, 12 (1978), 233–42

Spedding, Alison J., '"At the King's Pleasure": The Testament of Cecily Neville', *Midland History*, 35 (2010), 256–72

Straub, Richard E. F., *David Aubert: Escripvain et clerc* (Amsterdam: Rodopi, 1995)

Suydam, Mary A., 'Beguine Textuality: Sacred Performances', in *Performance and Transformation: New Approaches to Late Medieval Spirituality*, ed. by Mary A. Suydam and Joanna E. Ziegler (New York: St Martin's Press, 1999), pp. 169–210

Taylor, Andrew, 'Displaying Privacy: Margaret of York as Devotional Reader', in *Cultures of Religious Reading in the Late Middle Ages: Instructing the Soul, Feeding the Spirit, and Awakening the Passion*, ed. by Sabrina Corbellini (Turnhout: Brepols, 2013), pp. 275–95

Thomas, Marcel, 'Recherches sur les légendes françaises de Saint François d'Assise: Edition de la version anglo-normande (MS BN fr. 13505)' (Thèse dactylographiée, École nationale des chartes, 1942)

Tomasi, Michele, 'La pala d'altare di Maubuisson', in *Conosco un ottimo storia dell'arte...': Per Enrico Castelnuovo. Scritti di allievi e amici pisani*, ed. by Maria Monica Donato and Massimo Ferretti (Pisa: Edizioni della Normale, 2012), pp. 125–30

Van Hemelryck, Tania, and Stefania Marzano, eds, *Le Recueil au Moyen Âge: La Fin du Moyen Âge [3e colloque international du Groupe de recherche sur le moyen français de l'Université catholique de Louvain, 10, 11 et 12 mai 2007] avec la collaboration d'Alexandra Dignef... [et al.]*, Texte, codex et contexte, 9 (Turnhout: Brepols, 2010)

Van Hoorebeeck, Céline, *Livres et lectures des fonctionnaires des ducs de Bourgogne (ca 1420–1520)* (Turnhout: Brepols, 2014)

Walters, Barbara R., Vincent Corrigan, and Peter T. Ricketts, *The Feast of Corpus Christi* (University Park: Pennsylvania State University Press, 2006)

Walters, Lori J., 'Le Thème du livre comme don de sagesse dans le ms. Paris; BnF fr. 926', in *Le Recueil au Moyen Âge: La Fin du Moyen Âge*, ed. by Tania Van Hemelryck and Stefania Marzano, Texte, codex et contexte, 9 (Turnhout: Brepols, 2010), pp. 315–31

Warner, G. F., and J. P. Gilson, *Catalogue of Western Manuscripts in the Old Royal and King's Collections*, 4 vols (London: British Museum, 1921)

Warren, Nancy Bradley, *Women of God and Arms: Female Spirituality and Political Conflict, 1380–1600* (Philadelphia: University of Pennsylvania Press, 2005)

Waters, Claire M., *Translating 'Clergie': Status, Education, and Salvation in Thirteenth-Century Vernacular Texts* (Philadelphia: University of Pennsylvania Press, 2016)

Weightman, Christine B., *Margaret of York, the Diabolical Duchess*, 2nd edn (Stroud: Amberley, 2012)

Whitehead, Christiania, *Castles of the Mind: A Study of Medieval Architectural Allegory*, Religion & Culture in the Middle Ages (Cardiff: University of Wales Press, 2003)

——, 'Making a Cloister of the Soul in Medieval Religious Treatises', *Medium Aevum*, 67 (1998), 1–29

Wijsman, Hanno, 'Femmes, livres et éducation dans la dynastie burgondo-habsbourgeoise: Trois Marguerites à la loupe', *Publications du Centre Européen d'Etudes Bourguignonnes*, 44 (2004), 181–99

——, *Luxury Bound: Illustrated Manuscript Production and Noble and Princely Book Ownership in the Burgundian Netherlands (1400–1550)* (Turnhout: Brepols, 2011)

Zink, Michel, *La Prédication en langue romane*, 2nd edn, Nouvelle bibliothèque du moyen âge (Paris: Champion, 1982)

INDEX

Medieval Women: Texts and Contexts

All volumes in this series are evaluated by an Editorial Board, strictly on academic grounds, based on reports prepared by referees who have been commissioned by virtue of their specialism in the appropriate field. The Board ensures that the screening is done independently and without conflicts of interest. The definitive texts supplied by authors are also subject to review by the Board before being approved for publication. Further, the volumes are copyedited to conform to the publisher's stylebook and to the best international academic standards in the field.

Titles in Series

Jutta and Hildegard: The Biographical Sources, trans. and introduced by Anna Silvas (1999)

New Trends in Feminine Spirituality: The Holy Women of Liege and their Impact, ed. by Juliette D'Or, Lesley Johnson and Jocelyn Wogan-Browne (1999)

Medieval Women — Texts and Contexts in Late Medieval Britain: Essays in Honour of Felicity Riddy, ed. by Jocelyn Wogan-Browne, Rosalynn Voaden, Arlyn Diamond, Ann Hutchinson, Carol M. Meale, and Lesley Johnson (2000)

The Knowing of Woman's Kind in Childing: A Middle English Version of Material Derived from the Trotula and other Sources, ed. by Alexandra Barratt (2002)

St Katherine of Alexandria: Texts and Contexts in Western Medieval Europe, ed. by Jacqueline Jenkins and Katherine J. Lewis (2003)

Send Me God: The Lives of Ida the Compassionate of Nivelles, Nun of La Ramée, Arnulf, Lay Brother of Villers, and Abundus, Monk of Villers, by Goswin of Bossut, trans. by and with an introduction by Martinus Cawley OCSO and with a preface by Barbara Newman (2003)

Seeing and Knowing: Women and Learning in Medieval Europe, 1200–1550, ed. by Anneke B. Mulder-Bakker (2004)

Writing the Wilton Women: Goscelin's Legend of Edith and Liber confortatorius, ed. by Stephanie Hollis with W. R. Barnes, Rebecca Hayward, Kathleen Loncar, and Michael Wright (2004)

Household, Women, and Christianities in Late Antiquity and the Middle Ages, ed. by Anneke B. Mulder-Bakker and Jocelyn Wogan-Browne (2006)

The Writings of Julian of Norwich: 'A Vision Showed to a Devout Woman' and 'A Revelation of Love', ed. by Nicholas Watson and Jacqueline Jenkins (2006)

Les Cantiques Salemon: The Song of Songs in MS Paris BNF fr. 14966, ed. by Tony Hunt (2006)

Carolyn P. Collette, *Performing Polity: Women and Agency in the Anglo-French Tradition, 1385–1620* (2006)

Mary of Oignies: Mother of Salvation, ed. by Anneke B. Mulder-Bakker (2007)

Anna M. Silvas, *Macrina the Younger: Philosopher of God* (2008)

Thomas of Cantimpré: The Collected Saints' Lives: Abbot John of Cantimpré, Christina the Astonishing, Margaret of Ypres, and Lutgard of Aywieres, ed. by Barbara Newman, trans. by Margot H. King and Barbara Newman (2008)

Claire M. Waters, *Virgins and Scholars: A Fifteenth-Century Compilation of the Lives of John the Baptist, John the Evangelist, Jerome, and Katherine of Alexandria (2008)*

Jennifer N. Brown, *Three Women of Liege: A Critical Edition of and Commentary on the Middle English Lives of Elizabeth of Spalbeek, Christina Mirabilis, and Marie d'Oignies* (2009)

Suzanne Kocher, *Allegories of Love in Marguerite Porete's 'Mirror of Simple Souls'* (2009)

Beverly Mayne Kienzle, *Hildegard of Bingen and her Gospel Homilies: Speaking New Mysteries (2009)*

Mary Dockray-Miller, *Saints Edith and Athelthryth: Princesses, Miracle Workers, and their Late Medieval Audience: The Wilton Chronicle and the Wilton Life of St Athelthryth* (2009)

Living Saints of the Thirteenth Century: The Lives of Yvette, Anchoress of Huy; Juliana of Cornillon, Author of the Corpus Christi Feast; and Margaret the Lame, Anchoress of Magdeburg, ed. by Anneke B. Mulder-Bakker, trans. by Jo Ann McNamara, Barbara Newman, and Gertrude Jaron Lewis and Tilman Lewis (2012)

Nuns' Literacies in Medieval Europe: The Hull Dialogue, ed. by Virginia Blanton, Veronica O'Mara, and Patricia Stoop (2013)

June L. Mecham, *Sacred Communities, Shared Devotions: Gender, Material Culture, and Monasticism in Late Medieval Germany*, ed. by Alison I. Beach, Constance Berman, and Lisa Bitel (2014)

Partners in Spirit: Women, Men, and Religious Life in Germany, 1100–1500, ed. by Fiona J. Griffiths and Julie Hotchin (2014)

The Manere of Good Lyvyng: A Middle English Translation of Pseudo-Bernard's Liber de modo bene vivendi ad sororem, ed. by Anne E. Mouron (2014)

Nuns' Literacies in Medieval Europe: The Kansas City Dialogue, ed. by Virginia Blanton, Veronica O'Mara, and Patricia Stoop (2015)

Nuns' Literacies in Medieval Europe: The Antwerp Dialogue, ed. by Virginia Blanton, Veronica O'Mara, and Patricia Stoop (2017)